CELEBRITY HUMANITARIANISM

In the last two decades especially, we have witnessed the rise of 'celebrity' forms of global humanitarianism and charity work, spearheaded by entertainment stars, billionaires, and activist NGOs (e.g. Bob Geldof, Bono, Angelina Jolie, Madonna, Bill Gates, George Soros, Save Darfur, Médeçins Sans Frontières). This book examines this new phenomenon, arguing that celebrity humanitarianism legitimates, and indeed promotes, neoliberal capitalism and global inequality.

Drawing on Slavoj Žižek's work, the book argues that celebrity humanitarianism, far from being altruistic, is significantly contaminated and ideological: it is most often self-serving, helping to promote institutional aggrandizement and the celebrity 'brand'; it advances consumerism and corporate capitalism, and rationalizes the very global inequality it seeks to redress; it is fundamentally depoliticizing, despite its pretensions to 'activism'; and it contributes to a 'postdemocratic' political landscape, which appears outwardly open and consensual, but is in fact managed by unaccountable elites.

Ilan Kapoor is a Professor at the Faculty of Environmental Studies, York University, Toronto. He is the author of *The Postcolonial Politics of Development* (Routledge, 2008). His research interests include critical development studies, postcolonial theory/politics, psychoanalysis and Marxism, participation/democratic theory, and social and environmental movements.

Interventions

Edited by:
Jenny Edkins, Aberystwyth University and
Nick Vaughan-Williams, University of Warwick

'As Michel Foucault has famously stated, "knowledge is not made for understanding; it is made for cutting." In this spirit The Edkins–Vaughan-Williams Interventions series solicits cutting edge, critical works that challenge mainstream understandings in international relations. It is the best place to contribute post disciplinary works that think rather than merely recognize and affirm the world recycled in IR's traditional geopolitical imaginary.'
Michael J. Shapiro, University of Hawai'i at Mānoa, USA

The series aims to advance understanding of the key areas in which scholars working within broad critical post-structural and post-colonial traditions have chosen to make their interventions, and to present innovative analyses of important topics.

Titles in the series engage with critical thinkers in philosophy, sociology, politics, and other disciplines and provide situated historical, empirical, and textual studies in international politics.

Europe's Encounter with Islam
The secular and the postsecular
Luca Mavelli

Re-Thinking International Relations Theory via Deconstruction
Badredine Arfi

The New Violent Cartography
Geo-analysis after the aesthetic turn
Edited by Sam Okoth Opondo and Michael J. Shapiro

Insuring War
Sovereignty, security and risk
Luis Lobo-Guerrero

International Relations, Meaning and Mimesis
Necati Polat

The Postcolonial Subject
Claiming politics/governing others in late modernity
Vivienne Jabri

Foucault and the Politics of Hearing
Lauri Siisiäinen

Volunteer Tourism in the Global South
Giving back in neoliberal times
Wanda Vrasti

Cosmopolitan Government in Europe
Citizens and entrepreneurs in postnational politics
Owen Parker

Studies in the Trans-Disciplinary Method
After the aesthetic turn
Michael J. Shapiro

Alternative Accountabilities in Global Politics
The scars of violence
Brent J. Steele

Celebrity Humanitarianism
The ideology of global charity
Ilan Kapoor

Deconstructing International Politics
Michael Dillon

CELEBRITY HUMANITARIANISM

The ideology of global charity

Ilan Kapoor

LONDON AND NEW YORK

First published 2013
by Routledge
2 Park Square, Milton Park, Abingdon, Oxon OX14 4RN

Simultaneously published in the USA and Canada
by Routledge
711 Third Avenue, New York, NY 10017

Routledge is an imprint of the Taylor & Francis Group, an informa business

British Library Cataloguing in Publication Data
A catalogue record for this book is available from the British Library

Library of Congress Cataloging in Publication Data
Kapoor, Ilan.
Celebrity humanitarianism: the ideology of global charity / Ilan Kapoor.
p. cm. – (Interventions)
Summary: "This book examines the new phenomenon of celebrity
humanitarianism arguing that legitimates neoliberal capitalism and global
inequality"– Provided by publisher.
Includes bibliographical references and index.
() 1. Charities. 2. Celebrities. 3. Humanitarianism. 4. Capitalism. I. Title.
HV41.K276 2012
361.7–dc23
2012018127

ISBN: 978-0-415-78338-5 (hbk)
ISBN: 978-0-415-78339-2 (pbk)
ISBN: 978-0-203-08227-0 (ebk)

Typeset in Bembo
by Taylor and Francis Books

TO KENT, AS ALWAYS

CONTENTS

ACKNOWLEDGEMENTS

Many thanks to the following for their insightful comments and critiques on one or more of the chapters in this book: Michael Bach, Asef Bayat, Zsuzsa Gille, Kent Murnaghan, Ryan O'Neill, Anna Zalik, and three anonymous reviewers.

Thanks to my editor, Craig Fowlie, and to the Routledge production staff. I am very grateful to Nicola Parkin for her many efforts in seeing this book through to its publication. My thanks as well to the Routledge 'Interventions' series editors, Jenny Edkins and Nick Vaughan-Williams.

Thanks to my family and the Murnaghan family. And thanks to the following for their always warm and invaluable friendships: Usha Rangan, Rob Gill, Leesa Fawcett, Michael Bach, Anna Zalik, Nigel Barriffe, Radhika Mongia, Shubhra Gururani, Alok Johri, Anne-Marie Cwikowski, Geeta Uppal, Vasanthi Srinivasan, Zamil Janmohamed, Sherdil Hussain, Mohamed Khaki, Paul Yee, Prabha Khosla, Jennifer and Kevin Knelman, Cyril Thivollet, Patricia Kohen, and Gert ter Voorde.

Kent, I owe you more than I can possibly say – for your loving care, your unwavering support, and your wicked sense of humour!

I gratefully acknowledge permission from Kent Murnaghan to reproduce a close-up image of the following on the book cover: Kent Murnaghan, Untitled water colour drawing on paper, 10" x 7", 2011.

ABBREVIATIONS

AIDS	Acquired immune deficiency syndrome
BBC	British Broadcasting Corporation
BINGOs	Big international non-governmental organizations
CCTV	Closed-circuit television
CD	Compact disc
CEO	Chief executive officer
CEU	Central European University
CNN	Cable News Network
DATA	Debt Aids Trade Africa (advocacy group)
DOS	Disk operating system
DVD	Digital video disc
ERM	European Exchange Rate Mechanism
EU	European Union
FTSE	FTSE 100 Index (of highly capitalized UK companies on the London Stock Exchange)
G8	Group of Eight (of the world's largest economies)
G20	Group of Twenty (of the world's largest economies)
GDP	Gross domestic product
HIPC	Heavily Indebted Poor Countries
HIV/AIDS	Human immunodeficiency virus/Acquired immune deficiency syndrome
IBM	International Business Machines Corporation
IMF	International Monetary Fund
IPRs	Intellectual property rights
IT	Information technology
MSF	Médeçins Sans Frontières (Doctors Without Borders)

MTV	Music Television
NGO	Non-governmental organization
PR	Public relations
PVR	Personal video recorder
(RED)	Product (RED)
SDC	Save Darfur Coalition
SFM	Soros Fund Management
TV	Television
UN	United Nations
UNDP	United Nations Development Programme
US	United States (of America)
VCR	Videocassette recorder
WHO	World Health Organization
WTO	World Trade Organization

INTRODUCTION

Celebrity humanitarianism and ideology

Three celebrities are sitting around wondering what to do with all the money they collected for a charity.

The first says: 'I have an idea. Let's draw a circle, throw all the money up in the air, and what falls *inside* the circle, we give to the poor.'

The second says: 'I have a better idea. Let's draw a circle, throw all the money up in the air, and what falls *outside* the circle, we give to the poor.'

Then the third says: 'I have an even better idea. Let's draw a circle, throw all the money up in the air, and what falls to the ground – we keep!'

Celebrity humanitarianism

In the last two decades especially, we have witnessed the rise of 'celebrity' forms of global humanitarianism and charity work, spearheaded by entertainment 'stars', billionaires, and activist NGOs (e.g. Bob Geldof, Bono, Angelina Jolie, Madonna, Bill Gates, George Soros, Save Darfur, Médeçins Sans Frontières). This book examines this new phenomenon, arguing that celebrity humanitarianism legitimates, and indeed promotes, neoliberal capitalism and global inequality.

Drawing on Slavoj Žižek's work, the book shows how celebrity humanitarianism, far from being altruistic, is significantly contaminated and ideological: as in the above joke, it is most often self-serving, helping to promote institutional aggrandizement and the celebrity 'brand'; it advances consumerism and corporate capitalism, and rationalizes the very global inequality it seeks to redress; it is fundamentally depoliticizing, despite its pretensions to 'activism'; and it contributes to a 'postdemocratic' political landscape, which appears outwardly open and consensual, but is in fact managed by unaccountable elites.

This book focuses on three contemporary types of celebrity humanitarianism:

i the global charity work of entertainment stars such as Bono, Geldof, Jolie, and Madonna (Chapter 1);

ii the corporate philanthropy of billionaires (Gates, Soros) and big business – for example, in the form of celebrity-endorsed charity products sold under the Product (RED) brand, which raises funds for the fight against AIDS (Chapter 2); and

iii the humanitarian work of 'spectacular' NGOs (Save Darfur, Médeçins Sans Frontières), which not only pursue celebrity endorsements for their programs, but are increasingly able to achieve celebrity status themselves to boost fundraising and reach (Chapter 3).

I will attempt an ideology critique of all three types, showing how each strives to ignore, mystify, or disavow the dirty underside of the neoliberal global order, including the latter's tendencies towards depoliticization, imperialism, and inequality.

To illustrate the meaning of ideology critique, Žižek (2011a) often repeats the humorous story in Ernst Lubitsch's film, *Ninotchka*, in which the hero visits a cafeteria and orders coffee without cream. The waiter replies, 'sorry, we have run out of cream; we only have milk. Can I then bring you coffee without milk?' This dialectical joke illustrates how ideology functions: it doesn't only matter what you say (or see), it also matters what you don't say. Ideology critique consists, then, in uncovering the unsaid implied in what is said, in detecting the absences in what is in plain view. This is the case when, for example, Jolie's transnational adoptions are presented as benevolent, masking how this 'kind' act also helps improve her brand (cf. Chapter 1), or when Bill Gates, the 'world's greatest humanitarian', gives away spectacular sums of money, but sidelines how such enormous wealth was accumulated in the first place (cf. Chapter 2). This is also the case when celebrities disavow their significant economic investment in charity work (e.g. royalties, product endorsements, corporate partnerships), or when the 'spectacle' of humanitarian relief focuses only on the immediate and outward crisis, not its broader politics (cf. Chapter 3). My ideology critique in this book consists, therefore, in trying to uncover the *unconscious* of celebrity humanitarianism, to represent its absences.

What is significant about such an ideological landscape is that the contradictions of celebrity humanitarianism are in plain sight for all to behold, yet are so easily rationalized. In Chapter 2, drawing on Žižek, I refer to this phenomenon as 'decaf capitalism' – a sort of humanized capitalism that manages to hold together both enormous wealth accumulation and significant global inequality by attending to the worst manifestations of such inequality through charity. Thus, ruthless business practices stand alongside corporate 'social responsibility';

sweatshops and denuded forests alongside 'ethical' and 'green' shopping; and social havoc and financial crisis alongside celebrity 'caring'. The important implication – one that I emphasize throughout the book – is that it is celebrity humanitarianism that helps decaffeinate capitalism, doing the bare minimum to stabilize the system, preventing it from spinning out of control. Celebrity charity work, in this sense, is *integral* to the neoliberal global order: it helps cover over the latter's grimy foundations, acting as a 'safety net for [capital] to thrive' (Donini 2002: 261).

Also noteworthy are the depoliticizing tendencies of celebrity humanitarianism (another theme I will return to frequently in this book). By 'depoliticization' I mean the removal of public scrutiny and debate, with the result that issues of social justice are transformed into technocratic matters to be resolved by managers, 'experts', or in this case, humanitarian celebrities. Thus, when celebrities speak *for* the Third World[1] on issues of debt or poverty, or NGOs act as 'witnesses' on behalf of disaster 'victims', they reduce the Other into passive bystander, unilaterally representing her/his needs and desires. Similarly, when the spectacle of humanitarian relief focuses on the 'show', as it most often does, it ends up valuing the crisis's outwardly visible and photogenic aspects, diverting public attention away from the latter's long-term and structural causes. All such instances are depoliticizing because they tend to eliminate public deliberation, disagreement, and conflict, thereby upholding both a top-down politics and the status quo.

Celebrity humanitarianism, in this sense, conforms well to what some[2] have called our 'postdemocratic' liberal politics, in which largely unaccountable elites (technocrats, business tycoons, expert scientists or economists – and now celebrities) govern. This implies that celebrities increasingly have a powerful say on such significant global policy issues as debt, trade, famine, health, poverty reduction, or emergency relief. It also implies that mostly unelected private individuals and organizations have, for all intents and purposes, taken over what should primarily be state/public functions, which is itself revealing of the increasing current trend towards the neoliberalization of politics and economies.

Regarding my overall argumentation, several caveats are in order. While I sometimes focus on particular celebrities/humanitarian organizations such as Bono or Save Darfur, my purpose is not to emphasize their personal/institutional motives, idiosyncrasies, or failures, but to examine how their humanitarian work helps illuminate key structural characteristics of our contemporary global economic and political system. In other words, my contention is that the production of 'humanitarian celebrities' says something important about both global capitalism and its accompanying political arrangement – liberal democracy.

Moreover, my purpose is not to hold celebrities solely responsible for the ideological manoeuvrings of contemporary celebrity humanitarianism. On the contrary, as I make clear in all three chapters, we, the audience, are integral to, and complicit in, the process – through our fandom, our enjoyment of the celebrity spectacle, our consumption of charity products. We help prop up celebrities as powerful political figures through our beliefs and political passivity, which ultimately acquiesce to global neoliberalism. Re-orienting these beliefs and re-invigorating our politics, as I will argue in the Conclusion, is crucial if we are to begin to meaningfully scrutinize and dismantle the political economy of celebrity culture.

Finally, my purpose in arguing against celebrity humanitarianism is not to suggest that we should refrain from helping 'poor' and marginalized people, or abstain from 'rescuing' those affected by disasters. Of course we should come to their assistance! My point, rather, is that by focusing attention and resources on the immediate crisis and short-term emergency, the overwhelming tendency is to tackle the symptoms rather than the causes, the quick and efficient managerial fixes rather than more complex political struggles, the media-friendly 'personal stories' rather than the wider and recurring patterns of inequality and dispossession. In other words, humanitarianism, if it is to be meaningful (and meaningfully destabilized), needs to move away from the domain of unilateral and moralizing solutions such as those offered by celebrities, towards the much broader, long-term, and necessarily messy, terrain of politics.

A brief word about terminology: in common parlance, the terms 'charity', 'philanthropy', and 'humanitarianism' are often used interchangeably, and I will mostly follow suit. All signify assisting one's fellow human beings. But we need to keep in mind some notable differences in the meanings and genealogies of the terms. 'Charity' is a markedly Christianized concept associated with Christ-like 'love' for others (*OED* 2011). There is an unmistakeable stamp of this in contemporary celebrity humanitarianism – think, for instance, of Geldof's famous Band Aid song, 'Do They Know It's Christmas?', the lyrics of which refer to prayer, snow-filled Christmases, and our need to feed the world. 'Philanthropy', on the other hand, tends to have more secular associations: it means 'love of humankind', which is expressed through generous donations to 'good causes' (*OED* 2011). Perhaps it is because of this secular dimension that the term 'philanthropy' is most commonly associated today with the likes of business tycoons and the corporate sector (although there is no hard and fast rule here; 'corporate charity' is not an uncommon usage). This sense of civic responsibility is also present in 'humanitarianism' which is meant to express one's 'concern for human welfare' (*OED* 2011; cf. Barnett and Weiss 2008). Humanitarian NGOs typically universalize this civic responsibility, often underlining the need for impartiality or neutrality in their programming (whether they can and do live up to such ideals is, of course, debatable).

All three terms carry with them a strong sense of moral action (religious or secular). More often than not, such moral action creates a hierarchical distinction between the donor (a benevolent agent) and the recipient (a passive victim). It is the depoliticized nature of this relationship, as underlined earlier, that is so problematic. Moreover, all three terms concern moral actions carried out, for the most part, by private individuals or organizations: the actions may well be oriented towards a public or civic good, but the point is that the interests, management, and accountability involved in the actions remain private, not public (cf. Marshall 1997). It is this depoliticizing feature of celebrity humanitarianism that is, once again, so troubling.

Interestingly, the moral dimension makes humanitarianism out to be a transhistorical phenomenon: the fiction is that an act of generosity is being done without interest or return, and irrespective of circumstance. It is precisely this alleged purity, disinterest, and non-discrimination – doing the right thing regardless of the Other's position in space and time – that gives humanitarianism its moral weight. Yet, as we shall see, the problem with celebrity humanitarianism is that not only is it deeply contaminated by personal, institutional, commercial, and geopolitical interests, it is also highly circumscribed by its present historical time. Celebrity humanitarianism, as I have suggested above (and will argue through the book), is integral to the current global order, aiding and advancing postdemocratic governance and neoliberal economics. Hence, celebrities are 'doing the right thing', not for the Third World Other, but *in order for* capitalist liberal democracies to thrive.

The implication is that, far from being transhistorical, the moral dimension of humanitarianism has a historical–material basis. David Brion Davis argues (1975), for example, that contemporary forms of humanitarianism are the product of capitalist development and bourgeois market society. Their (Western) origins lie in nineteenth-century 'moral' movements such as the anti-saccharite and anti-slavery movements, when, for example, British housewives and Christian church groups organized boycotts and abstention campaigns against sugar and tea to oppose the use of slaves in plantations. But, as Davis points out, while such movements stood for abolishing slave-labour, they readily acquiesced to the use of wage-labour, betraying the need in many Western industrial economies to move away from slave-labour, which had by then become economically unviable.

Similarly, it can be said that celebrity humanitarianism is anchored in late capitalist political economy, which has seen increasing trends towards capital mobility, informatization, and global monopoly. As I will show, not only do humanitarian celebrities directly benefit from these trends (e.g. through corporate product endorsements, or global marketing and media campaigns), they also largely contribute to them (e.g. by helping sell products and brands, or promoting a culture of hyperindividualism; cf. Rojek 2001). Indeed, it is hard to imagine how celebrity humanitarianism could have arisen at any time other than now, particularly with such global reach and force. While celebrity culture may date back to the nineteenth-century expansion of the newspaper and book publishing industries (cf. Gamson 1994; Rojek 2001), it is the 1980s information revolution that has enabled it to become so globally pervasive. An important part of the story here is the emergence of a handful of global media giants such as AOL Time Warner, Disney, Viacom, Bertelsmann, and Sony, which integrate a wide range of functions, including advertising, merchandising, film, TV, software development, and publishing (McChesney 2008). Celebrities rely significantly on this broad global media empire for their humanitarian fundraising, advocacy, and advertising campaigns.

The three types of celebrity humanitarianism that I cover in this book – entertainment, corporate, and NGO – all emerge from this late global capitalist infrastructure. While older institutional forms of global humanitarianism (i.e. bilateral, multilateral, and non-governmental aid)[3] continue to operate, it is these new and increasingly powerful arrivals that I believe now require investigation: the privatized and highly celebritized nature of their humanitarian work exposes our networked and media-dominated societies, in which spectacle, style, personalization, and (neoliberal) hyperindividualism prevail (cf. Debord 1983; Stevenson 2010).

The Žižekian notion of ideology

The concept of ideology has been all but abandoned of late, especially since the fall of the Berlin Wall, but it is Žižek who has almost single-handedly renewed interest in it. For him, ideology critique is crucial at a time when the collapse of the Soviet experiment means that the global advance of capitalism and liberal democracy stands more or less unchallenged. Drawing on Lacanian psychoanalysis, he argues that there is a founding inconsistency or gap (i.e. 'the Real') in our structures of signification: reality is forever ruptured by contradictions, the human condition cannot escape imperfection, and the subject is always a subject of lack. Ideology, then, is that which attempts to obscure the Real, to cover over these gaps, contradictions, or imperfections (Žižek 1989: 45). Accordingly, when power attempts to naturalize itself, it is doing ideological work. When capitalist globalization and liberal democracy are sold by the likes of Bono or Bill Gates as the only horizons of economic and political possibility, as I will show, we have ideology.

This standpoint differs from the predominant Marxist notion of ideology, as well as from the postmodern tendency to reject ideology in favour of discursivity. The Marxist conception makes a distinction between an illusory world, where 'false consciousness' and superstition prevail, and an objective reality, to be apprehended by the critical and rational mind. Ideology critique, in this view, becomes a question of overcoming chimera, so that truth is revealed. In contrast, for Žižek, ideology is *not* a dreamlike illusion, but a

fantasy-construction which serves as a support for our 'reality' itself ...
The point of ideology is not to offer us a point of escape from our reality but
to offer us the social reality itself as an escape from some traumatic, real kernel.

(1989: 45)

In this sense, ideology should not be dismissed as an '"error" but regarded as an
unwitting indication of a truth' (Pfaller 2005: 108), so that the Real or the
unconscious is not so much hidden as obscured in plain view, disavowed even
as it is spoken, audible in the silences and gaps of language itself.

Part of the problem with the dominant Marxist conception is that it assumes
a neutral, pure place outside ideology from which one (i.e. the political 'van-
guard') can distinguish between objective and illusory reality. Foucault and
others (e.g. Rorty 1998) have pointed out that it yields to an elitism, if not a
heroic revolutionary idealism (Foucault 1980). Foucault argues instead for a
discursive reality in which there is no external consciousness or meaning; for
him, knowledge emerges out of historically-specific contexts and is always
imbricated with relations of power.

On the former point, Žižek agrees: we are all ideologically interpellated, so
there is no question of stepping outside ideology. He writes that 'in the predominant Marxist perspective the ideological gaze is *a partial* gaze overlooking
the *totality* of social relations, whereas in the Lacanian perspective ideology
rather designates a *totality set on effacing the traces of its own impossibility*'
(1989: 49). But on Foucault's latter point about the total negation of an outside, Žižek diverges. There may not be a positive outside, but this does not
mean there is no (negative) non-discursive core: for Žižek, the Real does not
pre-exist the symbolic order, but comes into being at the very same time,
which is to say that the Real is 'ext-imate' or 'internally external' to the
symbolic order (Vighi and Feldner 2007: 51).

Here, Žižek is advocating for a universality or truth-dimension, targeting
postmodernism's relativism, and in particular Foucault's historicism (i.e. the
view that everything is historical). As Vighi and Feldner (2007) point out,
Žižek distinguishes between 'historicism' and 'historicity', understanding the
latter to mean that the Real is an absent cause or imminent exception that always
returns in history: the Real is *not* 'an underlying Essence' but a 'rock that trips
up every attempt to integrate it into the symbolic order' (Žižek 1994a: 199).[4]
In other words, while for Žižek nothing is unhistorical, history is not everything,
and is itself ridden with gaps, exceptions, and exclusions. Ultimately, what is at
stake for him here is opening up possibilities for a radical politics (as the con-
cluding chapter in this book will illustrate). Foucault's discursivity and historicism give way to localized micro-politics and resistance, missing the universally
disruptive potential of the Real and the political possibilities of social antagonism
and contradiction (Vighi and Feldner 2007: 27).

According to Žižek, there are two crucial 'non-rational' elements upon which ideology relies – *belief* and *enjoyment*. Belief, for him, is ontological: it is impossible *not* to believe. From the moment we enter the symbolic order, we must yield to a master signifier – 'mother', 'parent', 'family', 'society', 'I' – in order to have meaning or indeed develop identities as subjects. We must give in, even if reluctantly, to parental or social commands in our continuing process of socialization. As Todd McGowan explains:

> The authority's injunction exists on its own, without any subsequent signifier that would provide completion and justification for the master signifier. The parent tells the child to obey, but no parent can ground this demand in an ultimate reason that would allow it to make sense. This is why, at some point, the parent must respond to the child's question 'Why?' with the unsatisfying response, 'Because I said so'. The ultimate justification for parental (and societal) authority is tautological. In the last instance, the child must obey simply because the parent says so, and this absence of a ground for the parental injunction is typically our first experience of the missing binary signifier that would provide a sense for the senseless master signifier.
>
> *(2010: 8)*

Belief, in this view, is nonsensical; it averts any rational argumentation or judgment. We believe unconditionally, without reason (Pound 2008: 53ff.), and it is upon this non-rational kernel, this incomprehensible submission, that ideology rests. We obey the Law or the logic of the market, despite protestations or resistance, because we have already unconsciously accepted them; reasoning or rationalization comes afterwards. In this sense, for Žižek, there is *belief before belief*:

> ... we find reasons attesting to our belief because we already believe; we do not believe because we have found sufficient good reasons to believe ... far from hiding its full authority, this traumatic, non-integrated character of the Law is a *positive condition of it* ... the reasons why we should believe are persuasive only to those who already believe.
>
> *(Žižek 1989: 37–38)*

Beliefs exist, moreover, not just in the realm of ideas, divorced from reality; indeed, the opposite is the case – they are always externalized, so that material reality is the very proof of their existence. As Žižek states, 'Belief is *always* materialized in our effective social activity: belief supports the fantasy which regulates social reality' (1989: 36). This is why, as mentioned earlier, ideological 'truth' is always 'out there', in plain view, as an embodiment of our unconscious beliefs.

Perhaps the most obvious manifestation of such exteriorization is custom:

> ... by following a custom, the subject believes without knowing it, so that the final conversion is merely a formal act by means of which we recognize that we have already believed. In other words ... the external custom is always a material support for the subject's unconscious.
>
> *(Žižek 1989: 37–38)*

We might well be responding to irrational injunctions and groundless authority when we follow custom or habit, but we proceed as if the contrary is the case. Ideological belief, in this sense, does not necessarily require violent force or threat; it can rely instead on the more gentle and gradual persuasion of ritual, tradition, routine, structure, repetition. Going along with the Law (e.g. the rule of law, liberal democracy, neoliberalism, celebrity charity), even if grudgingly, is already a step towards consent; but with repeated submission over time, the Law is finally confirmed as belief, and it is as though one already believed in it because it was always true, right, and just. These tendencies are magnified in our current information age, where sound-bytes, headlines, images, and advertising circulate so repetitively and pervasively.

Žižek often emphasizes how we outsource our beliefs, that is, allow an Other to believe for us, mostly because our busy lives leave us little time or energy to be politically active (he refers to this as 'interpassivity'; cf. 1997: 107–13). Thus, just as we outsource work or dating, so we delegate our humanitarian beliefs to celebrities. We allow them to make key policy decisions on our behalf regarding debt, health, disaster relief, or poverty reduction (cf. Chapters 1 and 3). But in so doing, we strengthen the ideology of humanitarianism: our political passivity translates into de facto consent to the status quo.

The second non-rational element on which ideology depends is enjoyment (*jouissance*). Part of the problem with Foucauldian discourse analysis, according to Žižek, is that it inadequately grapples with the subject's interior life, failing to confront the psychic inclinations that support ideology (Vighi and Feldner 2007: 24; Žižek 1999b: 66). Žižek makes the economy of human enjoyment central to his worldview, an emphasis now considered one of his key contributions to recent political theory. Drawing directly on Lacan, he takes *jouissance* to denote the libidinal surplus produced when we enter the social/symbolic order, a surplus that constantly drives yet troubles human pursuits. Enjoyment, in this sense, is not just pleasure or even pleasurable pain; it is *excessive* or *transgressive* pleasure/pain 'for the sake of which we do what might otherwise seem irrational, counterproductive, or even wrong' (Dean 2006: 4). Žižek has in mind here the deep comfort and satisfaction we get from bureaucratic processes, religious rituals, or social customs (i.e. the same customs that can become objects of belief – for there can be enjoyment in belief, too, according to Žižek). On this point, he is echoing Althusser, for whom ideology is exemplified in the institutional procedures of political parties, schools, churches, etc.

More pertinent to Žižek's argument though are the psychic investments we make in a range of ideological fantasies: the thrill we get from feeling unique (e.g. as celebrity, humanitarian, or activist); the enjoyment derived from what binds us as a nation, social community, or religious group; the pernicious draw of imperial triumphalism or aggressive militarism; and the often blind identification with national rituals (e.g. national holidays), sacrifices (e.g. the war dead or veterans), or myths (e.g. 'the US is the greatest country in the world', 'Canadians are very polite', 'Gandhi is the father of the Indian nation', 'Bill Gates is the greatest humanitarian in history'). Most often, the object of such enjoyment is delusional, dangerous, and without rational benefit or immediate self-interest, but nonetheless attractive and alluring. And quite often, the enjoyment in question is not just our own, but that of an Other: Žižek frequently uses the example of Nazi fascism, which faced with social and economic upheaval during the 1930s, blamed the Jews as the cause (1989: 96–97, 124ff.; 1994a: 79). The underlying narrative was, 'we must annihilate the Jews, because, instead of us enjoying (i.e. living well), *they* are; they have stolen *our* enjoyment'. Here, ideology is constructed around a stereotypical 'outsider' who threatens the German people's enjoyment, thus diverting from the country's real problems (in this case, its military defeat after the First World War and the crisis of capitalism faced by a good part of the world at the time).

It is important to note the relationship of enjoyment to desire and fantasy/ ideology. Human life centres on desire, which seeks enjoyment but can ultimately never be satisfied because of the ever-present and constitutive lack. Fantasy helps structure desire: we desire (the fantasy of) fullness and its promise of enjoyment – the perfect car, pure love, an ideal democracy, true humanitarianism. Desire thus involves the misrecognition of both fullness and promised enjoyment, and fantasy/ideology is 'the support that gives consistency to what we call "reality"' (Žižek 1989: 44).

Enjoyment for Žižek is not only irrational and arbitrary, but as just implied, also boundless: we keep on desiring, even when we fail to satisfy our desires. In fact, failure is written into the very economy of enjoyment, for we derive pleasure from the painful experience of never reaching our mark, from repeated failed attempts; and both this excess and lack are what ideologies often successfully imply and manipulate (Žižek 1989: 124–25; cf. Dean 2006: 12). Žižek frequently aligns enjoyment with the superego,[5] whose equally senseless and contingent injunction is to 'Enjoy!', as evidenced in the George W. Bush regime's command (read: permission) to enjoy torture, military aggression, or exceptions to the rule of law (e.g. in Guantánamo), or in late capitalism's bid for us to consume irrepressibly (Dean 2006: 31; McGowan 2004). This supergoic order to 'Enjoy!', in fact, feeds very well into the logic of the market and capital's continuous need to reproduce itself, a point Žižek often underscores (cf. 2006b: 297). Chapter 2 will examine, for example, how the consumer's enjoyment of charity shopping fastens her/him to global humanitarianism and capitalism. Charity products, in this sense, become more 'goods' for capitalism to manufacture in order to keep itself growing.

Belief and enjoyment are thus two key non-rational kernels of ideology. We tend to dismiss the nonsensical and arbitrary, for example in fascism or totalitarianism, yet Žižek points out that they are precisely what binds ideology and draws people to it. The crucial implication is that ideology operates not so much at the level of reason and knowledge, as we often assume, but at the level of the unconscious. This is why Žižek shifts the emphasis from what people know to what they do: ideology lies not on the side of knowledge but in the 'reality of the doing itself' (1989: 33), and it succeeds precisely because people continue to 'do', despite knowing better. Žižek describes this as the *fetishistic disavowal* (1989: 18, 32–33). For instance, we may know very well that Madonna's adoption of a Malawian boy is (at least partly) a publicity stunt, but we nonetheless believe she is good-hearted and donate to her charities; or I am aware these shoes were made in Indonesian sweatshops, but I still buy them because they are cheap. Belief and enjoyment are present in one's actions, so that one can know but still not renounce or refrain. And one can know (or know better) but still remain *within* ideology. Žižek is targeting here the postmodern tendency to think that ironic distance allows us to step outside ideology, giving way to a 'post-ideological age'. He argues that ideology does not need to brainwash us to be effective. Rather, it thrives on allowing us a certain distance from it, a space from which we can 'dis-identify' with the power regime. It is this ability to transgress, this enjoyment taken in a certain non-conformity with the law, that ultimately binds us to the prevailing ideology and keeps our loyal consent. Hence transgression, cynicism, or ironic detachment leave 'untouched the fundamental level of ideological fantasy' (Žižek 1989: 30).

Žižek thus provides us with a refreshing and critical perspective with which to decipher ideology – in this case, celebrity humanitarianism. What is compelling is that he helps us see that celebrity humanitarianism not only has a historical–material basis, but a psychic foundation as well: following Žižek, one could argue (as indeed I do) that the fantasy of celebrity charity is produced by late global capitalism to escape its traumatic kernel (inequality, unevenness, social marginalization). This fantasy is sustained by celebrities themselves, since they are so materially and libidinally invested in it. But it is also sustained by us as audience, fans, or consumers – our beliefs and enjoyment are crucial to helping produce celebrity culture. The challenge, then, is trying to identify and unravel these traumas, complicities, and libidinal excesses through ideology critique.

1

CELEBRITIES: HUMANITARIANS OR IDEOLOGUES?

There is a now famous Bono joke that goes something like this:

> In the midst of a U2 concert, Bono approaches the microphone earnestly, asking for complete silence. He proceeds to clap, slowly and steadily, and pronounces in a hushed voice: 'I want you all to think about something: every time I clap my hands, a poor child dies in Africa.' Upon which, someone in the crowd screams, 'Well, stop bloody clapping then!'

The joke, of course, lies in the gap between the metaphoric meaning of Bono's performance and the literalness of the audience member's understanding of it. But what if, speaking metaphorically, the latter understanding really were true – an African child is dying *because* Bono is clapping? That is, what if it is the performance of the celebrity's humanitarianism that *is* the show? What if staging the 'poor', dying African child is a cover for the structural violence leading to that death? And all said and done, what if the clapping is actually applause *for* that child's death (for otherwise, no one would profit)?

In this chapter, I want to take up many of these implied themes – celebrity self-promotion, diversion, propaganda, and profiteering, as well as audience adulation, accedence, and incredulity. Broadly speaking, I want to argue that celebrity humanitarianism legitimates late liberal capitalism and global inequality. Drawing on Žižek, I hope to show, in fact, that such charity work is deeply tainted and ideological. Its altruistic pretensions are belied by several notable accompaniments: its tendency to promote both the celebrity's brand and the image of the 'caring' (Western) nation; its entrenchment in a marketing and promotion machine that, willy-nilly, helps advance corporate capitalism, as well as the very 'poverty' it purports to remedy; its support to a 'postdemocratic' liberal political system that is outwardly populist yet, for all intents and purposes, conducted by unaccountable elites; and its use and abuse of the Third World, making Africa, in particular, a background for First World hero-worship and a dumping ground for humanitarian ideals and fantasies. All the while, I want to underscore Žižek's important point about our own complicity in this ideological work: as audience members and fans, or indeed even as detractors or critics, we too easily carry on our lives, consoled that someone is doing the charity work for us, just as long as we don't have to.

Celebrity humanitarianism

Celebrity humanitarian work has become de rigueur these days. Whether in the form of mediatized events (concerts, awareness campaigns, product/campaign endorsements, travel to crisis areas), personal charity (donations, volunteer work, child adoption), or lobbying (i.e. pressuring political leaders), do-gooding is a virtual career requirement for the established or aspiring star. Almost every day, it seems, George Clooney is organizing a fundraiser, Steven Spielberg is making a pledge, Scarlett Johansson is going on a mission, Jay-Z is touring Africa, a star like David Beckham is being appointed as UN Goodwill Ambassador, or *American Idol* is 'giving back'. Charity work has become so clichéd, in fact, that even Brüno (a.k.a. Sacha Baron Cohen) sees it necessary to adopt an 'African' baby to jump-start his Hollywood career!

I think it's important though to examine this phenomenon more closely, given that the pairing of humanitarianism with entertainment – commonly referred to as 'charitainment' or 'politainment' – is a potent combination, bringing to international development the enormous resources and reach of 'star-power' and the media. I will focus primarily, although not exclusively, on the humanitarian work of Bob Geldof, Bono, Angelina Jolie, and Madonna, outlining in this section some of their key accomplishments, and in the next, the ideological underpinnings of their work.

Geldof has become much more famous as a global activist than as a rock singer and leader of the 1970s band, The Boomtown Rats. This is mainly because, benefiting from the onset of the global information industry in the 1980s, he pioneered the charity-rock-concert-as-global-media-event. Although his activism follows in the footsteps of such entertainers as Woody Guthrie, Paul Robeson, George Harrison, Audrey Hepburn, Joan Baez, Danny Kaye, and others, he is often credited (along with Bono) with being the first to involve celebrities in large-scale global causes, thereby successfully galvanizing widespread public and media attention. Today, he has become a key player in global politics, especially concerning poverty, debt, trade, and HIV/AIDS. He is treated as a political leader in his own right, benefiting from one-to-one meetings with the likes of Barack Obama, Gordon Brown, and Stephen

Harper. In 2007, he persuaded Angela Merkel to include African development on the Heiligendamm G8 agenda, and he has been known to chide G8 leaders for not meeting their aid commitments, sometimes publicly shaming them into increasing their aid budgets. It is no wonder, then, that he and a few of his celebrity colleagues (Bono, Jolie) are labelled 'celebrity diplomats' (Cooper 2007, 2008a), engaging in what he himself calls 'punk diplomacy':

> I ... realised what enormous potential there was for me ... for saying the unsayable and confronting those in power ... They had to listen because I had not only the money but the constituency of support which that money represented. And it was a populist, non-governmental constituency ... Punk diplomacy ... was born ...
>
> *(Geldof quoted in Hague et al. 2008: 11)*

In 1984, responding to widespread news reports about famine in Ethiopia, Geldof co-wrote and recorded the song, 'Do They Know It's Christmas?' to raise funds for famine relief ('Band Aid'). What was particularly compelling for him and the wider British public at the time was a Michael Buerk BBC documentary showing chilling images of suffering Ethiopian babies with emaciated bodies and swollen heads, desperately being nursed by their mothers. Geldof's song echoed the 'biblical scene' staged in the documentary (Edkins 2000: 109), evoking Christian charity and the birth of the child-saviour. Recorded by forty-nine pop stars, the song became the fastest selling single of all time. It sold over three million copies and raised over £8 million (it was re-recorded and re-released in 1989) (BBC 2006).

After a visit to Ethiopia in early 1985, and keen to keep the famine in the spotlight, Geldof organized 'Live Aid', two live charity concerts in London and Philadelphia showcasing top musicians. The sixteen-hour concerts were broadcast in full on radio and TV channels in Britain and elsewhere. Dramatic video footage of the famine was aired, and public contributions were solicited (Geldof practically demanded public donations, declaring, 'There's people dying now, so just send us the fockin' money'; cf. *New Internationalist* 2006). Watched by some 1.5 billion people worldwide, Live Aid raised over £110 million for famine relief in Ethiopia (BBC 2006).

In 2004, British Prime Minister Tony Blair appointed Geldof to a newly set up Commission for Africa, whose mandate was to examine African development. The Commission's report called for better governance across the continent, with the need for support from the West on a range of issues, particularly debt reduction and development assistance (Commission for Africa 2005). These recommendations became the basis for the 2005 Gleneagles G8 summit.

At the same time, Geldof became the main organizer and de facto spokesperson of a broad-based global NGO effort (the Global Call to Action Against

Poverty, represented in the UK by the Make Poverty History campaign, and in the US by the ONE campaign) to compel G8 leaders to better address global poverty issues. A series of ten simultaneous Live 8 concerts was held across the globe. Eschewing fundraising in favour of political lobbying, the intent was to help focus world attention on the Gleneagles summit and, more specifically, to pressure G8 leaders into increasing Western foreign aid, reducing/cancelling the debt of the poorest countries (especially the so-called HIPC or Heavily Indebted Poor Countries), and improving the terms of trade for the South. The concerts were watched by some three billion people worldwide (Live 8 2005), while at the summit itself Geldof and Bono were received like political leaders, benefiting from exclusive meetings with George W. Bush, Tony Blair, and other G8 leaders.

The Live 8 events were a massive success in terms of garnering public and media attention. Large demonstrations, marches, and petition campaigns were organized across England and Scotland, with some 750,000 'Votes for Trade Justice' delivered to Tony Blair (Nash 2008: 170). In Britain especially, media coverage happened not just in the news, but also in such TV sit-coms as *The Vicar of Dibley*, an episode of which included a Make Poverty History campaign video. And in the run-up to the summit, the BBC aired an Africa TV series, including Geldof's own production, *Geldof in Africa*. But ultimately, Live 8 was largely a failure in terms of its primary aim of influencing G8 development programming and policy: I will develop this point further in the next section; suffice it to say for the moment that, to date, neither substantial debt cancellation nor much more Western aid has actually materialized, and WTO trade negotiations to improve the terms of trade for the South (especially in agriculture) have largely failed.

Like Geldof, Bono (a.k.a. Paul David Hewson) has become a force to reckon with in the global anti-poverty movement, although unlike Geldof he has successfully kept up his musical career as the frontman of the Irish rock band, U2. His foray onto the global stage began mostly in the mid-1990s, when he took a lead role in Jubilee 2000, the international NGO movement devoted to clearing Third World debt by the new millennium. He spoke about the issue of debt at the 1999 Brit Awards, and then, along with Geldof, led an NGO delegation to lobby Bill Clinton, the World Bank, and other policy-makers in Washington.

In 2002, Bono established DATA (Debt AIDS Trade Africa), an advocacy association headquartered at Universal Studios in London and financed mostly by the likes of George Soros and Bill Gates (Cooper 2008a: 51). In an effort to bring attention to some of the issues taken up by DATA, particularly HIV/AIDS, he convinced US Treasury Secretary Paul O'Neill to accompany him on a tour of Africa. A year later, he was instrumental (along with Geldof) in lobbying George W. Bush to create the largest ever aid commitment for a single disease – the $85 million Emergency Plan for AIDS Relief. Then, at the Davos World Economic Forum in 2006, he launched Product (RED), which brings together corporate brands and consumers to raise funds for the fight against HIV/AIDS in Africa (see Chapter 2 for details).

Bono has collaborated closely with Geldof on a number of fronts, including, as just mentioned, the 2005 Live 8/Make Poverty History campaign and the frequent lobbying of political leaders. Their joint efforts have also gone into publicizing development issues in the media: they have guest-edited several newspaper and magazine issues together, usually focusing on Africa – an issue of *The Independent* in 2006, *Bild-Zeitung* in 2007, and *The Globe and Mail* in 2010. In 2007, Bono guest-edited (this time without Geldof) the July 2007 volume of *Vanity Fair*. The aim of the issue was to 're-brand' Africa, with photos from Annie Leibovitz and contributions from Brad Pitt, Barack Obama, George Clooney, Oprah Winfrey, Desmond Tutu, Condoleezza Rice, and several others (*Vanity Fair* 2007).

Like Geldof, Bono has earned substantial credibility within global development circles. He has educated himself on North–South issues, and has not hesitated to surround himself with professionals: DATA, for example, is staffed by senior policy analysts and experienced development workers. He calls Jeffrey Sachs, the Columbia University economist and ubiquitous 'development advisor to the stars',[1] his 'mentor'; both have been frequent travel companions to Africa, especially on debt issues. Bono often uses the language of justice in his public forays on development and poverty, and frequently likens the experiences of colonialism, famine, and the displacement of his homeland, Ireland, to those of contemporary Africa. Typical of his views is the following excerpt from an interview he gave to Michka Assayas:

> Two hundred years ago, it appears that very little difference existed in living standards between the Northern Hemisphere and the Southern Hemisphere. Today, a very wide income gap exists: the North is many times richer than the South. What brought this gap? The answer seems to lie in colonialism, trade, debt. The reason ... is largely to do with us, and our exploitation of unfair trading agreements, or old debts. You can't fix every problem. But the ones we can, you must.
>
> *(quoted in Cooper 2008b: 258)*

Arguably, Bono has been a more effective diplomat than Geldof, whose opinionated views have sometimes rubbed people the wrong way. Bono is charming and versatile, adept at talking about scripture as much as colonialism, and conversing as much with such arch-conservatives as Jesse Helms and Pat Robertson as with liberals such as Clinton, Mandela, or Tutu (cf. Cooper 2008b). But while ready to compromise, he is no push-over: he has not hesitated to chide allies such as former Canadian Prime Minister Paul Martin for not living up to aid commitments, and in 2007, when Martin's successor, Stephen Harper, said he was too busy to meet Bono at the G8 summit, the latter only had to publicly chide Harper for the lagging Canadian record on African aid before a meeting was hurriedly organized (Rachman 2007).

If Bono and Geldof are quite business-like in their approach to global activism, Jolie and Madonna appear more empathetic and 'caring', although no less business- and media-savvy, in theirs. Jolie contributes significant personal time to her humanitarian causes, and often portrays herself as a 'witness' to disasters, conflicts, and other people's suffering. She reportedly became interested in development issues while filming in Cambodia in 2000. Since then, she has carried out several missions across the Third World, donating personal money for refugee causes and relief agencies, from Chad to Darfur to Haiti (the Jolie–Pitt Foundation was established in 2006 to continue this charity work). She has put a lot of effort into volunteering for the UN High Commissioner for Refugees, and was named its Goodwill Ambassador in 2001.

Like Geldof and Bono, Jolie has engaged in political lobbying, frequently pressuring members of the US Congress on human rights and refugee issues, speaking at the Davos World Economic Forum (in 2005 and 2006), and becoming a member of the US Council on Foreign Relations in 2007. Like Geldof and Bono, moreover, Jolie has deliberately tried to publicize her humanitarian work. In 2003, she published personal reflections from her field missions, entitled *Notes From My Travels* (Jolie 2003). With a view to reaching out to Western youth, she and economist Jeffrey Sachs agreed to a 2005 MTV documentary focusing on their visit to Kenya (*Diary of Angelina Jolie and Dr. Jeffrey Sachs in Africa*). Over the years, she has also accepted to do several magazine interviews/ articles, speaking about her personal goals and charity work – the 2007 *Marie Claire* article, 'Angelina – from the heart', is a well-known example (Connelly 2007).

But it is perhaps for her role as mother and transnational adoptions advocate that Jolie is best known. As Jo Littler points out, her charity work 'indicates a globalised sensibility and a cosmopolitan caring, an effect augmented by Jolie's high-profile Benetton-style adoption of a range of differently shaded children from a variety of countries' (2008: 238). In addition to her own three biological children (including twins), she has adopted children from Cambodia, Ethiopia, and Vietnam to much sought-out publicity and fanfare. She has given several interviews advocating for transnational adoptions (cf. Davidson 2007), so much so that following her adoption of Zahara from Ethiopia in 2005, there was a reported increase in US adoptions of African children, with one adoption agency spokesperson declaring that 'After Angelina Jolie adopted a kid from Ethiopia, agencies got a spate of calls from parents wanting to know how to adopt a kid from Ethiopia' (quoted in Magubane 2007a: 3; cf. 2007b: 377; ABC News 2005). Similarly, the birth of her and Brad Pitt's daughter in

Namibia in 2006 attracted considerable media attention. In fact, the Namibian government went to great lengths to keep the couple 'secure', banning flights over their residence and, along with the couple's own army of private security personnel, carrying out door-to-door searches to find and expel paparazzi (cf. Barron 2009: 224). Photographs of the baby and interviews were then sold to *People* magazine and *Hello* for millions of dollars (reportedly donated to charity), indicating that the couple was more interested in managing the media and the message than 'security' or privacy. A similar scenario followed the birth of the couple's twins in France in 2008.

Madonna's charity work mirrors Jolie's, although it has been much less extensive, and has focused mainly on Malawi. In 2006, she travelled there to help fund an orphanage. Soon after, she proceeded to successfully adopt a boy, David Banda Mwale, surrounded by much media hype and controversy. There were allegations that she used her celebrity status and personal donation to the orphanage of several million dollars to bypass Malawian adoption laws (adoptive parents are required to be residents for at least a year before adopting) and that the boy could have been better brought up in the country by his biological father. In 2009, she decided to adopt again, this time a girl, Mercy James. While the adoption was initially rejected by a Malawian lower court, it was finally approved by the Supreme Court on the grounds that it was overwhelmingly 'in the child's best interest', despite the residency requirement (cf. Saunders 2007). Since then, Madonna has continued to visit the country for charity tours (often joined by Jeffrey Sachs), funding orphanages and building schools (including the on-again, off-again Raising Malawi Academy for Girls[2]). The media frenzy over her adoptions and orphanage work has continued unabated, and she has often courted it, giving interviews and appearing on talk shows to defend herself and encourage adoption. Not surprisingly, news outlets such as the *Wall Street Journal* have reported that 'international adoptions by Americans have been escalating with stars such as Madonna travelling abroad to adopt' (quoted in Magubane 2007a: 3; cf. 2007b: 377).

We thus live in an age – the 'information age' – in which entertainment stars play a prominent role as 'humanitarians' in world politics. Geldof, Bono, Jolie, and Madonna have achieved notable stature and 'currency' (Singer 2002). They have significant access to the halls of power, and the ability to galvanize publicity on a global scale. Whether as charming diplomat, caring humanitarian, or provocateur, they each have the clout to help fundraise, increase audience awareness, and shape media perceptions on a range of global issues, from famine to transnational adoption. And much more than any mainstream politician or diplomat, they can connect with large and diverse audiences through a variety of media (news, MTV, blogs, Twitter, etc.).

But how are we to assess this new-found power? How are we to speak truth to it, that is, examine what it hides and excludes, for whom or what it speaks, and to what interests it is responding or beholden? These are the questions taken up by the next section.

Ideological underpinnings

To examine the ideological underpinnings of celebrity humanitarianism is, if one is to follow Žižek's advice, to uncover its unconscious. This means detecting its contradictions, exclusions, and imperfections – those it cannot fully avow, yet are in plain view; those it takes for granted or are beyond question; and those that return to haunt it in the form of symptoms, dreams, slips, or gaps. It also means exposing celebrity philanthropy's presentation of itself as pure, ideal, or unified, and the presentation of its flaws as minor, removable, or contingent. Finally, it means extracting the relevant kernels of enjoyment and belief – those irrational and unconditional elements that, according to Žižek, ground and bind ideology. In what follows, I will attempt this excavation by focusing on the self-serving nature of celebrity humanitarianism and its collusion with nationalism, capitalism, and liberal democracy. I will also point out how such self-promotion and collusion instrumentalizes the Third World, and how we, as audience members, are implicated in this ideological nexus.

Self-promotion

> Newly converted to Judaism, the celebrity steals her rabbi's snazzy gold watch.
> She doesn't feel too good about it, so she decides, after a sleepless night, to go to the rabbi.
> 'Rabbi, I stole a gold watch.'
> 'But that's forbidden! You should return it immediately!'
> 'What shall I do?'
> 'Give it back to the owner.'
> 'Do you want it?'
> 'No, I said return it to its owner.'
> 'But he doesn't want it.'
> 'In that case, you can keep it.'

Despite being presented to us (or at least implied) as a selfless and altruistic philanthropic act, celebrity humanitarianism is notably tarnished: it is deeply invested in self-interest and promotion, and in this post-Fordist industrial age, particularly in the creation and marketing of the celebrity 'brand'. Stardom, after all, is manufactured, backed by a massive marketing machine that includes management and talent agencies, entertainment lawyers, and advertising and public relations firms, each often tied to larger corporate media and entertainment interests. The integration of celebrity philanthropy and branding has enabled the creation of a brand-identity (the 'humanitarian celebrity'), with widespread and instant recognition that sells not just a product but also a lifestyle, value, aspiration. Thus, just as Nike is associated not merely with shoes but 'transcendence', Benetton not just with clothing but 'multicultural diversity', and Starbucks not just with coffee but 'community', so stars such as Jolie or Bono are associated not just with entertainment but 'caring', 'compassion', or 'generosity'.

It is for this reason that humanitarian celebrities (and their marketing backers), capitalizing on the apparently insatiable demand for celebrity stories, are keen to solicit media coverage that can show them 'up close', so they can 'confess' to really caring about global poverty, refugees, or orphans. It is also for this reason that they often rely on a slew of philanthropic advisors and 'cause marketing' firms that counsel them on which humanitarian causes are worthy and saleable. One cause marketing company explains its role this way, underlying the exchange value of charity work: 'Cause Marketing is when [you partner] with a worthy cause, usually a … non-profit organization, to raise money for the organization while raising your profile in your community and acquiring new customers' (Negen 2009).

Espousing humanitarian causes allows celebrities to build their brand-image in several ways. It can increase their profile by widening their media exposure and allowing them to remain in the public eye. It is surely no accident, for instance, that the Madonna and Jolie–Pitt adoption stories were repeatedly leveraged in the media; it helped keep them in the news even when there was no CD or movie to promote, while also marketing the image of the multicultural brood as trendy, sexy, or 'good looking' (the fact that Jolie and Pitt are frequently voted the 'most beautiful' and 'sexy' in the world only adds to their brand-mystique).

Charity work aids in humanizing the celebrity, too: it can soften the image of crassly mainstream and commercial entertainers, helping to make them compassionate and sympathetic. As *USA Today* states about Jolie:

> Being an activist provides a patina of class. Speaking to business leaders in Davos, Switzerland at the World Economic Forum, as Jolie does, gives people a new way of looking at you. It's a way to stand out and get attention from other kinds of people who don't read entertainment magazines.
>
> (quoted in Magubane 2007a: 4)

In some instances, philanthropic work can divert attention away from the more embarrassing or lurid elements of celebrities' lives – in the case of Madonna, her serial marriages and affairs, racy videos, or 'material girl' reputation; in the case of Jolie, her 'wild child' past, or her reputation as a marriage-wrecker (i.e. for allegedly having had an affair with Pitt while he was still married); and in the case of Geldof, his foul-mouthed character, or his troubled marriage and child custody battles.[3]

The branding of celebrity humanitarianism also brings significant economic returns, surely the source of deep satisfaction (i.e. ideological *jouissance*) to both the celebrities and the entertainment industry that supports them. First, before even engaging in humanitarian work, there are significant tax benefits to derive from establishing a charitable foundation such as the Jolie–Pitt Foundation (in the US and elsewhere, charitable gifts are tax-exempt for non-profit foundations). Several celebrities (e.g. Tyra Banks, Justin Timberlake) have set up foundations that have higher administrative expenses than the donations they disburse, and some celebrities even lend their name or brand to a foundation (for a fee), while providing no actual financial support of their own (Randall 2008). Next, there are the professional benefits to be drawn from carrying out the actual charity work. Jolie, for example, who can earn some $15 million per film, saw her 'Q score', a Hollywood quotient that measures a star's likeability, almost double between 2000 and 2006, due at least in part to her 'good works' (Swibel 2006: 118). Similarly, Geldof, while not performing at his live charity concerts, has nonetheless profited from them: he has re-released the entire back catalogue of his former band, The Boomtown Rats, and even attempted to resurrect his solo musical career with a British tour (*New Internationalist* 2006). And in 2006, riding high in the pop music charts and from Bono's notoriety as global humanitarian, U2 moved part of its corporate base away from Ireland to the Netherlands after the Irish government ended the tax exemptions that allowed the band to collect royalties tax-free (which angered many in Ireland) (Dieter and Kumar 2008: 263).

But probably the most pertinent example here is that of Live 8. Billed as the 'greatest show ever' in support of global humanitarianism, it was produced, as mentioned earlier, as a massive media event that sloganized and logoized debt and poverty (e.g. the 'Make Poverty History' advertising campaign) and served as a marketing platform for several corporate sponsors (AOL Time Warner, BBC, Nokia). It also provided 'unpaid' artists with wide global exposure, and subsequent rises in music sales. Thus, for example, the HMV and Amazon album sales of Live 8 artists Pink Floyd, The Who, Annie Lennox, Sting/ The Police, and Madonna increased by between 150 percent and 3,600 percent in the week following the concerts (see Table 1.1).[4] By any measure, this was indeed the 'greatest show ever', although not for poverty as much as self-promotion.

Complementing the economic benefits are the symbolic returns. Talking about Live 8 in a *Guardian* interview, Bono declares, for instance, that 'This is

TABLE 1.1 Live 8 stars' album boost

HMV album boost (1 week after Live 8)	Amazon album boost (1 week after Live 8)
1. Pink Floyd – *Echoes: The Best of Pink Floyd* – 1,343%	1. Pink Floyd – *The Wall* – 3,600%
2. The Who – *Then and Now* – 863%	2. Pink Floyd – *Wish You Were Here* – 2,000%
3. Annie Lennox – *Eurythmics Greatest Hits* – 500%	3. Pink Floyd – *Dark Side of the Moon* – 1,400%
4. Dido – *Life for Rent* – 412%	4. The Who – *The Ultimate Collection* – 1,400%
5. Razorlight – *Up All Night* – 335%	5. Pink Floyd – *Animals* – 1,000%
6. Robbie Williams – *Greatest Hits* – 320%	6. Velvet Revolver – *Contraband* – 1,000%
7. Joss Stone – *Mind, Body & Soul* – 309%	7. Robbie Williams – *Greatest Hits* – 800%
8. Sting – *The Very Best of Sting & The Police* – 300%	8. Pink Floyd – *Echoes: The Best of Pink Floyd* – 600%
9. Travis – *Singles* – 268%	9. Razorlight – *Up All Night* – 600%
10. Madonna – *The Immaculate Collection* – 200%	10. The Killers – *Hot Fuss* – 200%
	11. Kaiser Chiefs – *Employment* – 200%
	12. Dido – *Life for Rent* – 200%
	13. Joss Stone – *Mind Body & Soul* – 200%
	14. Scissor Sisters – *Scissor Sisters* – 200%
	15. Madonna – *The Immaculate Collection* – 150%

Sources: HMV (quoted in BBC 2005) and Amazon.co.uk (quoted in BBC 2005).

show business ... Years ago we were very conscious that in order to prevail on Africa, we would get better at dramatising the situation so that we could make Africa less of a burden and more of an adventure' (Bunting 2005). He admits that drawing attention to 'Africa' requires dramatization through show-business-as-adventure; but what he shies away from is that such dramatization often ends up centring the star, not Africa. So when Jolie speaks about Africa (as she often has – for instance in a June 2006 CNN interview with Anderson Cooper), the story ends up being not about Africans, but mostly about her – *her* experiences travelling there, *her* guilt, *her* sympathy: as Nickel and Eikenberry state, 'an uncritical celebration of philanthropy ceases to talk about poverty and instead talks about those who feel bad about poverty' (Nickel and Eikenberry 2009: 982).

Perhaps more poignant here are the instances of celebrities hijacking humanitarian campaigns. George Clooney's 2006 drive to 'save Darfur', for example, was criticized for being ill-advised and overly dramatic about the civil war (cf. Chapter 3). Aided by the likes of Don Cheadle and Mia Farrow, Clooney called for the immediate intervention of UN troops in Darfur, appearing before the UN Security Council and organizing public rallies in the US. While the campaign may have helped increase public awareness about the problem, it sensationalized and misrepresented the conflict (e.g. by overstating mortality rates and using inflated language such as the term 'genocide'), and called for unrealistic remedial measures (e.g. unenforceable no-fly zones over the region, overblown expectations of what UN troops could deliver). Many frontline NGO personnel and policy-makers, including some in the US State Department, believed the campaign ended up unnecessarily inflaming the Sudanese government, undermining slowly cultivated on-the-ground efforts at compromise (de Waal 2008: 45; Haeri 2008: 40, 44; Mamdani 2009).

A similar scenario unfolded as the Gleneagles G8 summit drew to a close, with several NGOs criticizing Geldof for misrepresenting the summit's accomplishments: keen to make the Live 8 pressure on the G8 leaders look fruitful, he boasted to the press about 'mission accomplished', declaring it was 'a great day for Africa', and giving Tony Blair a '10 out of 10' for his leadership and the G8 an '8 out of 10' on debt (*Guardian* 2005). Yet, many NGO leaders who had worked hard on the Make Poverty History campaign were much more critical, with one spokesperson declaring that 'Bob Geldof's comments after the G8 were very unhelpful, because they made people think everything had been achieved' (Dave Timms quoted in Littler 2008: 243; cf. Hague et al. 2008: 6).

Such celebrity urges to sensationalize, declare premature victory, or show moral outrage appear as self-centring strategies aimed at promoting their own brand-image. The unfortunate casualties are the humanitarian causes being espoused, often resulting in drowning out dissenting voices instead of heeding them, simplification instead of considered examination, razzle-dazzle instead of content.

Success, though, may not be the point at all; failure may in fact be fine, as long as the philanthropic effort comes off looking good. Thus, as briefly touched on in the last section, Band Aid/Live Aid raised significant funds for famine relief in Ethiopia, which was marketed as an outward success. Yet, some 1.2 million people still starved to death in the 1984–85 famine (BBC 2006); and the indiscriminate supply of aid may have helped prolong the civil war in 1991, with allegations of some aid being diverted to buy arms and a few aid agencies acting as accomplices to the crimes committed under President Mengistu Haile Mariam (de Waal 2008: 52; BBC 2010a; 2010b).[5] As Alex de Waal states, 'the rush was *to be seen* to deliver food. The public and politicians demanded visible action to salve their consciences. The pressure unleashed by Band Aid debased the currency of humanitarianism … advertising went up and quality went down' (2008: 52; cf. Cooper 2008a: 64).

The same is true of Live 8, which the above NGO criticisms of Geldof were alluding to: while the concerts garnered enormous public and media attention, the development outcomes were dismal (belying Geldof's declaration of 'victory'). The 0.7 percent aid target has not been reached by any G8 country, and may have actually declined in real terms if debt relief is excluded (World Development Movement 2006). The promise to cancel or reduce debt, especially for the poorest countries has not materialized, with only some 10 percent of pledges having been met a year later, much of this coming from already committed bilateral and multilateral aid (Shah 2005; Eurodad 2005: 4; World Development Movement 2006). Furthermore, the G8 commitment to greater trade justice has all but vanished in the face of the European Union's refusal to reduce farm subsidies, which bar agricultural exports from the South. Meanwhile, the G8 leaders, along with Geldof and his celebrity allies, have all emerged as heroes, announcing aid pledges and debt reduction schemes to much fanfare, and successfully spinning the failures as success – proving once again that what really matters is optics and image boost. Some have argued, in fact, that the entire Live 8/Make Poverty History campaign was a losing proposition from the start, because it chose to work with institutions dominated by the rich and powerful states of the North that have a continuing interest in the status quo (Monbiot 2005; Nash 2008: 176–79).

Consequently, although outwardly other-regarding, celebrity charity's first duty is to itself, helping to advance the star's brand-image and accrue spectacular economic benefits. The thrill of being the centre of attention, feeling unique, being handsomely rewarded – in short, the excessive and narcissistic enjoyment – is what binds stars to (the ideology of) humanitarianism, making them its champions and propagators. Their personal 'heroism' is hardly what matters. Backed by the power of corporate entertainment and media, their humanitarianism is choreographed and staged, so that it is not necessarily achievement that is rewarded, but presentation, sexiness, saleability, spin. This is not to say that their charity work is only about marketing and branding: as the cases of Geldof, Bono, Jolie, and Madonna illustrate, stars often do have some knowledge of the issues they espouse, putting in resources, time and effort, and undertaking field missions to gain on-the-ground experience. Michael Goodman puts it this way:

> We, as the audience, need to be convinced to some degree they, as the celebrity, do indeed know what they are talking about in order to be taken somewhat seriously and, thus, the celebritization of development is not just *simply* about marketing-driven photo-shoots designed to up the celebrity's exchange value.
>
> *(2009: 13)*

Yet, it must not be forgotten that their knowledge of development issues (like their public display of 'caring') is not pure or neutral, but motivated and invested; it is anchored in the expectation of generous economic and psycho-symbolic returns.

What is remarkable is that although the self-serving nature of celebrity charity is in plain view, it is never *fully* revealed or spoken about by the celebrity. And this attempt at covering up the embarrassing truth, at disavowing the dirty underside, is precisely why celebrity humanitarianism is a form of ideology, in the Žižekian sense. Although Jolie's *Notes From My Travels* (2003), for example, is a moving account of her experiences and impressions of the Third World, she makes almost no mention of her celebrity status, referring to herself as 'just an American who wants to learn about Africa', feeling 'stupid and arrogant to think that I know anything about these people and their struggles' (2003: 5, 11). On another occasion, in her 2006 CNN interview on Africa, she discloses only a little more, referring to her wealth as 'stupid income' (quoted in Nickel and Eikenberry 2009: 982). Yet, these attempts at 'anonymizing' herself (Barron 2009: 212, 218), this performance of the authentic and 'ordinary person', appears as little more than a ploy to ingratiate herself with her public, thus once again putting herself at the centre of the story. As Nickel and Eikenberry state, 'The truth is that most of the world does not have the luxury ... to participate in the discourse that is being narrated ... The only way to follow in Jolie's footsteps is to accumulate vast sums of money' (Nickel and Eikenberry 2009: 982).

Most often, when celebrities *do* publicly disclose something about their social privilege, it is in the form of humour and irony. Thus, Coldplay's Chris Martin (husband of Gwyneth Paltrow), appearing as himself in a charity advertisement on the sitcom, *Extras*, parodies the narcissistic celebrity: he'd rather promote his latest album than the charity, and exclaims, 'Can we get on with this? I've got AIDS and Alzheimer's and landmines this afternoon and I wanna get back to *Deal or No Deal*. Plus Gwyneth's making drumsticks' (quoted in Littler 2008: 245). Poking fun at both himself and the hypocrisy of celebrities appears progressive, yet as Žižek would point out, it is a case of 'fetishistic disavowal'. It allows celebrities to express a certain anxiety about their privilege or narcissism, about the contradiction between their dominant social position and the poor people they profess to be fighting for; but they still continue to go about their business. Ironic distance provides the illusion (and enjoyment) of critique, but leaves untouched the fundamental ideological fantasy of humanitarianism (cf. Žižek 1989: 30). The situation is even more dire in this case, since laughing at oneself, appearing honest and vulnerable, is yet another attempt at endearing oneself to the public; it smacks of a certain ideological desperation. As Littler argues, such satire 'entails both greater "debasements" and greater rewards for being a good sport. In other words: the stakes have become higher' (2008: 246).

Promoting the (Western) nation

A distinguishing feature of any nation, according to Žižek, is the way in which it organizes its enjoyment (*jouissance*), through festivals, sports, holidays, myths, and the like. Celebrity philanthropy is a case in point, since it allows Western nations to construct a political community around a heroic figure in the person of the humanitarian celebrity. When Jolie and Madonna donate large sums of money to charities, Geldof is repeatedly considered for the Nobel Peace Prize, or Bono is chosen as *Time* magazine's 2005 'Person of the Year', the nation – in this case, the US, Great Britain, and Ireland – feels and looks good. Celebrity humanitarianism is thus bound up with nationalist/Occidentalist discourse, since it helps produce a generous and benevolent national community or Western identity, building unity and pride. It is no wonder that politicians are keen to knight the likes of Geldof, or that in 2005 Tony Blair and Gordon Brown were eager to position themselves as the champions of the Make Poverty History campaign, promoting Britain as a 'great nation' that stands for cosmopolitan and humanitarian values (Nash 2008: 175). Their euphoria was supported and echoed, in turn, by celebrities such as Coldplay's Chris Martin, who during the same G8/Live 8 spectacle was quoted in the *Mirror* as saying, 'Britain is amazing – it really cares about this stuff [i.e. debt cancellation, more foreign aid, etc.]' (quoted in Nash 2008: 176). Such mutual self-congratulation and gratification is intoxicating, so much so that Western countries may well have become hooked on it, giving new meaning to the term 'aid dependency': as I have suggested elsewhere (Kapoor 2008: 89–90), it is not just that parts of the Third World may have got dependent on humanitarian aid, but also that the First World may be addicted to it because of its potent psycho-symbolic returns.

But several problems ensue. For one, nationalist intoxication is blinding. As underlined in the introductory chapter, enjoyment is irrational and arbitrary, appealing to feeling and passion and sometimes working against our own self-interest, so that we tend to 'enjoy our nation as ourselves' (Žižek 1993: 200; cf. Adorno 1990). It means that people identify with their national myths and heroes without really knowing or understanding them. We feel so proud and ennobled by our national icons (or our national 'Thing' as Lacan/Žižek would have it), it's as if we *do* know them intimately; we are willing, then, to overlook their imperfections, either through blissful ignorance or disavowal. Celebrity humanitarianism thus appears pure, altruistic, courageous, heroic – and it is advertised as such by entertainment stars and Western national leaders alike. What tends to get buried in this mêlée is the careerism and profiteering done in its name.

Another concern is the nationalist/Occidentalist attitude towards the 'outside'. Since enjoyment is what singles out any political community from its Others, the construction of humanitarian icons is a way to make the country unique and recognizable – in the manner of the 'compassionate' nation, for example. Humanitarianism allows the Western nation to gloat vis-à-vis its neighbours and competitors, or lord it over its aid recipients (i.e. the Third

World), a point I will return to later in this chapter. More troubling perhaps is when humanitarianism aligns itself with the nationalist proclivity to identify external threats and enemies. Thus, in an effort to sell the US on more aid to Africa, Bono has had no hesitation in linking aid to US national interests and the 'War on Terror', declaring in an NBC news interview, 'What's in it for America? ... Strategically making friends during a wartime. I think that might be smart. Africa is 40 percent Muslim country [sic]. There's extremists working to take advantage of that situation' (quoted in Magubane 2007a: 5). Such a view fits well with the increasing securitization of US and Western foreign policy, with growing amounts of foreign aid being devoted to fighting terrorism in 'front line states' such as Iraq, Afghanistan, Turkey, Pakistan, Yemen, and Indonesia (Tarnoff and Nowells 2005).

A notable feature of nationalist discourse is its preoccupation with gender, particularly the symbolic importance given to mothering and child-bearing, something Jolie and Madonna's humanitarianism aligns itself with. In fact, the philanthropic causes they have espoused appear stereotypically gendered, equating femininity to motherly caring and transnational adoption (the charity work of Mother Teresa and Princess Diana would also fit the bill here; cf. Rajagopal 1999).[6] Such gendered humanitarianism mirrors idealized nationalist (and Christianized) notions of womanhood, wherein mothers are entrusted with ensuring the stability of home and hearth, and with the preservation and reproduction of family and kinship. (In light of her adoptions, Madonna's erstwhile 'racy' and 'un-Christian' life stands in ironic contrast to her new-found association with the iconic 'Madonna and Child' image.) Indeed, in the US during and after the Cold War, to adopt a child was to serve the nation and its national security/foreign policy priorities, especially in the aftermath of the Korean and Vietnam wars (cf. Eng 2003). Madonna and Jolie may thus be said to be continuing this US national tradition: their transnational adoptions aid the nation by encouraging others to adopt, while also constructing themselves (and other adoptive parents) as saviours of orphaned Third World children. To echo Gayatri Spivak (1988), it's another case of white (wo)men saving coloured babies from coloured (wo)men, in the service of the nation.

The celebrity preoccupation with children acts as an equally conservative and imperializing force on the nation. Just as it does for motherhood, the nation invests a lot in the notion of childhood, which is constructed as innocent and pure, a symbol of the very future of the land. Such symbolism takes on added significance in the West today, with declining birth rates and the environmental crisis seen as threatening our future. Transnational adoption helps assuage this apocalyptic vision, while making the family a key socionational building block. As David Eng points out, the adoptee is used to perform 'a type of crucial ideological labour: the shoring up of an idealized notion of kinship,

[and] the making good of the [mostly] white heterosexual family' (2003: 11). In order to rationalize adoption, the child adoptee is typically portrayed as an innocent victim of a crisis (i.e. war, displacement, starvation, infanticide), dependent and helpless; hence the need for its rescue. Not surprisingly, investing the child with rescue fantasies and feelings of redemption/guilt ends up centring the adoptive Western parent as responsible guide and saviour (especially in relation to the 'absent' and 'irresponsible' Third World parent), while once again instrumentalizing the child.

But in addition to being a symbolic support, Madonna and Jolie are also a material support to the (Western) nation: their example as transnational adoptive parents helps address critical bottlenecks in Western country demographics and labour markets. Declining birth rates (themselves the result of such factors as improved health, or the increasing presence of women in the workplace), and the rising labour requirements of ever-expanding economies – all translate into the need for greater immigration and adoption. In this regard, Western governments have been quick to encourage international adoptions, many of them providing tax incentives. In the US, for example, adoptive parents can claim up to $10,000 in tax credits (cf. Saunders 2007: 8; Eng 2003: 10). As a result, some 50,000 transnational adoptions happen globally every year, most in the US and Europe (Saunders 2007: 2). Such a phenomenon has become big business globally (so much so that one of its nefarious by-products is child trafficking), correlating with similar other contemporary global phenomena such as mail order brides, domestic servants, and illegal immigrants.

Reflecting these structural dynamics, adoptive parents in the West have come to see parenthood as an 'economic entitlement and legal right' (Eng 2003: 8). Subject to eligibility, many adoption agencies allow them to shop and colour-coordinate their adoptions by paying differential rates depending on the choice of race/colour and health/disability. Yet, far from yielding a multicultural brood (à la Madonna and Jolie–Pitt), their selections have been gendered (most adoptees tend to be girls) and highly racialized. In the US, for example, the first main wave of adoptions was Asian children, in the aftermath of the Korean and Vietnam wars. But after the collapse of the Soviet Bloc, there was a significant rise in adoptions from such countries as Romania and Russia, with a corresponding decline in adoptions from Asia: 'as soon as white children were available, prospective international adopters opted for race over all other considerations' (Gailey 2000: 5).

There also appears to be a marked preference for transnational over *domestic* adoptions. In the US and Canada, black and aboriginal children are over-represented in the welfare system,[7] yet most adoptive parents favour adopting from abroad. As Ortiz and Briggs suggest (2003: 40, 181; cf. Waldinger and Lichter 2009), this is due partly to the pathologizing of black and aboriginal 'welfare mothers' and 'crack babies'; partly to rescue fantasies and the sentiment that foreign babies can be more easily transplanted and moulded to suit the new nation/home; and partly to the more complex legal environments in the West that make it more difficult to adopt at home (i.e. more strict eligibility criteria, the risk of custody battles). The consequence is a racialized discursive practice on transnational adoption.

Aided and abetted by celebrity humanitarianism, transnational adoption is therefore nothing short of neocolonial. When privileged white Western parents deracinate Third World children, deprive a country of significant social/intellectual life-potential, select the most 'desirable' children (based on race, health, ability), all the while failing to address the root causes (inequality, social strife, high birth rates), we have relations of domination and dependency.[8] It is for this reason that critics such as Twila Perry have argued that 'rather than transferring the children of the poor to economically better-off people in other countries, there should be a transfer of wealth from rich countries to poor ones to enable the mothers of poor children to continue to take care of their children themselves' (quoted in Eng 2003: 10). True, Madonna and Jolie *are* doing some of this, by funding orphanages in Ethiopia and Malawi for instance; but their efforts address individual and personal humanitarian causes, rather than broader structural problems.

Celebrity humanitarianism is thus at the service of the (Western) nation. It helps construct the image of national beneficence, singling out the nation as unique, while also setting it apart from its Others. It aids in strengthening nationalist/Occidentalist and racialized discourses on mothering and childhood. And in the form of transnational adoption, it facilitates the West's economic/labour agenda, organizing the nuclear family 'as a supplement to capital' (Eng 2003: 12), often at the expense of the Third World. Hence, celebrity humanitarianism is blighted by its collusion with the nation … and capital.

Promoting capitalism

Celebrities' involvement with capital has already been alluded to above, but I want to develop the point further in this section. I will argue that celebrity humanitarianism isn't just entrenched in capitalism, but actually promotes it, thereby rationalizing the very 'poverty' that such humanitarianism seeks to rectify. And if this rationalization is ideological in the Žižekian sense, so is the anti-poverty agenda that lies at the heart of celebrities' global charity work.

Celebrities are already tied to the corporate world through their professional work (commercial film and TV, music industry, sports corporate sponsorships, PR and marketing firms, etc.), earning some of the highest incomes globally, as reported by the likes of *Forbes* magazine (2011), for example. They also profit tremendously from their brand-image, a point I underlined earlier. In the movie industry, whereas stars used to be tied exclusively to the studios, they now legally own their own image or 'publicity rights', which function like a trademark or copyright (Drake 2008). This means they have a monopoly over their brand-image and can control who profits from it, including the studios when the latter do movie promotions or DVD releases. Philip Drake puts it this way:

> the political economy of celebrity is one that firmly favors the rights of celebrities over their fans. Celebrities propertize themselves by drawing upon a discourse of achievement associated with traditional notions of the hero, in order to exclusively claim the intellectual property of their images, extending a former privacy right (available to all) to a property right (the right of publicity, available only to the famous).
>
> *(2008: 450)*

It is these exclusive intellectual property rights that enable celebrities to take advantage of corporate product endorsements, lending their name and image to a corporate brand for a fee that can amount to several million dollars (Stephen Adair calls this 'excessively valorized labour'; cf. 2010: 243). Table 1.2 illustrates the extent of such endorsements, focusing particularly on humanitarian

TABLE 1.2 Product endorsements by humanitarian celebrities (illustrative list)

Humanitarian celebrity	Product endorsement
Ben Affleck	Axe, Burger King, Alpro, Morellato
David Beckham	Coty, Giorgio Armani, Motorola
Bono/U2	BlackBerry, Apple iTunes, Skol, Louis Vuitton
George Clooney	Toyota, Nestlé, Martini, Fiat, Emidio Tucci
Bill Cosby	Jell-O, Kodak
Leonardo DiCaprio	Orico, Suzuki, Honda, Marc Jacobs, Tag Heuer, Bubble Yum
Michael J. Fox	Pepsi-Cola, Shimano, Kirin, Lipton
Bob Geldof	Kleenex, Telstra, Wilkinson Sword
Richard Gere	JAL, Dandy House, VISA
Bob Hope	American Express
Jay-Z	Rocawear, Hewlett Packard, Budweiser, Chevy, Armadale Vodka
Scarlett Johansson	Calvin Klein, Estée Lauder, Louis Vuitton, L'Oréal, Mango
Elton John	Coke, VISA, Verizon, Cadbury's, Orange
Angelina Jolie	St. John Knits, Shiseido, Arnette, Louis Vuitton
Madonna	Pepsi-Cola, Mitsubishi, The Gap, Versace, Panasonic, H&M, Shochu
Paul Newman	Lux, Fujicard
Gwyneth Paltrow	Tod's, Estée Lauder, Bean Pole
Brad Pitt	Rolex, Honda, Levi's, Heineken, Edwin Jeans, Roots Coffee, SoftBank, Tag Heuer, Pringles
Sharon Stone	Christian Dior, Vernal, Badgley Mischka
Sting	Jaguar

Sources: Google and YouTube searches, Creswell 2008.

celebrities, including Geldof, Bono, Jolie, and Madonna. It is telling that several stars (e.g. Clooney, DiCaprio, Pitt) do product advertising abroad, especially in Japan, presumably so that such crass commercialism does not taint their image back home. I was not able to locate data on the corporate profits derived from product placements made specifically by some of these celebrities, but the following information gives us a sense: Michael Jordan is estimated to have contributed about $10 billion to the US economy through his many endorsements (Nike, Coke, McDonald's, etc.) during his fourteen-year NBA career in the 1980s and 1990s; and PepsiCo attributed a 1 percent rise in its market share (worth several million dollars) to its Spice Girls endorsements in the late 1990s (Erdogan et al. 2001: 39).

Of course, some humanitarian celebrities are entrepreneurs in their own right. Bono, for instance, owns a luxury hotel and is the managing director and co-founder of Elevation Partners, a private equity firm with some $1.9 billion of capital invested in intellectual property and media, including shares in the conservative business publishing conglomerate, Forbes (Dieter and Kumar 2008: 262–63). Jay-Z owns and manages a billion dollar empire, including an urban clothing brand (Rocawear), a stake in a beauty products franchise (Carol's Daughter), a global investment firm (Gain Global Investment), luxury hotels, and real estate (Curan 2010). For his part, Geldof co-owns a TV production company (Planet 24) and a media/publishing firm (Ten Alps).

Significantly, humanitarian celebrities bring their business acumen and experience to their charity causes. Already in 1985, when organizing Live Aid, Geldof saw himself more as entrepreneur and fundraiser than entertainer, emphasizing the commercial and media, rather than the artistic, aspects of the event. He is even reported to have declared, 'the more multimillion record selling acts the better' (quoted in Hague et al. 2008: 10). As Hague et al. argue, '[h]is role was not that of the perceptive artist shaping popular sensibility, but rather of enterprising entrepreneur staging events to raise cash. He was branding and marketing a cause' (2008: 10).

The same commercial branding was visible ten years later during Live 8, with its logoization of poverty ('Make Poverty History') and its corporate sponsorships (outlined earlier). Describing his and Geldof's role in that event, Bono affirms, 'we're adventure capitalists' (quoted in Bunting 2005). And in a *New York Times* article, entitled, 'Citizen Bono Brings Africa to the Idle Rich', he goes further, advertising Africa as a business opportunity in the manner of an agent of capital:

> One of the things I have learned of in Africa is the crucial role that commerce will play in taking its people out of extreme poverty. Everyone talks about China being the next big thing, but if you spend any time in bars or hotels in Africa, you see a lot of Chinese doing deals

there. There is tremendous opportunity there ... Africa is sexy and people need to know that.

(Carr 2007; cf. Magubane 2007a)

Not only are humanitarian celebrities deeply immersed in capitalism, but their charity work is entangled with it and unquestioningly promotes it. Yet, what they fail to realize (or admit) is that it is this very capitalism that is so often the root cause of the inequality they seek to address through their humanitarianism. The historical development of global capitalism has produced abundance alongside deprivation, and capital dispersal and concentration alongside inequity and unevenness (cf. Wallerstein 1974, 1980, 1989, 2004; Harvey 2006). In its latest 'neoliberal' phase (mid-1980s onwards), supported by market and trade liberalization regimes, capitalism's unquenchable thirst for surplus value and new markets has meant the super-exploitation of labour reserves (e.g. sweatshops, primarily composed of women), depriving many social groups from adequate access to socioeconomic and environmental resources, particularly in the Third World. We are witnessing today the continued growth of an underclass, which as Žižek states, is excluded 'sometimes even for generations, from the benefits of ... society ... Today's "exceptions" (the homeless, the ghettoized, the permanent unemployed) are the symptom of the late-capitalist universal system, the permanent reminder of how the immanent logic of late capitalism works' (1997: 127).

This increasing global socioeconomic marginalization is reflected in readily available statistics. The UNDP (1999: 3), for instance, has published historical estimates of the income gap between the fifth of the world's population living in the wealthiest countries and the fifth in the poorest, showing the following ratios: in 1820: 3 to 1; 1870: 7 to 1; 1913: 11 to 1; 1960: 30 to 1; 1990: 60 to 1; 1997: 74 to 1. That such inequality has intensified in some parts of the Third World since the onset of neoliberal globalization is further evidenced by the fact that, in Sub-Saharan Africa, the majority of the population is poorer now in absolute terms than it was thirty years ago (Kiely 2000: 1064).

It is important to note that several of the multinational corporate firms that humanitarian celebrities are associated with have contributed directly to social marginalization and exploitation. Of the firms listed in Table 1.2 above, for instance, a few are worthy of mention: Nestlé is famous for its baby formula fiasco in the 1970s–1980s, but is also reputed as one of the worst violators of labour rights, ranging from its use of child and forced labour on cocoa farms in West Africa to its worker mistreatment and union busting in Colombia (Curtin 2005: 164); Coca-Cola also has a questionable labour record in several countries (including Colombia), and has contributed to global water depletion (e.g. in India) through its over-use of ground-water and its drive towards water privatization (Killercoke 2010); and finally, Gap is well known to have sold items produced in sweatshops (e.g. in Cambodia, India) (DeWinter 2001). To add insult to injury, Jeffrey Sachs ('development advisor to the stars'), rather than being critical of certain corporate labour practices in the Third World, has defended them, declaring in the *New York Times* that '[m]y concern is not that there are too many sweatshops but that there are too few' (Myerson 1997).

Therefore, humanitarian celebrities tend to be ideologues, sustaining and upholding capitalism even as it causes inequality and unevenness. Andrew Cooper, writing approvingly about the strengths of 'celebrity diplomats' in publicizing issues of debt and poverty, affirms that they are 'filling gaps of neglect' (2008b: 271); my Žižekian response is to say: 'yes, and that is precisely the problem'. In that they help capitalism fill its gaps and disavow its social antagonisms, they are apologists for the system. Celebrity charity work is ideological work: it not only masks the causes of inequality, but handsomely profits from this deception, too. The very emergence of celebrities as diplomats on the world stage is tied to the development of late capitalism (cf. Introduction), which promotes individual initiative and philanthropy as a panacea for structural problems.

The humanitarianism of celebrities proceeds as though equality/justice can be achieved without confronting power, including their own. Such depoliticization is the strategic function of any ideology – to resolve, contain, and manage trauma, and where required, to soothe and comfort, so as to avert or disavow social antagonisms (i.e. the Real). As noted earlier, very rarely do celebrities implicate their own privilege and authority in their work, and if they do, it is in the form of irony or liberal guilt. Referring to Jolie, Nickel and Eikenberry write that her 'story [of humanitarianism] is fiction ... because she has not actually challenged the power dynamics that made her story possible in the first place' (2009: 983). Moreover, almost never do celebrities challenge capital; at most, Bono and Geldof will decry Third World debt, but they refrain from criticizing the IMF or other banking capital that underwrites it.[9] Ostensibly, this is because they are leery of alienating their audiences, but mostly it is because they have little incentive in confronting the corporate power they so profit from. Yet, it is this depoliticization of capital that causes its presence to be unspoken and invisible.

Enjoyment (*jouissance*) has much to do with why capital is left unspoken. Capitalism relies on the production of excess, and the glamorous lives and brand-image of celebrities are one of its best advertisements. No wonder that stars such as Madonna or Elton John are so often equated with lavishness, hedonism, hyperindividualism, hyper-consumerism. In turn, celebrities' defence and promotion of capital is the result of their excessive enjoyment of it. Even their charity work is sustained by such enjoyment (or the eternal promise of it) in the form of material and symbolic returns, as discussed earlier. Humanitarianism, in this sense, is the gift that keeps on giving *back*, blinding capital's production of inequality.

But perhaps humanitarian celebrities are not quite so blinded: given the pleasure/pain dimension of the Žižekian notion of *jouissance*, perhaps they are sadists, secretly enjoying, not just the excessive pleasures of capital, but also the pain and degradation that capitalism inflicts on the Other. Despite public expressions of guilt, perhaps they derive obscene satisfaction and fascination from the global system of inequality which places *them* as the dominant. Perhaps they get off on humanitarianism's ideological deceptions, cover-ups, and disavowals.

I think there is something transgressive about *jouissance* that needs to be reckoned with here. People can derive pleasure from pain, for example in seeing one's neighbour or competitor fail or stumble; yet such an indiscretion must remain publicly unacknowledged and unutterable. In regard to humanitarian celebrities, I cannot help but wonder about their outwardly compassionate yet potently voyeuristic/sadistic gaze on the Third World: the eagerness with which they will go on 'missions' to 'witness' the plight of refugees or the suffering of HIV/AIDS patients, for example, all the while occupying the dominant position; or the lengths that their fundraising activities will take in dramatizing the victimhood of, say, famine casualties in the form of emaciated bodies and swollen heads. The suffering Third World functions as fetish, to which the celebrity (and the sensationalist media) become disproportionately attached, perversely enjoying her/his assertive and privileged relationship to it.

If celebrity humanitarianism is deeply ideological, so is the anti-poverty agenda that it so readily espouses. Indeed, the Live 8/Make Poverty History campaign championed by Bono and Geldof was an explicitly anti-poverty, not an anti-capitalist or anti-globalization, campaign – it took for granted that current global governance structures can help end poverty (Nash 2008: 169). Yet, the very concept of 'poverty' covers up the inequality wrought by capitalism. It tends to assume being poor is a question of unfortunate circumstances or inappropriate cultural characteristics. By so isolating poverty, it mystifies the close relationship between surplus extraction and impoverishment, wherein wealth in some parts of the world (i.e. the affluent centres of the North and South) is the historical result of the pauperization of others. In this regard, Issa Shivji is right to ask, 'how can you make poverty history without understanding the "history of poverty"?' (2006: 43). The mainstream discourse of poverty dehistoricizes by privileging the 'now' of poverty, eliding the West's (neo)colonial immiseration of the Third World.

This poverty discourse deploys several ideological strategies worthy of note. The first is indeed the attempt to individualize and isolate problems. In the case of celebrities, this is evident in their tendency to focus on issues near and dear to their hearts (and brand-images) such as famine or adoption, without adequate attention to the relevant structural causes, as discussed earlier. Most often, the problems are displaced by blaming them on particular individuals or values – rogue civil servants, corrupt leaders (one of Jeffrey Sachs's favourite themes; cf. Sachs 2005b), uneducated or irresponsible mothers, 'ethnic' or 'traditional' practices – so that the solution becomes the need for better (i.e. modern, Western-style) leadership, norms, and codes of conduct. The Westernized capitalist system is taken as a given, with people/institutions having to adapt to *it*.

A distinct moral tone pervades this discourse. Celebrities mete out a 'politics of pity' that portrays poverty as an issue of unfortunate circumstances and chance (Boltanski 1999), while their 'expert' policy advisors (e.g. Sachs) stand as arbiters of the 'right' values of governance. Both celebrity and 'expert' are thus positioned as unique and heroic: Michael Goodman writes in this regard that

> wider structural cultural and social problems are forcefully refracted through the neo-liberal lens of the 'heroic individual' taking responsibility off the shoulder of, in the case of development, international financial institutions, states, and the economic structures of inequality more generally.
>
> *(2009: 13)*

The tendency is to focus on 'visible' and soundbite-friendly problems – sick children, weeping mothers, derelict housing – sidelining the often complex and not immediately perceptible structural inequality and domination that have often caused them (cf. Chapter 3). Thus, Žižek asks,

> [i]s there not something suspicious, indeed symptomatic, about this focus on [visible and] subjective violence … Doesn't it desperately try to distract our attention away from the true locus of trouble, by obliterating from view other forms of violence and thus actively participating in them?
>
> *(2008a: 10–11)*

A second ideological strategy of the celebrity anti-poverty agenda is that of 'distancing'. As Nickel and Eikenberry note, 'celebrity philanthropy is an uncritical celebration of celebrities and their production of an elite society that can only be philanthropic by virtue of its ability to distance itself from poverty' (2009: 981). The celebrity's humanitarianism is a form of evasion, since it focuses attention on the Third World, while avoiding the material complicity of the star – how her/his privilege might contribute to the spaces where suffering takes place (Littler 2008: 248). But this discourse on poverty is also a way of keeping the 'poor' at bay. Aid and charity provide just enough to cater to the worst manifestations of poverty so that not too many poor people try to escape it. Meanwhile, the West's socioeconomic comforts are protected through the enforcement of immigration walls (real walls in the form of concrete barriers, and legal walls in the form of immigration laws and crackdowns) to keep out Third World migrants. Under capitalism, 'it is "things" (commodities) which freely circulate, while the circulation of "persons" is more and more controlled' (Žižek 2008a: 102).

A final ideological strategy is (once again) depoliticization. As we have seen, celebrities tend to champion 'safe' and marketable topics, shying away from anything too politically controversial. Usually, this means that they focus on 'symptoms rather than core problems, providing, for example, tools for illiteracy rather than addressing the problem of core funding in schools or economic equality' (Littler 2008: 243). Moreover, despite the ineffectual G8 record, the celebrities' favourite topics – 'debt' and 'aid' – could be accomplished through (perhaps politically difficult but not insurmountable) financial measures. In contrast, WTO reform or transnational regulation of multinationals stand as much greater political hot potatoes, threatening corporate power, Western farmers, and economic growth (cf. Nash 2008: 178). Small wonder that the latter issues are rarely if ever broached by celebrities.

But the fundamentally depoliticizing move here is that, by trying to cure the symptom rather than the cause, the discourse on poverty ends up prolonging poverty. The remedy itself becomes part of the problem because, rather than making inequality impossible, it merely tries to keep poor people alive, by enabling them to survive (cf. Žižek 2009a). By framing the problem through the depoliticized lens of poverty, it strives to bracket out the notion that inequality is unjust. And perhaps fearful that poor communities might revolt, it suspends such emancipatory human passions as envy, hostility, and rage. Thus, Žižek (2009a), drawing on Oscar Wilde, argues that the worst slave owners were those who were 'kind', because they ended up rationalizing slavery under the pretence of their enlightened goodness, but in so doing they may have prevented the politicization of the slaves and prolonged the very institution of slavery.

Promoting a 'postdemocratic' order

The rise of humanitarian celebrities is emblematic of what Žižek and Jacques Rancière have termed a 'postpolitical' or 'postdemocratic' order. The terms describe our current capitalist liberal democratic landscape, in which 'all parties are known and … everything is on show, in which parties are counted with none left over and … everything can be solved by objectifying problems' (Rancière 1998: 102). This is a world where all is ordered and given a place (Rancière 1994: 173). Democracy is reduced to periodic elections, and people choose between mostly politically indistinguishable parties and platforms.

The liberal democratic regime is accepted as given without any fundamental re-thinking or critique, so that political change actually means the status quo. Politics becomes what Žižek calls 'the art of the possible' (1999a: 199).

The postdemocratic state is a managerialist one: technocrats, expert policy-makers (polling specialists, economists, scientists), and corporate oligarchs interpret people's demands and translate them into practical policy decisions. 'Good governance' replaces politics through the use of expert analysis and 'enlightened' policy-making. The phenomenon is particularly acute in supra-national bodies such as the WTO, IMF, UN, or World Bank, where administrators and legal experts, who claim to be doing what's best for everyone, can override national sovereignty and decide what member states should do, or can be used by the member states themselves to get around the will of the people to achieve the government's desired policy priorities (Rancière 2006: 81–82).

Politics, in this state of affairs, is really the lack of it, with disagreement and dissent foreclosed. Enemies, outsiders, 'fundamentalists', and radicals are vilified, and state power is used with impunity to neutralize them by resorting to the declaration of emergencies and the suspension of the rule of law, which subsequently becomes the norm (i.e. what Agamben calls the 'state of exception'). With dissension and conflict defused, political regimes can afford to engage in 'consensus building', outwardly including and valuing 'all' points of view. For Rancière, such consensual politics is the hallmark of the postdemocratic order:

> Consensus refers to that which is censored ... there is no contest on what appears, on what is given in a situation and as a situation. Consensus means that the only point of contest lies on what has to be done as a response to a given situation ... Consensus is the dismissal of politics as a polemical configuration of the common world.
>
> *(2003: paragraphs 4–6)*

Consensual politics is mediated not through party politics as much as the corporatized and technocratic state managers. As a result, the state becomes a kind of 'police agent servicing the (consensually established) needs of market forces and multiculturalist tolerant humanitarianism' (Žižek 2006b: 72; cf. 1999a: 198). Indeed, neoliberalism and multiculturalism are the order of the day: the former enables late global capitalism to proceed without disruption or upheaval; and so does the latter – it accedes to the individualized cultural demands of various groups, but is careful to prevent the universalization of any emancipatory or economic claims so as not to obstruct the smooth circulation of capital (cf. Žižek 2006c: 151ff.).

Humanitarian celebrities strengthen, and fit well into, this postdemocratic order. Advised by managerial experts such as economist Jeffrey Sachs, they have become, as emphasized earlier, the pundits of global altruism and a 'go-to' on global policy questions ranging from debt and HIV/AIDS to adoption and famine. They command exclusive access to the global corridors of power, with the ability to influence G8 leaders, US Congressional representatives, captains of industry, or senior policy-makers from the World Bank or IMF. In their capacity as 'celebrity diplomats' they serve as a support to the work of state technocrats, purporting to represent popular consensus and dispensing 'enlightened' policy.

The legitimation of celebrities as policy-makers can be seen, for example, in Live 8, which was framed as though Bono and Geldof (along with the G8 leaders) were the exclusive representatives and change agents of such causes as debt and poverty, in spite of the fact that the Make Poverty History campaign was primarily an NGO effort. It can also be seen in the Sharon Stone incident at the Davos World Economic Forum in 2005: after the Tanzanian President had expressed the need for mosquito nets because people were reportedly dying from malaria, Stone rose up and pledged $10,000, challenging other business and political leaders in the audience to match her pledge. Over $1 million was eventually pledged, but only a portion was actually honoured, with the UN having to step in to make up the difference (Littler 2008: 242–43). As a result, several observers questioned Stone and other celebrities' legitimacy and credibility as policy-makers, asking how they can determine on what the likes of the UN should be spending its limited resources. The issue, as Littler explains, is that 'the power of celebrity can pull aid towards a particular cause that appeals to them and away from others' (2008: 243).

The Stone incident is characteristic of the elite political landscape of post-democracy. In this age of neoliberalism and widespread belief in the merit-rewarding society, it underlines the heroization and 'hyperindividualisation' of humanitarian celebrities (Littler 2008: 246). Backed by powerful interests (corporate, nationalist), celebrities are positioned to act as political brokers and decision-makers, and feel entitled to do so under the guise of well-intentioned altruism, despite their lack of accountability. As Hague et al. argue, '[t]he logic of ... [celebrity humanitarianism] echoes post-democracy in that, despite the rhetoric of populism, it is elite-focused. The emphasis ultimately is not on mass public action but on elite action' (2008: 19). Meanwhile, as audience members, we become the means by which celebrity charity work is legitimated, acting as witnesses to such celebrity media events as Live 8. Politics thus becomes mediated spectacle, with citizens transformed into fans, consumers, and bystanders.

Using and abusing Africa/the Third World

I have already underlined how celebrities act as direct or indirect agents of capital. Whether through their professional work (in music, film, sports), product endorsements, or personal business ventures, they help extend global corporate power to the Third World. In reference to the film industry, Lee Barron points out that

> studios do not merely transmit film product to the 'South' ... but also use Southern countries to make their films. For example, Jolie's *Tomb Raider* ... which was shot at the Angkor Wat temple in Cambodia, opened up the country to numerous subsequent productions that took advantage of the lower costs of filming there.
>
> *(2009: 223)*

But such economic imperialism is complemented and supported by cultural imperialism, with the Third World being used by celebrities as both cultural backdrop and dumping ground. Despite best intentions, celebrity visits to the South on observer or philanthropic missions are most often self-promoting and voyeuristic endeavours: as journalists look on and cameras roll, the spectacle of smiling/suffering children or thankful/crying mothers serves as an excuse to showcase the celebrity's do-gooding. Africa, in particular, is constructed as desperately in need (of philanthropy). With the celebrity as the audience's guide, the 'dark continent' becomes a museum or tourist attraction and, to recall Bono's earlier-quoted remark, 'less of a burden and more of an adventure'. Sometimes, such instrumentalization is plainly crass. For example, Madonna has used images of AIDS-stricken African children as a backdrop for her concert performances. Commenting on such a practice, *The New York Times* opines that she 'has always known how to spot a trend. And much as it may strain the limits of good taste to say it, Africa – rife with disease, famine, poverty, and civil war – is suddenly "hot"' (Williams 2006; cf. Magubane 2007b: 376–77; 2007a).

If the Third World serves as a background for the purposes of instrumentalization and appropriation, it also acts as a dumping ground for a range of First World fantasies. There are, to begin, the rescue fantasies we touched on earlier, which construct the West as dominant and Africa, in particular, as an aberrant space – a construction which conveniently mobilizes a rationale for external intervention (in the form of charity, aid, adoption, guidance, etc.). These celebrity fantasies are not much different from the colonial 'white man's burden' or the missionary visions of salvation of yesteryear; indeed, they may even be tinged with a Christianized message of deliverance, as witnessed by Geldof's famine relief song, 'Do They Know It's Christmas?'.

There are also the strong celebrity tendencies to romanticize the Third World. In her travel writings, for example, Jolie declares she is in 'awe of these [African] people' and proclaims she 'loves' her very simple and basic travel lodgings (2003: 37). Similarly, in his 2005 BBC TV series, Geldof pronounces

Africa to be 'quite simply the most extraordinary, beautiful and luminous place on our planet', and depicts 'Africans' as having a 'captivating grace of elegance and gesture' (2005). Yet, while outwardly sympathetic, such romanticized and aestheticized fantasies about the Other mask a colonizing gaze: they aim, first and foremost, at consolidating the Self by ingratiating the celebrity to the audience and rationalizing her/his humanitarianism. They also aim at managing the Other, by exoticizing it and, where necessary, passing judgement on it to put it in its place. Thus, even as she strives to come across as empathetic to Africa and Africans, Jolie records her indignation towards the use of the bur-quah (2003: 164), saying that it allows for 'no individuality ... I bought one and tried it on. I felt like I was in a cage. They are horrible' (2003: 220; cf. Barron 2009: 221). Likewise, having pronounced Africa to be a 'luminous place', Geldof feels entitled to proffer a slew of orientalist characterizations such as 'conflict bedevils Africa' or Kinshasa is the 'capital of chaos' (2005). Žižek calls such posturing a thinly disguised racism that parades as 'multiculturalism': privileged, deracinated Westerners declare their respect for other cultures, yet maintain a definite distance – a racism with a distance – by proclaiming them to be strange and exotic. One 'retains this position as the privileged *empty point of universality* from which one is able to appreciate (or depreciate) other particular cultures properly – multiculturalist respect for the Other's specificity is the very form of asserting one's own superiority' (Žižek 1999a: 216).

Therefore, just as the Third World already serves as a dumping ground for hazardous materials and e-waste, or for dangerous products such as milk substitutes and contraceptive implants, so it serves as a disposal site for self-promoting and colonizing fantasies that cover up or disavow the celebrity's power and privilege (cf. Kapoor 2008: 65–66, 72). First World humanitarian celebrities, in this sense, need the Third World, since it serves as a receptacle through which they can organize their enjoyment.

The problem, however, is that in this process, the Third World is rendered silent. As self-declared global representatives of famine victims, poor people, orphaned children and the like, the stars end up speaking *for* the Third World subaltern. Thus, Jolie has no compunction about going on CNN to comment on 'Africa' in an hour-long program in which not a single member of the African public is heard. In her 2006 interview with Anderson Cooper, she states that the 'borders were drawn in Africa not that long ago. These people are tribal people. We ... colonized them. There's a lot we need to ... under-stand and be tolerant of, and help them to do. They have just recently learned to govern themselves' (quoted in Magubane 2007a: 6). And such orientalist constructions are reproduced time and again by the likes of Geldof as well: his 1985 Live Aid fundraising concerts displayed images of the Ethiopian famine as a backdrop. As Jenny Edkins notes, the images showed the people caught up in the famine only as victims. No African aid workers were shown, only white Europeans, giving the impression that the West was coming to the rescue of incompetent Africans. People were not allowed to speak for themselves — the voice-over of a commentator replaced interviews.

(2000: 109)

A similar pattern ensues in *Geldof in Africa*, which aired on TV some years later. Geldof is present in almost every frame, either visually or verbally through his (paternalistic) voiceover commentary, opining about poverty and conflict, or how the 'Maasai are an extraordinarily successful people' (Geldof 2005). Yet once again, very few Africans are actually interviewed, and when they are it is mostly cute children, or quaint or 'exotic' hunter-gatherers and village elders. Missing in this idealized and sentimentalized account are any contemporary urban people, as though the whole of Africa is stuck in some ancient rural backwater.

Even charity advertising campaigns, presumably advocating for the Third World subaltern, can easily fall prey to such orientalist and disempowering tactics. For example, in a 2006 *Harper's Bazaar* issue, an ad for Keep A Child Alive, an NGO devoted to helping HIV/AIDS-affected children and families, has Gwyneth Paltrow dressed with face paint and an African-style bead necklace, declaring 'I am African'.[10] The campaign recalls the minstrel blackface phenomenon in nineteenth-century US and Britain, with all its racist dimensions; and it prompts Hannah Pool, a *Guardian* columnist, to ask: 'what does it say about race today when a quality newspaper [sic] decides that its readers will only relate to Africa through a blacked-up white model rather than a real-life black woman?' (quoted in Magubane 2007a: 3; cf. 2007b: 378).

This exclusion of Africans pervades many of the celebrity-organized charity programs and institutions as well. For instance, most Southern NGOs refused to join the 2005 Make Poverty History campaign because it was so dominated by Geldof and Northern NGOs (Hague et al. 2008: 20). They were not wrong, as it turned out, since the concerts themselves included practically no African musicians, with Geldof justifying his decision by asserting that 'African acts do not sell many records' or have much 'political traction' (quoted in Hague et al. 2008: 16; and Magubane 2007a: 6). Dismayed with such a position, one human rights activist, Kofi Mawuli Klu of the Forum of African Human Rights Defenders, declared that Geldof had 'acted in his own self-interests. It was all about self-promotion, about usurping the place of Africans. His message was "shut up and watch me"' (quoted in Cooper 2008a: 67).[11] Even Bono, who has explicitly tried to forge close links with African musicians, is not immune here: his organization, DATA (Debt AIDS Trade Africa), has exclusively Anglo-Westerners on its board, and only one of five of its offices is located in Africa (Dieter and Kumar 2008: 263); and the board of the ONE campaign, with which he is closely associated, is conspicuous by the absence of any Africans (cf. Cooper 2008b: 271).

Celebrity humanitarianism thus constructs the Third World, and Africa in particular, as voiceless and invisible. Because Africans are shown to be passive, without knowledge or agency, the stars can ventriloquize and paternalize them. The ideological resort to stereotypes – 'Africans' are simple, noble, tribal, incompetent, politically naive – aims at fixing and naturalizing them, diverting attention away from the real nexus of problems (i.e. inequality, domination). The employment of the term 'Africa'[12] attempts to elide or homogenize the continent's complexity and difference in order to contain it, to make it manageable. The ubiquity of images of deprived women or abandoned children helps reinscribe paternalistic–colonial relationships, through which the African subject is treated as a victim or a child in need of guidance and representation.

All of these are deeply depoliticizing ideological moves. They try to keep the Third World, particularly Africans, subordinate and submissive in the global economic and political system. They invest Africa with sentimentalized cultural stereotypes and unconscious desires of salvation to stitch up the production of inequalities, in which the celebrity is complicit. And they rationalize, or prepare the ground for, further domination through the 'need' for improved governance, better values, or more market liberalization. This is not to say that such ideological strategies necessarily succeed, or that Africans do not actually resist or have agency (cf. Kapoor 2008: chs. 7, 8). But it does point up the dominant position of the celebrity ideologue; the psychic, cultural, and economic resources s/he draws on; and the hegemonic relations of power that African subjects are pitted against.

Our complicity

Part of the problem is that as audience members, fans, or consumers (of celebrity-endorsed products, for instance), we are complicit in this ideological nexus. We support and maintain the celebrity fantasy of humanitarianism through our beliefs. We believe *through* the star; that is, we delegate our belief in political change or charity to the celebrity. Žižek illustrates this phenomenon by way of several examples, of which here are two:

> It is similar to Tibetan prayer wheels: you write a prayer on a paper, put the rolled paper into a wheel, and turn it automatically without thinking … In this way, the wheel itself is praying for me, instead of me – or, more precisely, I myself am praying through the medium of the wheel. The beauty of it all is that in my psychological interiority I can think about

whatever I want, I can yield to the most dirty and obscene fantasies, and it does not matter because – to use a good Stalinist expression – whatever I am thinking, *objectively* I am praying … In so-called primitive societies we find the same phenomenon in the form of 'weepers', women hired to cry instead of us: so, through the medium of the other, we accomplish our duty of mourning, while we can spend our time on more profitable exploits – disputing the division of the inheritance of the deceased, for example.

(1989: 34–35)

Like the prayer wheels or the weepers, humanitarian celebrities become standins for our feelings of beneficence or compassion for the Third World. Žižek calls this 'interpassivity', wherein not only do others believe for us, but through this transference we no longer need to believe (1997: 113; cf. Pfaller 2005: 114). The stars incarnate our urge for humanitarianism, and by delegating such work to them, we are relieved of doing charity, or indeed even of feeling charitable. Instead, we can go about our busy lives and daily grind, without overly concerning ourselves with inequality or famine. We can enjoy watching 'charitainment' events such as Live 8 or Idol Gives Back, which give the illusion that something humanitarian is being done. It is as though by watching we are doing. Celebrities save us from having to change our world and allow us to be vicarious humanitarians without actually confronting global problems. We are saved, too, from the guilt and helplessness caused by watching the tragedy of the starving child or family in distress (cf. Edkins 2000: 115).

And the curious thing about believing through the Other is that we believe the Other *knows*, in spite of the fact s/he may not, and often doesn't. So often, we are uninformed about global issues such as debt or structural adjustment, and if we are they are often too complex to understand; but our identification with humanitarian celebrities helps us get around this conundrum. We might well not know, but our deep belief (i.e. trust) is that there are others – celebrities in this case – who do. Political belief is mediated precisely through such identification. Žižek often cites the example of the priest reciting mass in Latin: the congregation understands next to nothing, but believes the priest does, which is sufficient to keep the faith (Žižek 1997: 107). So it is with celebrity charity work: in our postdemocratic order, we trust in 'the Other supposed to know', believing in her/his (often self-proclaimed) position and knowledge.

Now some of us may be ardent fans and admirers, enjoying the stars' entertainment and glamour, and believing indiscriminately and sometimes blindly in what they represent and do. But of course we may also be cynical and suspicious, tired perhaps of the celebrity's over-exposure, self-promotion, or narcissism (e.g. there is an online campaign and Facebook webpage devoted to 'Make Bono History'!). Yet, Žižek reminds us that such reluctance need not be antithetical to ideology, and in fact may be part and parcel of its operations: 'its successful functioning requires a minimum of distance towards its explicit rules' (1999b: 99), so that I may actually enjoy my status as cynic or critic, feeling unique or privileged as a consequence. Ideology thrives on providing us with a sense that we are not totally brainwashed. But the crucial point is this: though appearing to maintain a distance, secretly we may still enjoy watching (and identifying with) celebrity shows and charitainment; ultimately, then, humanitarian celebrities carry the day. It is once again a case of 'fetishistic disavowal', that allows for ironic distance but leaves untouched the ideological fantasy. We may not trust celebrities' global charity work outwardly, but we still believe in it inwardly. All said and done, we can go about our daily lives feeling consoled that, despite everything, at least someone is doing something about poverty or starving children.

Yet the moment we delegate our beliefs to others, ideology is externalized and materialized. When we don't have to think or do, because an Other thinks or does for us, we have acquiesced to the capitalist and postdemocratic order. We partake in empty rituals and so allow the prayer wheels or hired weepers to believe for us, cry in our place, or maintain or change the world according to designs that are not our own. Transferring social and political activity to others, even acrimoniously or reluctantly, may well allow us to escape a measure of trauma, but it is a highly depoliticizing move that only strengthens ideology, making us into passive and disinterested spectators.

Conclusion

I have argued that celebrity humanitarianism is an ideological phenomenon of the times: one way in which late capitalist liberal democracies cover over their structural tendencies towards domination and inequality is through celebrity charity work, which is sold as a solution to addressing Third World poverty, debt, famine, etc. Relying on their star-power, celebrities draw significant public attention to development problems, but their tendency to individualize and isolate such problems means that their own socioeconomic complicity, as well as broader issues of political economy and cultural imperialism, are glossed over or depoliticized. I have also tried to argue that, as audience members, we support the ideological production of humanitarianism. Although we may know better, we still tend to believe in celebrities as do-gooders or heroes/ heroines, propping them up as ideologues.

At least two questions arise from this analysis. First, if we are all complicit in the construction of humanitarianism-as-ideology, why single out celebrities? And second, are some humanitarian celebrities 'better' (i.e. more progressive in their charity work) than others? In regards to the first question, it is true that we are all – audience members *and* celebrities – ideologically interpellated. But celebrities are much more powerfully positioned in this ideological nexus. As I have emphasized above, the stars are backed by strong global economic and institutional forces, from which they derive their star-power, but for which they are also active promoters. This is why they, much more than we, are 'ideologues'. It is they who propagate humanitarianism, covering over, rather than challenging, the social antagonisms of the global order, from which they benefit tremendously both socioeconomically and symbolically. As audience members, we are much less powerfully positioned in this ideological web, and hence we are not so much propagators as followers, supporters, consumers. But we are nonetheless tainted, and hence unable to claim innocence or purity. In short, none of our hands are clean ... but the celebrities' hands are particularly dirty.

In regards to the second question: William Easterly, Andrew Cooper, and Zine Magubane all appear to answer with a definite 'yes'. Easterly (2010) champions John Lennon over Bono, because the former was a rebel who challenged power, whereas the latter is a conformist, interested more in technical and policy solutions than political activism. Cooper makes a slightly broader claim, arguing against the 'one-image-fits-all' treatment of celebrities because it misses the importance and complexities of 'celebrity diplomacy' in the present global conjuncture (2008b: 266). Thus, for him, Bono cannot be 'dismissed outright as an amateur' or as a 'moral entrepreneur or instrumental agenda setter' (2008b: 267); instead, he is a significant actor on the global policy stage, and in many respects 'far more astute' and effective than Geldof, who sometimes lacks charm and diplomacy (2007: 7, 18; 2008b: 269; cf. 2008a: 36ff., 52ff.).

For her part, Magubane takes a similar tack, although she argues against Bono in favour of Oprah: for Magubane, Bono may be critical in his humanitarian work by evoking such issues as 'colonialism' but, importantly, he avoids the issue of race; whereas Oprah, despite her 'dominant position in the American media', does charity work that is a type of 'counterpublic' because it challenges the prevailing stereotypes of black people (2008: 11; 2007b: 374). The uniqueness of Oprah's philanthropy can be seen, according to Magubane, in the Oprah Winfrey Academy for Girls in South Africa, which prioritizes the needs of African girls, was established in a consultative way (drawing on local South African expertise), and is motivated by Oprah's own experience and awareness of sexual abuse and racial discrimination (2007b: 378).

What all three analysts conveniently sideline is that all of their heroes[13] are deeply entrenched and invested in late capitalist liberal democracies which, as I have argued, severely contaminates their humanitarianism or indeed rebelliousness. I agree with Cooper that we should not dismiss celebrity diplomats, that they perform a significant and powerful role on the current global policy stage. I even agree with the fact that Bono could be construed as a more 'effective' diplomat than Geldof. But while performing unique roles, what binds these stars, in my view, is their deep complicity in the global capitalist and postdemocratic system (an analysis of which is sorely missing in Cooper's and Easterly's work), which makes them *all* powerful ideologues. Lennon may be 'better' than Bono, and Bono 'better' than Geldof, but to turn Cooper's (or Easterly's) position on its head, my Žižekian stance would lead me argue that the more 'effective' the celebrity diplomat, the more powerful the ideologue because the more s/he helps cover up the holes of our current global order.

Similarly, what Magubane conveniently sidelines, even as she emphasizes it when referring to other celebrities (cf. 2007a: 4–5), is that Oprah's philanthropy happens not despite but *because* of her 'dominant position in the American media'. And I think this positioning decidedly taints the star's humanitarianism. It is visible in Oprah's branding of her charity work, which Magubane discusses in relation to Jolie (cf. 2007a: 4), but ignores when it comes to Oprah. Indeed, the very name of the Academy – the 'Oprah Winfrey Academy for Girls' – is a brand, something confirmed by a visit to the Academy's website (http://www.oprahwinfreyleadershipacademy.org), which has photos and quotes of Oprah displayed prominently on practically every page. Such branding is perceptible in the very idea of a 'Leadership Academy' which, as the website states, is meant to equip girls with skills necessary to assume 'positions of leadership'. To the extent that this mission statement reflects Oprah's own rise to prominence as a leader during the age of neoliberalism, it smacks precisely of neoliberalism, with its connotations of individual initiative and heroism. All of this casts doubt on Magubane's claims: how consultative could the establishment of the Academy have been, given such branding and personalization? Can philanthropy qualify as a 'counterpublic' when it is so entrenched in dominant material and symbolic systems? How progressive or critical could a project be, even one that emphasizes problems of race and gender, if it has a penchant for neoliberal values and an apparent lack of any critique of market institutions?

Therefore, my short answer to the question as to whether some celebrities are 'better' than others is this: it seems improbable, since to be a 'celebrity' is already to be invested in dominant power structures.[14] But much more important, I claim, is that it is a mistake – indeed an ideological displacement – to seek a redemptive or radical politics in 'good' celebrities when it is the broader structures which produce celebrity culture that require scrutiny and dismantling.

2

BILLIONAIRES AND CORPORATE PHILANTHROPY: 'DECAF CAPITALISM'

A businessman is caught red-handed shoplifting a gold watch from a jewellery store. Ashamed, he pleads with the store owner: 'How about I just buy the watch and we forget about this embarrassing incident?' The owner relents, and proceeds to write up a bill. The businessman looks at the bill and says: 'This is much more than I wanted to spend. Can you show me something less expensive?'

The moral of this joke, as I see it, is that you can't take the 'business' out of the businessman: even in a tight spot, he can't resist wheeling and dealing. He may well be red-faced, but he nonetheless remains an unabashed entrepreneur, trying to extract advantage in a moment of compassion.

The same appears true of contemporary corporate philanthropy. Whether it's the Bill and Melinda Gates Foundation or the philanthropic arm of American Express, each tries to turn a charitable proposition into a business opportunity. The 'business model' is sold as a panacea, applicable to government programs as much as philanthropic causes. Bishop and Green have famously called this 'philanthrocapitalism', which aims at 'harnessing the profit motive to achieve social good' (2008: 6).

But why is the one a joke and the other a socially appropriate practice? Or rather, how has the joke, which turns surely on the expression of social *unac*ceptability (i.e. the gall of the businessman-thief trying to profit from generosity!), become *acceptable* social practice today? The answer, it seems to me, lies in the naturalization of global neoliberal capitalism. When social ethics become a form of entrepreneurship, when gifts, meant precisely to interrupt market relations and the cycle of profit and exchange, are unproblematically infused with business calculations, then the hegemony of neoliberalism stands increasingly unchallenged.

This chapter will attempt an ideology critique of contemporary corporate charity. To this end, I will trace two main ideological paths (cf. Žižek 2009a). The first, exemplified by the work of celebrity billionaire-humanitarians such as Bill Gates and George Soros, consists of giving away spectacular sums of wealth along mostly entrepreneurial lines, yet forswearing how such wealth was accumulated in the first place. Indeed, I will show that this charity is often tied to (disavowed) ruthless business practices, a phenomenon I will refer to as 'decaf capitalism'. The second, newer form of corporate philanthropy consists of the integration of (celebrity-endorsed) charity with shopping, enabling all of us as consumers to do our bit for global humanitarianism. I will focus on the Product (RED) campaign to illustrate how such a coupling of ethics with consumerism helps further bind us to capitalism. My argument, in this sense, is that both of these ideological strategies, through their construction of the social fantasy of celebritized philanthropy, are attempts at repudiating their 'dirty' underside. Which is to say that both aim at stabilizing and advancing the global neoliberal capitalist order.

Billionaires and philanthropy

Q: Why is Bill Gates so keen on funding treatments for HIV/AIDS and malaria in Africa?
A: To keep Africans alive long enough so they can buy Windows 9!

My focus on Gates and Soros as billionaire-humanitarians in this section is meant to help illustrate the broader structural features of our current cultural and political economy. It should not be forgotten that both men are products of the neoliberal de-regulation of financial markets of the 1980s and 1990s, accompanied as it was by the emergence of the 'new information economy' and the dot.com boom. This is the period that witnessed notable economic growth in much of the West. But such growth was highly skewed, showing up in the form of a remarkable rise in the ranks of the super-rich, on the one hand, and growing social inequality, on the other. Thus, while the number of American billionaires during the last two decades has risen twenty-fold, the erstwhile economic boom has failed to 'trickle down'. In the US, the top 1 percent of the population owned about 20 percent of the country's wealth in the mid-1970s, almost as much as did the bottom 80 percent; while in the late 1990s, the top 1 per cent owned 40 percent, which by then was almost two-and-a-half times what the bottom 80 percent owned (Collins et al., quoted in Adair 2010: 245). (It is precisely this socioeconomic disparity that the global Occupy movement has been trying to highlight.)

In the midst of such concentrated wealth creation and rising social inequality, Gates and Soros have emerged as celebrities, partly for their status as two of the richest people on earth, and partly for their spectacular generosity, giving away hundreds of millions of dollars to a host of charities. They join the ranks of several other similar corporate billionaire-humanitarians such as Ted Turner (media mogul), Warren Buffett (investor), Pierre Omidyar and Jeff Skoll (of eBay fame), Richard Branson (Virgin Group), and Sergey Brin and Larry Page (Google co-founders). What is peculiar about Gates and Soros (as well as some of their billionaire colleagues) is their appearance as 'progressive' philanthropists: Žižek ironically refers to them as 'liberal communists' (2006d: 10) because they tend to espouse outwardly Left and cosmopolitan causes such as democratic reform and global health. But of course their progressiveness is decidedly liberal in that their view of social responsibility, as we shall see, is circumscribed firmly within a thriving global capitalist order. They are, Žižek continues, 'true citizens of the world. They are good people who worry' (2008a: 20).

Giving with one hand …

Bill Gates co-founded Microsoft Corporation in 1975. Under him, the company developed into the largest global software business, dominating personal computer operating systems worldwide. He stepped down as CEO in 2000 (although he remains non-executive Chairman), devoting his time to his charitable foundation, the Bill and Melinda Gates Foundation. Apart from being one of the world's richest men (his current net worth is assessed at $56 billion), he is also one of the most 'generous' philanthropists in history, estimated to have given, along with his wife Melinda, close to $30 billion to date in charity (*Forbes* 2011; *BusinessWeek* 2010).

Gates believes in what he calls 'friction-free capitalism' (2006), total transparency in global networking and communication, which is what he thinks the information revolution (pioneered by Microsoft) has made possible. But business and technological innovation, harbingers of a friction-free world, must be integrated creatively with social responsibility, according to him. He states that 'We have to find a way to make the aspects of capitalism that serve wealthier people serve poorer people as well' (2008: 9). We can bring self-interest and 'caring for others' together by using 'profit incentives whenever we can' (2008: 10). This he calls 'creative capitalism', another term for what others have termed 'philanthrocapitalism'. It is 'an approach where governments, businesses, and nonprofits work together to stretch the reach of market forces so that more people can make a profit, or gain recognition, doing work that eases the world's inequities' (Gates 2008: 10; cf. Bishop and Green 2008).

Private enterprise, in this view, allows creativity to flourish in business as much as social programs and charity work. The implication is that state regulation needs to be kept in check so as not to undermine human creativity. In fact, for Gates, private philanthropy, unencumbered by red tape, can be more successful, sustainable, and results-oriented than state social programs (Bishop and Green 2008: 12). But the private sector, large corporations in particular, must also do their bit, according to Gates. They must view corporate philanthropy (i.e. Corporate Social Responsibility) as making good business sense. And they must give more to fill the gaps left by declining state and nonprofit social funding (Bishop and Green 2008: 13ff.).

Inspired by this 'let's not be greedy, but instead help the world along creative business lines' motto, the Bill and Melinda Gates Foundation was set up in 1999 (as a merger of two previous foundations). In 2005, the Foundation's endowment stood at $35 billion, but was further replenished by a $37 billion pledge by Warren Buffett. Today, with an endowment of close to $60 billion, which is larger than the GDP of several countries, the Foundation is the biggest private charity in the world (cf. Gates Foundation 2011b; Piller et al. 2007; Okie 2006: 1084).

The Foundation disburses grants in the order of about $3 billion annually in three main areas: global health, global development/poverty reduction, and US education (Gates Foundation 2011a). Global health programs take up by far the largest share of grants (about $14.5 billion disbursed to date), focusing mainly on immunization and vaccine research, HIV/AIDS, and maternal and child health. Global development programs (about $3.3 billion disbursed to date) centre on financial services for the 'poor' (i.e. microcredit), agricultural development (including funding for a 'Green Revolution' in Africa), and water and sanitation. Finally, US education programs (about $6 billion disbursed to date) include support for schools, university scholarships, and computer access in public libraries (cf. Gates Foundation 2011a-b).

George Soros, like Bill Gates, is also one of the world's richest and most 'generous' entrepreneurs. Trained as an arbitrage trader in London, he moved to New York in the 1960s. There, he set up Soros Fund Management (SFM), which includes his now famous Quantum Fund, the hedge fund that has been the source of his enormous personal wealth. SFM holdings are currently estimated at $4.2 billion, with the billionaire's own net worth assessed at some $14.5 billion (Opalesque 2009; BBC 2010c; *Forbes* 2011).

Soros is an avid supporter of human rights, while also an opponent of 'market fundamentalism' for its unquestioning promotion of 'free' and unfettered markets (cf. Soros 2002a-b). He has openly condemned the likes of Vladimir Putin for his anti-democratic rule, while also funding US political organizations to help defeat George W. Bush's 2004 re-election bid. He is thus often seen as a strong critic of neoliberalism and authoritarianism, which may be taken as a Left critique. Yet, influenced by Karl Popper, Soros is in fact a strong defender of liberal democracy, believing, as did Popper, in the frailty of liberal institutions and the need to protect them (Soros 2002b: ix). He is more appropriately a 'liberal reformist', advocating for strong legal frameworks and a modicum of state regulation to make global capitalism more stable and equitable. In *On Globalization*, he writes:

> Of course I am a supporter of the capitalist system ... I am not advocating the abolishment of the capitalist system but I am arguing that it is *imperfect* and it has deficiencies ... we actually do need democracy to make capitalism stable, because we *need a social counterweight* to offset the excesses of capitalism ...
>
> *(2002b: 26, 24; cf. 2002a: 1–7)*

This worldview has translated into several notable philanthropic initiatives. In 1991, Soros provided Europe's largest ever educational endowment (€420 million) to create the Central European University (CEU) in Budapest, with the purpose of educating 'a new corps of Central European leaders' (CEU quoted in Guilhot 2007: 449). During the last two decades, the university has successfully trained a whole generation of economists and policy-makers. As well, in 2010, he donated $100 million to Human Rights Watch over the next ten years (BBC 2010c).

Aside from these singular initiatives, Soros has established a network of international charitable groups or Open Society Foundations, whose goal is to influence public policy and promote human rights and multi-party elections. With a total annual budget of between $400 million and $500 million (Open Society Foundations 2011), this network has supported a diverse array of local causes in more than seventy countries – from human rights in Zimbabwe and independent media building in Burma, to support for democratic change in Eastern Europe (including the 'Orange Revolution' in Ukraine and the 'Rose Revolution' in Georgia).

... Having taken with the other

The catch, as Žižek points out, is that 'in order to give, first you have to take' (2008a: 20). And indeed, as I will try and show, Gates and Soros's engagements to 'save the world' are premised on the prior accumulation of personal fortune in questionable, if not unsavoury, ways.

Of course, such accumulation has not been as overtly or directly exploitative as that of some of the pioneers of corporate philanthropy such as Andrew Carnegie or John D. Rockefeller, Jr. We have come to associate the latter industrialists with their largesse and support for educational and cultural causes, yet it is all too easy to forget their ruthless corporate tactics. Carnegie's Pittsburgh steel empire, for instance, was built on the suppression of worker rights, including on the occasion of the notorious 1892 Homestead strike against layoffs and long working shifts, when private security agents were ordered to fire on unarmed workers (cf. Krause 1992; Žižek 2006d). The same is true for Rockefeller, whose industrial and oil empire was associated with often brutal labour management tactics including, for example, the 1914 massacre of striking miners in Ludlow, Colorado (cf. Andrews 2008).

Gates and Soros might have averted such outwardly harsh methods, yet their business practices are not without serious social consequences. For exploitation under late capitalism has not disappeared; it has simply taken on different, and sometimes veiled, forms.

Gates: accumulation by enclosure

Simply put, Bill Gates's enormous wealth derives from the privatization of what should be an integral part of the commons – knowledge. Information/knowledge forms the very symbolic substance of our lives, yet by appropriating it he has made it into tangible property. This privatization of our 'general intellect' is 'a decisive battle which triggered the battle for the "enclosure" of the common domain of software' (Žižek 2008b: 422).

As Stephen Adair (2010) explains, while in our information age the conditions and relations of production have not disappeared, what has changed is that commodities are increasingly being informatized, transformed into bits that can easily be electronically reproduced and exchanged. Theoretically, this should lead to greater abundance for all through the free exchange of digitized knowledge, but such is not the case. Instead, the creative labour that goes into the initial design and display of software has been privatized and highly valorized by the likes of Microsoft: 'When use value can be copied with little or no labor, then valorizing labor … may be the only counteracting factor available for capital to prevent prices from falling to a level determined by the commodity's exchange value' (Adair 2010: 251). This means that software companies pay a relatively small initial cost for creative labour, but because digital copying is so easy and cheap, they are able to keep reproduction costs at a minimum, thus profiting from very large economies of scale. They are also able to add a price premium through product branding and logoization, which gives software its cachet and identity. Add to this Microsoft's continuous product updates to keep ahead of technological obsolescence, and you have the makings of massive wealth accumulation.

It is not surprising, then, that the dot.com boom of the 1990s saw the creation of mega-fortunes by such corporations as Netscape, Oracle, Microsoft, and Google. The wealthiest people in the world used to be steel magnates and oil barons such as Carnegie and Rockefeller; they are now the sultans of digitized intellect. And they are so successful, not because they have been able to extract traditional surplus value, but because they can use the creative labour of a relatively few employees to extract 'monopoly rents' (Adair 2010: 254).

Critical to the extraction of monopoly rents are intellectual property rights (IPRs) (i.e. royalties, trademarks, copyrights, licensing agreements). It is IPRs that enable the creation of exclusivity and scarcity, allowing Microsoft to collect rents from mostly anyone who wishes to participate in global networking and the intellectual commons. In fact, Microsoft's monopolization of the software industry depends crucially on the strict protection and enforcement of IPRs. Gates has been their ardent defender, supporting patent protection not only for the software sector but also the drug industry by declaring: 'I think if you invent drugs, you should be able to charge for them' (quoted in Rimmer 2010: 328). After all, IPRs insulate his company, permitting it to protect its brand; they help increase his company's market share, squeezing out competitors and potential threats. No wonder, as Adair underlines (2010: 250), that we are witnessing today the increasing corporate use of the likes of digital security and signal scrambling (in the face of file-sharing and pirating), as well as a clamouring for stronger libel and defamation laws (in the face of blogging and paparazzi journalism).

Many have called the novel mode of extraction and accumulation engendered by IPRs the 'new enclosure movement'. Rather than being socially managed and available in the public domain, IPRs are mostly monopolized and privatized. Žižek opines that if Gates were allowed a full monopoly over information, 'we would reach the absurd situation in which a private individual would literally own the software texture of our basic network of communication' (2009b: 53; 2008b: 429; cf. 1999a: 356). Such a problem is not exclusive to the software sector; it is prevalent in many other areas, particularly biotechnology. Thus, farming communities in Northern India may suddenly learn that the *basmati* rice they have been cultivating and sharing for centuries has been patented by a US biotech corporation (cf. Shiva 2005: 147–48), while we ourselves may discover that parts of our own bodies, 'our genetic components, are already copyrighted, owned by others' (Žižek 2007).

Microsoft has been able to maintain almost absolute control over the computer software market as a result of its copyright and licensing arrangements. Its operating systems are used by more than 85 percent of personal computers sold worldwide, with only minimal competition from Apple and open-source Linux. It also has a history of eliminating its competition, squeezing out WordPerfect and Lotus 1-2-3 in the late 1980s, and buying out an average of six companies a year since its creation in 1987, including those responsible for DOS, FrontPage, Internet Explorer, Hotmail, WebTV, and more recently, Skype (cf. Stross 1997). In this regard, it is worth noting that, in the 1990s, Netscape controlled 90 percent of the global browser market share, but by bundling its browser (Internet Explorer) with its operating system, Microsoft was able to squeeze out Netscape and gain market dominance. Thus, Žižek writes, 'The cruel businessman [Gates] destroys or buys out competitors, aims at virtual monopoly, employs all the tricks of the trade to achieve his goals' (2006d: 10).

In the late 1990s, the US government took out an anti-trust case against Microsoft for engaging in anti-competitive behaviour (in particular against Netscape and Java). After a series of rulings, in 2000, the corporation was found guilty of violating the Sherman Act (i.e. engaging in an illegal monopoly). In 2004, it was handed a record fine of some $666 million by the European Court for its breach of EU competition law, and in 2008 European anti-trust regulators fined it again, a record $1.3 billion, for failing to comply with the 2004 judgment (Castle and Jolly 2008).

Apart from Microsoft's anti-competitive conduct and extraction of monopoly rent, it is important to underline the significant global structural changes that it has helped bring about in the information industry, most often to the detriment of many in the Third World. True, it may not be fair to pin these changes directly or solely on Gates/Microsoft, but as pioneers and powerful leaders in the global software industry, they are far from blameless. The key issue here is the new global division of labour produced by the growing information revolution, in particular its creation of unevenness and new labour hierarchies and inequalities.

To be sure, the onset of post-Fordist and networked global production processes, which has seen the rapid growth of outsourcing and offshoring during the last two decades, and the valorization of 'creative labour' in the software industry (at the expense of other types of labour), has entailed the increasing fragmentation and flexibilization of production processes. Information technology (IT) companies have sought out cheap skilled and unskilled labour in the Third World. This has meant that those countries with low-cost, educated workforces and strong IPR protections have been favoured (parts of South and Southeast Asia), mostly ignoring others (parts of the Middle East and Sub-Saharan Africa) (cf. Carmel and Tjia 2005: 69ff.). The result is the creation or reinforcement of geographic inequalities globally – ironically, the very ones that Gates's charity work is responding to. Such global unevenness is matched by regional and local unevenness, with growth in the software sector restricted mainly to large cities (e.g. Shanghai, Beijing, Singapore, Bangalore, Chennai). The consequence here is the heightened development of highly modern, Westernized enclave economies alongside inner-city slums and impoverished peri-urban and rural areas (cf. Brenner and Keil 2005).

In addition, the globalization of the IT industry has yielded impressive wealth and job creation, but at a substantial labour cost. The offshoring and outsourcing of IT to India, for example, has seen a profusion of new small and medium sized subcontractors. As a consequence, the industry grew at a rate of

50 percent per year in the 1990s, and in 2005–6 earned \$17.6 billion and employed about 1.3 million people (Upadhya and Vasavi 2008: 13). But such a boom has been accompanied by notable inequalities between higher-end-and-paid software development/programming jobs and low-end-and-wage service jobs in data entry, clerical work, and call centres (e.g. for after-sales assistance or the processing of banking, insurance, and airline claims).

IT development has also produced the flexibilization of labour, which affects all jobs, whether high or low end. For instance, Indian software companies prefer to hire engineering graduates, who are often ill-suited and over-qualified but can be trained easily and quickly for a variety of software tasks (the same is true of call centre work) (Upadhya and Vasavi 2008: 17). Much of this is part-time, shift work, with employees often lacking job security and benefits, and their employment being subject to the vagaries of dot.com booms and busts. Those lucky to have full-time jobs are required to be mobile (to be sent onsite for travel abroad) and frequently work double shifts. Their work environments tend to be competitive and stressful, characterized by high job attrition rates (Upadhya and Vasavi 2008: 18–19). Most often, they are subject to 'normative' controls (the need for self-managing, self-motivated, cooperative, loyal, and adaptive workers), cultural assimilation (e.g. the need to speak and act 'American'), and surveillance (e.g. the use of cameras, swiping machines, and attendance records to monitor employee performance, communication skills, tact, etc.) (Upadhya and Vasavi 2008: 22–32). While team work is greatly encouraged at the workplace, it is deterred in terms of collective bargaining, with unionization mostly absent or discouraged.

Women have not fared too well in this situation (relative to men): in fact, the IT boom has witnessed a worsening of the gender division of labour. Men tend to dominate skilled labour positions (management, design, programming), with women relegated to less skilled jobs (data entry, call centre work) and, increasingly, informal labour in the form of home-based employment (Gillard et al. 2008: 268–71). It is thus mainly women's IT work that tends to be low-skilled, lower-paid, dispensable, temporary, and routinized. And this 'feminization of labour' is prevalent not just in Asia, but more and more in Latin America (e.g. Brazil, Chile) and the Caribbean (e.g. Barbados, Jamaica). By and large, then, women are the ones who supply the IT boom (and late capitalism, generally) with cheap, flexible and unprotected labour (Gillard et al. 2008: 263, 273; Upadhya and Vasavi 2008: 34).

Such a state of affairs gives new meaning to Gates's much trumpeted ideal of 'friction-free' capitalism. For, it seems, his fantasy of smooth and transparent global networking is made possible only by a grimy underbelly – by outsourcing and offshoring the inconveniences of the IT industry. This is ideology at its purest, and Žižek offers a scathing critique of it: 'You export the (necessary) dark side of production – disciplined, hierarchical labour, ecological pollution – to …

[the] Third World ... The ultimate liberal communist dream is to export the entire working class to invisible Third World sweat shops' (2006d: 10). The notion of an immaterial and seamless cyberspace is premised on material inertia, on an obstacle-free capitalism, where the traumatic Real or the social antagonism (i.e. one's own social privilege, the materiality and power of labour, poor working conditions, gender inequality, environmental degradation) is disavowed. The fiction is to make capital movement free and unencumbered, so that software can win over hardware (Žižek 2008a: 17), and the exploitation of labour can be relegated out of sight: 'in the social conditions of late capitalism, the very materiality of cyberspace automatically generates the illusory abstract space of "friction-free" exchange in which the particularity of the participants' social position is obliterated' (Žižek 1997: 156).

But it's not just that Gates gives with one hand and takes with the other (or, dare I say it, exhibits sleight-of-hand!); it's also that the very hand he gives with is sullied. Indeed, the Gates Foundation, through which he channels his charity, has been the object of significant criticism in a number of areas. One key problem is that the Foundation tends to fund programs too narrowly, especially in the health field, where it has now become a major global player. It tends to take a technological approach to health, supporting programs that are frequently narrowly science-based (e.g. biomedical research, discovery of new medicines) (cf. Rimmer 2010: 330; Cooper 2008a: 85). One journalist revealingly describes Gates's zeal for health issues in the following way: 'The way [Gates] talked about wiping out malaria was how he used to talk about wiping out Netscape' (quoted in Cooper 2008a: 83). The technical aspects of health end up being too easily separated from larger political economic and social issues (Birn 2005), so that not enough attention is paid to the more intractable issues of health delivery or the broader structures of inequality and patriarchy. Most often, it is not the lack of new drugs, but such obstacles as food insecurity, political repression, or unequal land tenure that impact maternal and child health (Edwards 2009: 41). A notable fallout from its search for quick-fix technological solutions is that, because the Foundation is a leader in the global health field, it diverts energy, resources, and commitment away from other important areas such as primary health care, training of health workers, and so on (Edwards 2009: 38).[1]

A second target of criticism is that the Gates Foundation lacks transparency and accountability. Indeed, it is run by three trustees – Bill Gates, Melinda Gates, and Warren Buffett, and its main other officers are Gates family members (Bill Gates, Sr.) or former Microsoft executives (Eisenberg 2006). The Foundation is thus directed by a closed, inner circle of family and friends (*Lancet* 2009; Rimmer 2010: 330). Its decision-making lacks outside or public scrutiny of any kind, and even excludes representation from program 'beneficiaries'; yet, the Foundation plays such an influential global role in health, poverty reduction, and education, impacting policy-making, research, funding, and thousands of people's lives.

Finally, there is the issue of the Foundation's investments. The problem here is not simply that Gates avoids paying taxes on his charitable donations, as does the Foundation on the investment income from its endowments (Bishop and Green 2008: 11); all charitable donations and foundations do (in the US). The more serious difficulty is that the Foundation invests in ways that contradict its own programming goals. Piller et al. (2007) report that it spent $218 million on polio and measles immunization and research, including for programs in the Niger Delta. But at the same time, they find that the Foundation has invested $423 million in such oil companies as Royal Dutch Shell, Exxon Mobil, Chevron, and Total, companies responsible for serious environmental pollution in the Delta that would not be tolerated in Europe or the US (cf. Zalik 2004). In fact, many local Delta leaders blame the oil exploitation in the area for the very health infections the Foundation is combating – malaria from mosquitos in the stagnant water in oil bore holes, cholera from rivers clogged from oil spills, and lower health immunity among residents (including greater child suscept- ibility to polio and measles) from breathing in sooty gas flares that contain benzene, mercury, and chromium particulates. Piller et al. estimate, in fact, that some 41 percent of the Foundation's assets are invested in companies whose activities run counter to the Foundation's social and health programs. They state that its portfolio managers are provided with little direction other than to maintain a diversified portfolio. As a consequence, the Foundation has sizeable holdings in major US and Canadian polluters such as Dow Chemical, ConocoPhillips, and Telco; and it has forged partnerships with several phar- maceutical companies (e.g. Merck, GlaxoSmithKline), many of which resist the move to generic drugs, pricing medicines beyond the reach of the very patients that the Foundation is trying to help (cf. Bishop and Green 2008: 64–65; Cooper 2008a: 85).

In response to these criticisms, the Foundation announced a full review of its investments, only to later cancel the review, declaring that it stood by its initial policy but would use its shareholder voting rights to influence companies' practices from within (*Austin Statesman* 2007). Of course, in the absence of public scrutiny of the Foundation, there is no way of verifying if such influence is being exercised, and if so, whether companies are indeed complying.

Soros: accumulation by destabilization

It is ironic that George Soros talks of socioeconomic stability and the need to 'offset the excesses of capitalism' (quoted earlier), yet his hedge funds are pre- cisely a source of instability and excess. As Žižek avers, 'The same Soros who gives millions to fund education has ruined the lives of thousands thanks to his financial speculations' (2006d: 10).

Soros has been, and remains, a pioneer and leader in the hedge fund business, profiting from neoliberal globalization (of which he has nonetheless been critical), in particular from market deregulation, which saw an explosion of financial leveraging instruments such as his Quantum Fund. The result has been global capital flows and financial markets that today are complex, obscure, highly interdependent, and difficult to monitor (trillions of dollars are traded on markets almost every day). Many hedge funds are virtual or even fictitious, and can be moved around at lightning speed. This post-Fordist 'dematerialization' of financial assets has enabled a greater exchange of financial and economic information, but it has also been accompanied, as we shall see below, with the heightened risk, speed, and contagion of financial crises. Thus, slight changes in inflation rates or currency values can mean massive capital flight (Aslanbeigui and Summerfield 2001: 10).

The number of hedge funds used to be small in the 1990s, but has increased substantially since, with currently over eight thousand of them (Soros's is one of the biggest and most influential), managing about $1,000 billion globally (Holmes 2009: 434). Hedge fund investors used to be almost exclusively very wealthy investors, but this too has changed, with the investor pool broadening of late and even some public sector unions investing their pension money (itself the product of declining state support for social security).

But what exactly are hedge funds? They are pools of money that are leveraged in various ways to make very high returns in as short a time as possible (Caliari 2007). They make for a form of opportunistic financing, taking advantage of the vast complexity and size of global financial markets. They exploit the discrepancies of these markets, hedging (i.e. betting) against undervalued or overvalued interest rates, currencies, or company stocks. They often borrow shares to temporarily inflate prices and then re-sell them, or bet on the success or failure of company takeovers. They are also often able to borrow up to twenty times their value from banks to take leveraged positions, enabling hedge fund managers to buy assets without paying full cost (a practice directly related to the recent financial crisis) (cf. Harmes 1999: 16).

Hedge funds have revolutionized the entire approach to risk under late capitalism, particularly through their use of derivatives, which help magnify risk in an effort to make as much money as possible very quickly (Bryan and Rafferty 2006: 62; cf. Holmes 2009: 437; Dodd 2002). Derivatives 'provide a mechanism to link assets in the present to prices in the future (e.g. a tonne of wheat today to its price in 3 months). They also link prices of one asset form to another asset form – for example, interest rates to share prices' (Bryan and Rafferty 2006: 10). They are thus a kind of fictitious capital, which allows risk to be traded without the actual assets being traded.[2] They have become so complex, in fact, that they now use sophisticated computer models that factor in multiple financial indices, future energy prices, or even long-range weather forecasts.

One of the main reasons hedge funds have been so successful is because of the lack of adequate regulation. They are subject to few legal constraints, little fiduciary responsibility, and no disclosure requirements, a situation from which they have taken full advantage (Holmes 2009: 433). Several operate from off-shore centres, and most use tax havens to capitalize on investment gains. All of this erodes governments' tax bases, as well as the ability to monitor transactions or protect against financial crises (cf. Tanzi 2002).

Since hedge fund managers are interested only in quick, short-term returns, they frequently harm the long-term interests of people, governments, or companies. Bryan and Rafferty (2006) explain, for example, how derivatives, because they provide the real-time value of a company's assets, can put tremendous pressure on a company to intensify its competitive edge by lowering costs and increasing productivity. As a matter of fact, derivatives are frequently used to raid 'underperforming' businesses and turn them around ('leveraged buyouts'). Assets or plants not meeting profit goals are then depreciated, restructured, or sold. Most often, such pressure ends up on the backs of labour: the demand to cut costs, increase profits, and deliver on share values means extracting greater labour flexibility and wage competitiveness. Hence, derivatives tend to erode job security and worsen working conditions:

> Labour that cannot deliver globally competitive levels of productivity must compensate, as it were, for its less than frontier productivity by accepting longer hours and lower wages ... The widely documented intensification of labour over the past two decades, centring on flexibility in skills and working conditions, longer working hours, and wage increases less than productivity, follows directly.
>
> *(Bryan and Rafferty 2006: 176; cf. pp. 5, 32, 103)*

The most recent trend is for hedge funds to engage in 'land grabs': they have been identified as a major source of land acquisitions in parts of Africa, presumably to hedge against current food and energy insecurity and help raise profits in the agricultural and biofuels sectors (BBC 2011a). Hedge funds have acquired large tracts of land in such countries as Ethiopia, Tanzania, South Sudan, Sierra Leone, Mali, and Mozambique, mainly for the cultivation of cash crops (e.g. cut flowers) or sugarcane for use as biofuel. In the process, however, they are estimated to have displaced millions of farmers (Oakland Institute 2011), threatening Sub-Saharan Africa's long-term ability to grow food (as opposed to cash crops).

Of course, we may not be able to attribute full or direct responsibility for all of this to Soros; but as a major global player in hedge funds, his hands are certainly dirty. Part of the problem of attributing responsibility in this case is that hedge funds evade public scrutiny and specific information about them is hard to come by. There are nonetheless at least two relatively recent events with which Soros has been notoriously associated, both involving serious financial destabilization. The first is the 1992 European Exchange Rate Mechanism (ERM) crisis, precipitated by Soros. Believing that the pound sterling was overvalued, he bet massively on the fall of the currency, dumping the pound to the tune of about $10 billion, with other hedge funds following suit. The result was what came to be known as 'Black Wednesday' (16 September 1992), when the British government was forced to leave the ERM, costing taxpayers billions of pounds, while profiting Soros to the tune of $1 billion or more (Harmes 1999: 16–17).

Perhaps more serious was Soros's involvement in the 1997 Asian financial crisis. As Thai property and asset markets began to weaken earlier that year, several hedge funds, including Soros's Quantum Fund, dumped the baht, which created investor panic and rapid capital outflow, spreading to four other countries in the region (South Korea, Indonesia, Malaysia, and the Philippines). The Bank of Thailand saw most of its foreign reserves depleted, the baht went on to lose 50 percent of its value, and the government was forced to lift the currency's peg with the US dollar (Bello et al. 2000: 15).[3]

There has been much debate about whether hedge fund speculation caused this crisis or was one link in a chain of events contributing to the crisis. The IMF blames the troubles mainly on weak regulation of real estate and financial markets, rather than on private financial speculation (although, ironically, it is the IMF that had pushed for the deregulation of these very markets only a decade earlier; cf. Aslanbeigui and Summerfield 2001: 11–12). Others argue that hedge funds played a key role, outmanoeuvring regulatory safeguards and throwing caution to the four winds (cf. Dodd 2002: 447–48, 465, 471; Caliari 2007; Stiglitz 1998: 32). The point in either case is that while there may have been bad investments, over-valued exchange rates, and weak regulatory oversight, derivatives did what they are designed to do – exploit these weaknesses in pursuit of rapid profits, thus quickening and deepening the crisis. Part of the issue here is that hedge fund managers tend to engage in 'herd behaviour': they hunt for profits in packs, following the lead of key investors, collectively manipulating markets for quick gain (Holmes 2009). They may not be able to influence markets for more than a short time, but often that is all the time they need to make sizeable profits (Harmes 1999: 12).[4] This herd-like behaviour was certainly significant in the Asian financial crisis, as it has been in other similar crises such as the above-mentioned ERM, the 1994–95 Mexican peso crisis, or Greece's current economic woes.[5]

Meanwhile, the social impacts of the 1997 Asian crisis were significant and widespread, reversing several decades of socioeconomic gains in the region.

Thailand, Indonesia, South Korea, the Philippines, and Malaysia all witnessed an increase in unemployment, poverty, malnutrition, and a deterioration in access to education, with women and the poorest sections of society hit the hardest (Hill and Chu 2001: 13–18; Bello et al. 2000: x). In less than a year, Indonesia's currency depreciated by 72 percent and its real wages dropped by 40 percent, while South Korea's real GDP declined by 13.7 percent and its unemployment rate, particularly in urban areas, tripled. Overall, more than 50 million people moved under the poverty line in the region (Aslanbeigui and Summerfield 2001: 9).

It is only in the wake of the most recent global financial crisis and massive rescue of financial institutions that world political leaders have been forced to reckon with the need for much stronger hedge fund regulation and oversight. The G20 and EU, in particular, have begun to make moves in this direction, though falling short of their initial strong commitments.[6] The fact remains that hedge funds, Soros's included, will continue to operate, albeit perhaps in a manner less ruthless and unregulated than before.

A last point on Soros's philanthropic initiatives: for, like those of Bill Gates, they are not without reproach, even as they are paraded as humanitarian. While some of the funding from his Open Society Foundations may be channelled towards organizations that are critical of states' human rights and democratic records, most of Soros's charity is geared towards the political and economic status quo. This is particularly true of his patronage of the Central European University, which, like many other neoliberalizing universities, favours tech-nocratic training and positivist social science methodologies (e.g. econometrics, political modelling) for the education of state administrators. Several university training modules, for instance, are associated with the World Bank, involving seminars on such issues as privatization, corporate governance, or the creation of business schools (Guilhot 2007: 465–66). Even Soros's backing for 'critical' human rights groups (e.g. Human Rights Watch) is barely a threat to the system; at most, it is reformist – establishing and defending individuals' civil and political rights, but steering clear of the much more politically difficult area of collective socioeconomic rights (i.e. labour, land, or indigenous peoples' rights). Nicolas Guilhot thus writes that Soros's philanthropy is a 'privileged instrument for reinforcing international institutions and producing scientific, professional, social and political infrastructure needed for managing globalization' (2007: 464).

Decaf capitalism

That Gates and Soros give with one hand all the while having taken with the other is an attempt to produce what I will call, drawing on Žižek, 'decaf capitalism'. Indeed, Žižek sees the recent appearance of consumer products that endeavour to remove risk or danger, that try to cleanse their poison or sweeten their astringent, as indicative of the ideological make-up of our age:

> This brings to mind a chocolate laxative available in the US, publicized with the paradoxical injunction: 'Do you have constipation? Eat more of this chocolate!'. In other words, eat the very thing that causes constipation in order to be cured of it. This structure of a product counteracting its own essence containing the agent of its own containment is widely visible in today's ideological landscape.
>
> *(2009c: 14)*

There are many consumer products that fit Žižek's description – decaffeinated coffee, cream without fat, sugarless beverages, non-alcoholic beer – just as there is a range of contemporary social phenomena that do – phone sex, cybersex, and sexting (i.e. sex without sex); green mining and environmentally 'friendly' or 'ethical' oil exploration (i.e. ecological damage without degradation); and war without war, or war without casualties (i.e. distance technological war, on the basis of which we can bomb, say, Gaddafi's bases without involving Western ground troops in Libya, or use armed robots and unmanned drones that may well kill Afghan or Pakistani civilians, as long as no American soldiers' lives are lost) (cf. Žižek 2004a: 507–8). All are ideological attempts to evacuate from reality the dimension of the Real, to purify life, rid it of its inherent dangers and inconveniences.

And so it is with Gates and Soros. They balance out their ruthless profit-making with charity work, thus deploying a sort of 'decaf capitalism': a capitalism with a human face – a system that exploits but still cares, wreaks social havoc but really worries, institutes a Wild-West entrepreneurialism but also a welfare state.[7] Decaf capitalism enables them to rationalize away their mono-polistic corporate behaviour and cut-throat financial speculation, or their co-responsibility in labour exploitation and the production of feminized sweatshops. It allows them to continue with business as usual, 'giving back' to counteract the ills of capitalism, all the while becoming the globe's greatest humanitarians. Thus, Žižek writes:

> Soros stands for the most ruthless financial speculative exploitation com-bined with its counter-agent, the humanitarian worry about the cata-strophic social consequences of the unbridled market economy. Even his daily routine is marked by a self-eliminating counterpoint: half of his working time is devoted to financial speculations, and the other half to humanitarian activities – such as providing finances for cultural and democratic activities in post-Communist countries, writing essays and books – which ultimately fight the effects of his own speculations. The

two faces of Gates parallel the two faces of Soros ... Meanwhile, the greatest philanthropist in the history of mankind quaintly asks: 'What does it serve to have computers, if people do not have enough to eat and are dying of dysentery?'

(2009c: 14)

Today's corporate ethics or environmentalism (e.g. Corporate Social Responsibility, green capitalism) follows the same ideological route. The giant corporations that embrace it also engage in decaf capitalism, on the one hand grabbing as much money as possible, on the other returning a portion of it in the form of charity or green products. They, like Gates and Soros, see no contradiction, or perhaps even a relationship, between profit-making and inequality creation, between wealth accumulation and ecological crisis. They fail to discern their own complicity in the very 'poverty' or pollution they seek to redress. In fact, they often rationalize the latter through the practice of what Gates calls 'creative capitalism', making business itself the solution to poverty reduction or environmentalism. The attempt once again is to conveniently duck the ills of capitalism, to disavow its production of inequalities, injustices, and unevenness.

The implication is that it is charity that helps decaffeinate capitalism. It masks and purifies corporate ills, acting as a countermeasure to socioeconomic exploitation. For Žižek, it not only temporarily redistributes wealth, but also helps avoid war or stems revolution by tempering people's resentment (arising from generalized social inequality):

> ... it [charity] is the logical concluding point of capitalist circulation, necessary from the strictly economic standpoint, since it allows the capitalist system to postpone its crisis ... This paradox signals a sad predicament of ours: contemporary capitalism cannot reproduce itself on its own. It needs extra-economic charity to sustain the cycle of social reproduction.
>
> *(2008b: 374; cf. 2010a: 240; 2008a: 23–24)*

If charity is capitalism's necessary decaffeinating agent, allowing the latter to sustain itself while averting rebellion or crisis, it means that Gates and Soros are not philanthropists out of mere personal choice, religious belief, or Good Samaritanism; they are businessmen–humanitarians acting in the service of capitalism, tranquilizing its worst manifestations, or, to stick with the coffee metaphor, preventing it from overly percolating. They are, so to speak, coffee-pusher philanthropists, keeping people hooked but not wild (or wired), stimulated but not strung out. Their charity work is integral to the logic of capitalism; it helps regulate the system, calming it down when it runs amok. The irony, of course, is that it is the philanthropists' own business activities that help hyper-activate the system in the first place.

What is noteworthy (and implied in the two previous sections) is that the tycoons' decaffeinating philanthropy targets, not systemic problems or institutions, but what Žižek calls 'secondary malfunctions' – narrow science-based health, technocratic policy-making, corrupt and inefficient state institutions, and so forth. 'Precisely because they want to resolve all these secondary malfunctions of the global system, liberal communists [such as Gates and Soros] are the direct embodiment of what is wrong with the system' (Žižek 2009d: 10; cf. 2008a: 23, 37). They end up trying to address only the more outwardly perceptible or 'subjective' violence in the form of poverty, corruption, or individual rights abuse, as opposed to the slower, more tortuous, and less immediately tangible structural or 'objective' violence of social inequality, corporate monopoly, dehumanizing working conditions, unequal land tenure, or gender discrimination (cf. Žižek 2006d: 10). It is most often these latter broad malfunctions that lead to the former symptomatic subjective violence taken up by the billionaire-philanthropists. Thus, pointing to the need for ideology critique to uncover, not the latent meanings of social antagonisms (e.g. poverty), but their disguised meanings (e.g. inequality), Žižek often repeats Bertolt Brecht's famous quote: 'What is the robbery of a bank compared to the founding of a new bank?' (Žižek 1989: 30).

The problem about structural violence though is precisely that it appears abstract, so that Gates and Soros are able both to hide behind and to profit from the facelessness of decaf capitalism. They are able to maintain a certain distance and anonymity from the social impacts of corporate monopoly or ruthless financial speculation, yet at the same time benefit from a system that privileges individual effort, initiative, philanthropy. Such individualization is further magnified by the rise of media hype and celebrity culture. The tendency there is to personalize 'super-successful' businessmen such as Gates and Soros. Žižek notes, for instance, the propensity to appeal to Gates's familiarity as a friend: he is made out to be not an enigmatic, evil Big Brother, but an ordinary, geeky, nice guy, someone just like us, albeit tremendously talented: 'the notion of a charismatic "business genius" reassert[s] itself in "spontaneous capitalist ideology", attributing the success or failure of a businessman to some mysterious *je ne sais quoi* which he possesses' (Žižek 1999a: 349, 347). In the process, the power, influence, and unsavoury practices of these business leaders are further sanitized (i.e. decaffeinated), naturalizing and familiarizing corporate neoliberalism.

Such decaffeinating predilections are magnified in this instance because the tycoons in question don't simply give (millions of dollars), they give spectacularly (billions of dollars). Mary Phillips (2008) sees such orgiastic and excessive charity as a modern form of potlatch, with the mediated public display of it as a crying out for status, glory, honour. She quotes Marcel Mauss to reinforce the point: 'The rich man who shows his wealth by spending recklessly is the man who wins prestige' (2008: 252). The spectacle of giving, and of giving so much, aims at constructing Gates and Soros as celebrity-heroes, providing them with an instantly recognizable brand. For Phillips (as for Žižek, as noted above), such a phenomenon is an attempt by Gates and Soros to ward off their own mortality, but also, more importantly, the crisis of capitalism itself: the tycoons' excessive philanthropy helps defuse 'the potential of explosive surplus produced by the US in order to avert [social, environmental] catastrophe' (2008: 261).

A final consideration regarding decaf capitalism is its proclivity towards a 'decaf state' (or perhaps a 'decap state' – as in 'decapitated'!). To be sure, the billionaire-philanthropists' spectacular giving fits well with the neoliberal gutting of the state: their gifts, like those of the thousands of charitable foundations that have cropped up under neoliberalism, fill a few (among many) of the gaps in state social funding. The problem, however, is that private decisions are being made for public goods (health care, education, human rights, poverty reduction, etc.). Elites decide, according to their own priorities, prejudices, or idiosyncrasies, what causes matter, how much to spend on them, and in what manner. Enlightened benevolence and individual heroics thus replace collective will, with the (decaf/decap) state sidelined into adulation and gratefulness. As Nickel and Eikenberry point out, we have got to the point now where 'we rarely contest the social policy made by philanthropists because we mistakenly identify government wealth as being political and individual wealth as being apolitical' (2010: 271).

The related issue here is the lack of political legitimacy and accountability: state-funded programs have at least a modicum of public oversight and recall; their deregulation and privatization means they now answer only to a clique of private individuals. Not only are we left with the corporate world deciding what 'poor' or marginalized communities need, but we must also trust in corporate 'voluntary' self-regulation (e.g. accountability or certification codes that are part of Corporate Social Responsibility). Yet, isn't something amiss when private organizations such as the Gates Foundation have annual budgets greater than that of the World Health Organization and can more or less dictate policy on such issues as HIV/AIDS or malaria immunization? 'Wealthy individuals like Bill and Melinda Gates have the governing capacity to decide which diseases are eradicated – who lives and who dies – not because they represent the public collective will, but because they have accumulated massive profits' (Nickel and Eikenberry 2010: 272).

The flip side of the decaffeination of the state, of course, is not just that it cannot step up, but also that so often it *will* not. Private philanthropy appears to have sanctioned governments (in both the North and South) to abrogate their social responsibilities, letting them off the hook. The state can thus shirk its duties towards marginalized communities, human rights, or health, because the likes of Gates and Soros are there to fill in. It can ignore the lack of adequate regulation of big corporations or hedge funds, even though this might negatively impact jobs, consumers, business competition, or old-age pensions. The postpolitical landscape of decaf capitalism is one in which magnanimous elites spearhead both social programming and rabid entrepreneurialism without account, while the state is content to sit back and even applaud, equally without account.

The new corporate philanthropy: Product (RED) and charity shopping

Q: What's the latest on Starbucks?
A: The word is that it got some fair-trade coffee for its employees – not a bad swap that!

Of late, corporations have been rushing to claim their ethical responsibility. Starbucks sells fair-trade coffee, Marks & Spencer introduces a new line of non-sweatshop and fair-trade clothing, Whole Foods presents a sizeable 'ethical' section on its shelves (in addition to its regular organic food), and for every pair of Tom's shoes purchased, another is given to a 'child in need'. Businesses such as these are 'voluntarily' incorporating social and environmental concerns into their production processes, so much so that we can now buy ethical stocks on the Dow Jones Sustainability Index or the FTSE Socially Responsible Investment Index (called 'FTSE4Good').

Such a trend is new, and it raises the charity stakes to new heights. Whereas Gates and Soros's philanthropy is symptomatic of classic corporate charity, in which you first cold-bloodedly accumulate wealth and then give some of it away, this new form of it – charity shopping – integrates both gestures (cf. Žižek 2009a), in addition to making us complicitous as shoppers: by selling 'ethical' products, corporations are able to include charity in their business operations; and by buying these products, we as consumers are induced to become de facto philanthropists. In what follows, I will try and uncover the ideological operations of charity shopping, based mainly on the Product (RED) campaign.

Bono and the Product (RED) campaign

Established by Bono and lawyer and philanthropist Bobby Shriver, the Product (RED) campaign was unveiled at the 2006 Davos World Economic Forum, and subsequently launched across much of the Western world. The campaign involves teaming up with large corporations to sell (RED) products, with participating corporations donating about 1 percent of all purchases to a privately run foundation – The Global Fund to Fight AIDS, Tuberculosis and Malaria. Licensing deals have been made with many of the most prominent brands, including Apple, American Express, Gap, Hallmark, Starbucks, Nike, Motorola, Penguin, Microsoft, Emporio Armani, and Dell. (RED) products range from iPods and credit cards to T-shirts and fashion wares. Gap T-shirts, for example, have such mottos as 'INSPI(RED)' and 'ADMI(RED)' emblazoned on them, while Apple iPods and American Express credit cards are coloured red.

(RED) sees itself as a 'win–win' campaign, with businesses making profits while doing 'good', consumers buying what they 'need' for a worthy cause, and the Global Fund receiving sustainable funding. The Product (RED) 'manifesto' thus states:

> We believe that when consumers are offered a choice [to buy (RED) products that] ... meet their needs, they will choose (RED) ... more brands will choose to become (RED) because it will make sense to do so. And more lives will be saved ... (RED) is not a charity, it is simply a business model. You buy (RED) stuff, we get the money, buy the pills and distribute them. They take the pills, stay alive, and continue to take care of their families and contribute socially and economically in their communities ... All you have to do is upgrade your choice.
>
> *(Product (RED) 2008)*

The campaign attributes symbolic meaning to its registered trademark, (RED), stating that the parentheses represent 'embracing brothers and sisters dying of AIDS in Africa' (Product (RED) 2008). In this regard, the campaign website used to offer an online impact calculator with which one could track how many people in Africa one's purchase was helping keep alive, although it has now been removed (cf. O'Manique and Labonte 2008: 1562).

At its initial launch especially, (RED) carried out a massive media campaign, including TV commercials, promotions on Facebook and YouTube, charity art auctions, magazine advertisements (notably in the prestigious medical journal, *The Lancet*), and new song releases by U2 and Elton John. Bono made full use of his global celebrity for marketing purposes, appearing on *The Oprah Winfrey Show* and *Larry King Live* among others. Along with Giorgio Armani, he guest-edited an issue of *The Independent*, while garnering a host of celebrity endorsements for (RED) from the likes of Oprah Winfrey, Bill Gates, Nelson Mandela, Kanye West, Julia Roberts, Penelope Cruz, and Scarlett Johansson (Gates notably praised Bono's initiative as a case of 'creative capitalism'; cf. Product (RED) 2008). Meanwhile, (RED)'s corporate partners carried out their own advertising campaigns, with companies such as Gap reportedly spending

$58 million on its (RED) operations, $7.8 million of which went on marketing (Frazier 2007).

Between 2006 and 2011, (RED) claims to have raised $170 million for the Global Fund, affecting some 7.5 million persons living with HIV/AIDS (Product (RED) 2011). It should be noted though that this dollar figure represents less than 1 percent of the Global Fund's total income to date (Global Fund 2011). In addition, there have been accusations that (RED) and its corporate partners have spent more on advertising than they have taken in from sales (Frazier 2007; Rosenman 2007), although determining the veracity of such accusations is difficult given the noteworthy lack of transparency from all concerned about net sales, profits, and advertising budgets (Rimmer 2010: 323–24).

The production and consumption of charity

Product (RED) is a manifestation of 'cultural capitalism', wherein businesses incorporate cultural values or identities – in this case, charity, compassion, justice, caring – into their merchandise. (RED)'s corporate partners may thus be said to be producing a 'charity good', that is, charity as both commodity and good cause. Bono accurately describes it as 'hard commerce' charity, as opposed to 'bleeding-heart' philanthropy (*Daily Telegraph* 2006). Selling charity in this way is a rather cheap and easy method for corporations to boost their brands, since it gives them sizeable public profile, cachet, and legitimacy. It also aids them internally: a positive company image and reputation helps in corporate recruitment, and in workforce motivation, loyalty, and morale building. No wonder that more money might have been spent on marketing (RED) than raised for the Global Fund, or that only a measly 1 percent of corporate sales from (RED) is donated; the long-term value-added of branding and increased market share far outweighs the cost of publicity or donations (Littler 2008: 63–64, 242).

In the case of (RED), corporations build their brands by associating not just with charity but also celebrity – Bono's celebrity, as well as endorsements from the likes of Oprah. As a consequence, charity goods instantly gain a charismatic and auratic dimension. Adair notes, in this regard, that 'celebrity creates a sense of exclusivity, and appears to restore value to commodities that might otherwise be cheapened by reproduction' (2010: 250). And it is precisely on the basis of the 'excessive valorization of labour' made possible by celebrity that companies such as Microsoft or Gap can extract a tribute for their logoized yet cheaply produced commodities.

Such auratic branding is part of a key post-Fordist strategy – product differentiation and personalization. In the short term, these help make familiar commodities unfamiliar, if not magical, enabling mass-produced consumer items to appear unique and customized. More importantly though, in the long term, they allow capitalism to incessantly reproduce itself, through a limitless and constant search for novelty. (RED)'s production of auratic charity goods needs to be seen as integral to such renewal.

But the corporate production of charity goods also has many hidden costs. Although (RED) encourages its business partners to respect employees and work with local African producers (Youde 2009: 218), there is nothing contractually binding for either party and certainly no attempt to systematically address corporate labour and environmental practices. As Ponte et al. put it, Corporate Social Responsibility is 'separated … from the operations in which … corporations are involved. RED does not attempt to change or improve the normal functioning of business or trade' (2009: 312). As a result, at the same time that (RED)'s corporate partners are commodifying caring, their production processes could be involved in abuse of various kinds. Gap and Nike, for instance, are notorious for their resort to sweatshop labour (cf. Chapter 1), and we have just examined how Microsoft privatizes the knowledge commons, charges monopoly rents, and is associated with labour exploitation in the form of outsourcing, flexibilization, and gender discrimination.

But there is more: (RED) partner Motorola's phones have been criticized for their use of trafficked and environmentally tainted natural resources (gold, tin ore, coltan) originating from war-torn Eastern Congo (cf. Richey and Ponte 2008: 722). American Express cannot extricate itself from its global financial business, which depends on high-interest returns, including the repackaged debt of some of the most marginalized people and countries on the planet (Littler 2009: 32–33). And Starbucks leverages itself as an ethical company devoted to fair-trade coffee, yet only 1 to 2 percent of its coffee beans are actually fair trade (Fridell 2006: 20).[8] Meanwhile, despite the (RED) campaign's exhortation to work with local companies, (RED) companies have little direct involvement with Sub-Saharan Africa. Ponte et al. report that only Gap, Hallmark, and Motorola have one to two of their (RED) products made in the region, with a few of Gap's shirts manufactured from African cotton. Even this limited corporate engagement with the continent has seen no visible attempt to improve socioenvironmental practices. Thus, 'RED improves a company's brand without challenging any of its actual operations and practices' (Ponte et al. 2009: 314, 312–13).

Such has been the typical approach of most 'ethical' corporations, whether (RED)-related or not. In the fair-trade area, for example, the major food and coffee producers have heavily marketed ethical products but have yet to implement meaningful environmental and labour standards. The 'big four' food corporations (Nestlé, Kraft, Procter & Gamble, and Sara Lee) have voluntarily put into place several labour and environmental certification systems, but these tend to be weak, barely improving production processes or wages for small-scale farmers (Fridell et. al 2008: 20, 25). In fact, Fridell et al. (2008) show how the 'big four' have actively discouraged attempts by the alternate fair-trade movement to work towards organizing farming cooperatives or meaningful environmentally sustainable practices. They are able to maintain a monopoly on access to supermarkets, for example, by making new fair-trade entrants pay dearly for supermarket shelf space, or creating confusion among consumers by using labels that compete with those of alternate fair-trade brands (2008: 30–31). Instead, as if to make up for their weak production process record, the 'big four' fund charity programs for Third World farming communities in the form of schooling and medicines.

What emerges, therefore, is that charity goods such as those produced by (RED) don't live up to that name: they incorporate caring only on their sur-face – at the level of their branding, advertising, labelling, packaging – not in their content – at the level of their social and environmental relations of pro-duction. In fact, the former is deployed to cover up the latter, so that compa-nies can claim social responsibility while at the same time working against it, or they can re-brand themselves to recoup a scarred public reputation (as in the cases of Gap and Nike, for example). Such practices are the very mark of ideology as we have defined it: the creation of social fantasy to obscure social antagonisms and contradictions. Just like Gates and Soros's philanthropy, then, (RED)'s production of auratic charity 'goods' helps whitewash (greenwash?) the stain of global capitalist 'bads'. (RED) can even be said to be premised on these bads, given that its corporate partners would not be able to produce their affordable consumer items without low wages, ecological degradation, unjust trade relationships, or global unevenness. Not unexpectedly, the appearance of Product (RED), like the appearance of Corporate Social Responsibility gen-erally, coincides precisely with the global spread and hardening of neoliberal-ism, to which we owe increasing capital mobility, sweatshop production, lax environmental regulation, etc.

But this is only part of the picture: the production of charity cannot be divorced from its consumption. (RED) products, after all, are not just made and marketed, they also call forth a certain type of subject – an ethical con-sumer, a charity shopper. When one buys (RED) – a cell phone, shirt, greeting card, book, or computer – one is doing a number of things, apart from benefiting from the utility of the item itself. One gets the thrill of owning a brand, none other than a celebrity-endorsed brand. This is the 'cool factor' in auratic charity shopping (cf. Ponte et al. 2009). But by buying (RED), one is also buying *into* ethics (cosmopolitan caring, compassion, social responsibility), so that the purchase of a Starbucks *latte* enjoins one to a certain sympathy with the practice of fair trade (Žižek 2009a). With (RED) shopping, one is able to purchase the cachet of social responsibility *and* consume one's way to caring and compassion.

Richey and Ponte call this 'low-cost heroism', since we can do good with little effort by buying a relatively cheap consumer product that we would likely have bought anyway (2008: 723; cf. Littler 2009: 24; O'Manique and Labonte 2008). For his part, Žižek calls it (low-cost) 'redemption', because the very act of egotistic consumption already includes its opposite – freedom from guilt (2009a). We can engage in individualistic and materialistic (RED) shopping to our heart's content in the knowledge that we are doing our bit to save AIDS-stricken 'Africans'.

By buying (RED), therefore, we get bling, thrill, compassion, and redemption all in one. But is not such taunting and mesmerizing simply a powerful strategy to get us to shop more? Is (RED) not another manifestation of late capitalism's need for more consumption so that it can reproduce itself? In short, is (RED) not the latest display of 'commodity fetishism'? Marx coined the term to show how, under a capitalist regime, inanimate objects take on a strange and mysterious power to the point of their fetishization. As a result, commodities become more meaningful and important than people or social relations (1867: 163–65). Baudrillard draws on Marx to argue that such fetishism has become a key feature of late capitalism: 'humans of the age of affluence are surrounded not so much by other human beings ... but by objects ... We live by object time' (1998: 25). The myriad consumer items that fill our lives constitute a system of signs with significant cultural mystique (1998: 22–24), so that a car is not simply a car, it is the possibility of having fun with friends, racing through the city; or a (RED) T-shirt is not just clothing, but represents the ability to help those in need. Such a cultural mythology steers us towards identifying with the product, buying it, and going back for more. It is propagated and sustained, of course, by a massive corporate promotion and branding machine, but also, as Baudrillard emphasizes, by credit. Easy and cheap access to credit enhances consumer culture (i.e. 'buy now, pay later'), and like advertising, orients us towards more consumption 'so that society can continue to produce' (Baudrillard 1996: 160; cf. McGowan 2004: 34).

What is intriguing about such cultural capitalism, where objects are transformed into mythologies, is that it presents itself as having increased our freedom. The variety of commodities available, their mystique, their personalization and customization, all seduce us into thinking we have innumerable choices (about lifestyle, identity, social change). By shopping (RED), after all, I have the freedom to buy a range of products, while also contributing towards fair trade, malarial vaccination, and/or antiretroviral drugs. But closer inspection reveals how limited these choices actually are:

> Our freedom to choose causes us to participate in a cultural system willy-nilly. It flows that the choice in question is a specious one: to experience it as freedom is simply to be less sensible of the fact that it is imposed on

us as such … Choosing one car over another may perhaps personalize your choice, but the most important thing about the fact of choosing is that it assigns you a place in the overall economic order … 'personalization' … is actually a basic ideological concept of a society which 'personalizes' objects and beliefs solely in order to integrate persons more effectively.

(Baudrillard 1996: 141)

What looks like choice among (RED)'s innumerable charity shopping options, then, is more accurately its opposite: the seeming variety only imprisons us, further binding us to commodity fetishism. As Žižek reminds us, there is a big difference between formal freedom, in which one chooses from an already given background of choices, and actual freedom, in which one can change the very coordinates of available choices (2001: 121). (RED) charity shopping (and cultural capitalism generally) only does the former, making us think we have multiple ways of meaningfully helping others.

Commodity fetishism has several implications, especially in the case of Product (RED). It means that caring, compassion, and social justice are commodified so they can be easily and cheaply bought and sold. No wonder that AIDS and Africa have become 'hot'; they have been successfully marketed and logoized by the likes of Bono, Gap, and *Vanity Fair*, and readily consumed by the rest of us. But commodity fetishism also means that, by charity shopping, we continue to add to the problems of over-consumption by the North, wherein Americans can be the greediest consumers and biggest environmental polluters on the planet, while many in the South continue to suffer from (constructed) material scarcity and environmental degradation. All of this only ends up further orientalizing and disempowering those that the (RED) campaign is putatively trying to help: the commodification of AIDS or 'Africa' winds up reinforcing stereotypes about the continent (e.g. Africans are 'hypersexualized' and 'helpless victims'), while we in the North take for granted the privilege and time we have bought over the South (through our colonial history) so that we can continue to consume much more than most do in the South (Richey and Ponte 2008: 715, 721). In this sense, imperialism and environmental racism are integral to commodity fetishism and written into the very fabric of (RED).

But we must consider, too, the properly political implications of commodity fetishism. For one, by merging activism with shopping, Product (RED) reduces citizenship to consumerism. We as Western consumers get to determine the fate of anti-malaria and HIV/AIDS programs in the Third World through our purchasing decisions; global social change thus depends, not on political struggle or state intervention, but on Western shopping habits. The benevolent imperialism of such a stance aside, it means that the burden for structural global transformation is pinned on individuals, underlying once again the neoliberal faith in individual initiative and markets to solve social problems.

While not uncritical, Jeremy Youde (2009) defends such ethical consumerism, arguing that nay-sayers assume that 'markets are simply imposed on people. They deny any agency to citizens to respond to or reorganize in the face of markets' (2009: 211). The problem, it seems to me though, is not the denial of agency but the (neoliberal) limitation of agency to consumerism. Youde goes on to assert that 'political consumerism may be a person's *starting* point for action rather than its endpoint' (2009: 215). Perhaps, but it may also be the starting *and* endpoint, which in the case of (RED) amounts to 'low-cost heroism' (see above); that it should be the *starting* point at all, however, is highly revealing of today's neoliberal constriction of our political choices. Youde admits as much when he writes: 'Citizens may not have the time, energy, or skills necessary to engage in such lobbying and more overt political actions. However, nearly everyone goes shopping' (2009: 215). Precisely, and the fact that such commodity fetishism determines our political decisions should give us pause.

What Youde is hopeful about, evidently, is that ethical consumerism 'allows people to send a message to those with political and economic power about their choices and priorities' (2009: 216). As examples, he cites the effectiveness of the 1970s/1980s consumer boycott movement in dismantling South Africa's apartheid, and Walmart's recent decision to include organic products in response to customer pressure. In the first case, as Youde is well aware, there is no direct line between the consumer boycott and the undoing of apartheid. The boycott was a small part of a much wider global and domestic political movement, in which the African National Congress's own struggle was key. In the second case, Youde appears to have blind faith that individual purchasing choices necessarily or automatically add up, that is, that corporations respond to consumer pressure voluntarily, and that if they do, this pressure outweighs such corporate demands as keeping costs low, satisfying shareholders, and increasing profits and market share. Almost always, as I have been arguing, (capitalist) corporate logic tends towards the co-optation and compromise of social causes, with the result that carrying, say, organic food only happens if it makes business sense. Consequently, only safe and feel-good causes are taken up, with (RED) for instance funding the limited provision of vaccines and drugs, rather than engaging in the much more difficult struggle against the big pharmaceuticals for the provision of generic drugs.

My larger point here is that consumerist ideology makes invisible its background, the result being that by charity shopping, not only are we buying into the system (i.e. commodity fetishism), but our political options are also thereby severely limited and compromised (i.e. we have many choices except the choice of determining the range of choices; that is, we have formal but not actual freedom, as noted earlier). To put it still differently, for ethical consumerism such as that advocated by (RED) to be truly political, it would need to tie consumerism to production (and for that matter, redistribution) so that decisions are not made narrowly, impersonally, or in isolation. This would involve, not getting into bed with corporations, but struggling to bring them to account for their social and environmental actions. It would mean not uncritically catering to (RED) shoppers, but educating them about the North–South or ecological impacts of their consumption. The inability to make these political and relational connections is what mainstream ethical consumerism suffers from and commodity fetishism thrives on (cf. Littler 2009).

Anti-consumerist and fair-trade movements, which appear outwardly political, tend to be wanting for similar reasons. Critical of the intemperance and over-consumption of our times, anti-consumerists advocate extreme abstinence and frugality. Yet, is this not a perverse reproduction of the logic of commodity fetishism, replacing one excess with another (cf. Žižek 2008a: 89)? The withdrawal from consumption does nothing to fight against, and in fact only protracts, the social and environmental exploitation of global capitalist consumerism. By isolating consumption from production and social relations, anti-consumerism ends up, ironically, in compliance with the status quo. The same goes for the mainstream fair-trade movement, seen by some as an alternative to capitalist globalization. Gavin Fridell (2006) examines the key global group working on this issue, the fair-trade network, loosely composed of a range of organizations supporting fair trade and active mainly since the 1980s. He finds that, despite its rhetoric, it relies on corporate voluntarism on issues ranging from fair-trade labelling to socially responsible production processes. Many of its NGO members, in fact, receive funds from private corporations and the World Bank. The network is thus far from a direct challenge to neoliberal globalization, and is, in fact, highly compatible with it (Fridell 2006: 19). This depoliticization of fair trade certainly explains why the likes of Starbucks or Nestlé embrace it.

A final political implication of commodity fetishism is its tendency towards distancing (cf. Ponte et. al 2009: 312). In the case of (RED), the act of shopping alienates the shopper not simply from the campaign's purported beneficiaries (e.g. people living with HIV/AIDS), but also the production processes of (RED) commodities (e.g. wage-labour or environmental pollution). Product (RED) allows us to feel good about our charity consumption without any real connection to workers, 'Africa', or Africans. We can have fun shopping, without questioning our own complicity in the global political economy, oblivious to such issues as dehumanizing working conditions, low wages, union busting, unjust trading relationships, or corporate monopoly in the global health sector.

Such distancing is reinforced by the phenomenon of online shopping, a key aspect in the (RED) campaign: with a mere push of a button, one can shop, help, and 'share' (e.g. through (RED)'s blogs on Twitter and Facebook). Online chatting gives the impression of public interaction and virtual communities, but as Todd McGowan notes, it is a public world 'that seems to have everything save actual physical interaction ... [It] merely increases the range of the subject's private world' (2004: 156–57). In the case of (RED) this is doubly the case, since the egotistic act of shopping is compounded by the atomized and narcissistic act of chatting about it.

Product (RED)'s distancing and alienating qualities reveal once again what we have previously called 'decaf capitalism': a capitalism that one can engage with, but from the security of a store or the privacy of one's home; a regime that is easy and fun, and makes you feel good without having to get involved with other people (especially not workers or HIV/AIDS patients); a system that is 'frictionless' and safely insulated from the frontlines of suffering or struggle; in short, a capitalism stripped of its problems and dangers, permitting you to experience the Other without the Other (cf. McGowan 2004: 157; Žižek 2004a: 507).

Consequently, despite its novel approach to philanthropy, in which charity is not an ex-post activity but integrated into the system itself, Product (RED) ends up being yet another stop-gap measure. Youde believes this is not necessarily a bad thing: although (RED) is not critical of neoliberalism, it is an effective way of working within the system. He writes that (RED)

> finds a way to generate something positive out of the currently existent system ... It provides an avenue for promoting progressive political change – increasing access to life-prolonging antiretroviral drugs (ARVs) to HIV-positive persons in Africa – within the very framework that often impedes such progress ... Product (RED) is not *the* solution to the AIDS crisis in Africa, but it can provide one avenue for involving citizens in correcting the current imbalance ... [It is] an effort to make do with a less-than-ideal situation.
>
> *(2009: 202, 208, 220)*

But isn't this the usual liberal blackmail? 'We need to do something, or else the system will be out of "balance"'; 'the situation is bad, but we need to make do'. Liberals recognize there are major structural problems, but they invariably shy away from addressing them. Instead, they 'make do'. What they disavow is that 'making do' is precisely part of the logic of the system; it is the way that global capital ensures its maintenance and reproduction.

Product (RED), as a result, is not special, strange, or resistant to the system, it is fully compliant with it. It increases our distance from the Other, enables corporations to brand and advertise in a way that obscures socioenvironmental antagonisms, and further binds people to consumerism and commodity fetishism so that society can carry on producing. It may well help provide needed drugs and vaccines, but as is the case with all charity, it addresses only the short-term and secondary malfunctions. Rather than delivering just medicines, why does (RED) not help reverse the neoliberal cutting of social programs, and pressure states and global institutions such as the World Bank into providing adequate and accessible health services for all? Instead of partnering with the big corporations, why does it not join forces with global movements trying to fight the corporate patenting of drugs so they are made cheaper and more accessible? (RED) does not, and because it is wholly acquiescent to capital, dare not, address the structural issues underlying Africa's AIDS pandemic. In this sense, it is not so much that (RED) or its liberal proponents (e.g. Bono, Gates, or indeed Youde) ignore the root causes of the problem as much as obfuscate and forswear them, an ideological strategy par excellence (if Žižek ever saw one!).

The enjoyment of charity shopping

We have already examined the way in which charity shopping pulls us into consumption by incorporating into its products the thrill of celebrity branding, the satisfaction of cosmopolitan caring, and the feeling of redemption from the guilt of shopping itself. In the Lacanian/Žižekian view, there is but one term to describe this 'pull' – enjoyment (*jouissance*). Charity shopping of the Product (RED) kind entices and taunts us, and extracting its kernel of enjoyment is key to Žižekian ideology critique.

For Lacanians, capitalism's demand to enjoy – the demand upon which charity shopping rests – is a relatively recent phenomenon. As McGowan explains (2004), early capitalist societies used to prohibit enjoyment, prodding people instead to renounce the satisfaction of their desires in favour of a range of social duties (e.g. 'work hard', 'save', 're-invest your wealth', 'put off enjoyment now for later'). Such prohibition was geared towards a productivist society: individual sacrifice and an entrepreneurial work ethic became vital to building capitalism (McGowan 2004: 2–3). But of late, especially since the 1990s, things have changed dramatically. Prohibition has become a limit to the emergence of monopoly capitalism and consumer culture, with the result that, rather than curbing enjoyment, late capitalism *commands* it (McGowan 2004: 31; cf. Žižek 1991: 102). Whereas enjoyment used to be a threat to productivist society, it is now essential to late capitalist consumerism.

Indeed, late capitalism's productive engine depends on the superegoic command to enjoy (cf. Introduction); its strength and success hinges on the extent to which it can elevate enjoyment 'into the very principle of social life, the speculative movement of money begetting more money' (Žižek 2006b: 297). This means that, as citizens, we cannot postpone enjoyment. We must obey our superego's injunction to 'express' ourselves, have satisfying sexual lives or careers, or seek out products that promise enjoyment or instant gratification. The result is excess: '*enjoyment as such emerges only in this surplus, because it is constitutively an "excess"*. If we subtract the surplus we lose enjoyment itself', in the same way that if we remove capitalism's ability to incessantly revolutionize its own material conditions, it ceases to exist (Žižek 1989: 52). In fact, late capitalist societies are characterized not just by excess, but the normalization of excess – the desire for the best, biggest, tallest, richest, most original; the pervasiveness of 'super-sized' everything, from coffee to art; the orgiastic show of wealth; the rise of sexual promiscuity and 'extreme' sports; or the overabundance of 'choice', whether in TV channels, restaurants, or even university programs (cf. Dean 2006: 37–38).

The problem, however, is that we are promised enjoyment but can never attain it. For, if an end to dissatisfaction *were* possible, that would spell the end of the capitalist system. Instead, the aim of the system is always to solicit and activate desire, but never allow it to be satiated; this is what enables ever-increasing growth, profit, or market share. Capitalism, in this sense, is driven by insatiable lack, so that try as we may to satisfy our enjoyment, we always miss our mark (i.e. what Lacan calls *objet petit a*). As McGowan states, 'the problem with the society of enjoyment is not that we suffer from too much enjoyment, but that we don't have enough' (2004: 8).

Not all of us necessarily or always succumb to the command to enjoy. Žižek is at pains to emphasize (e.g. 1999b: 88) that ideologies work, not by expecting us to identify fully with the social fantasy, but by allowing us a certain distance, that is, by sanctioning or even stipulating modes of quasi-transgressive enjoyment such as, say, engaging in 'extreme sports' or subscribing to alternative identities or sub-cultures (e.g. anti-consumerism). As pointed out earlier though, often these end up reproducing the excesses they are purportedly trying to escape, thus conforming to rather than rebelling against the status quo. Of course, *not* enjoying may also be an option, but most frequently the result is (socially imposed, superegoic) guilt, anxiety or depression – guilt for not enjoying, anxiety about not owning, say, a cellphone or car, depression from not being part of the mainstream. The superego under late capitalism is one that bombards us with impossible or contradictory demands, leaving us free yet constrained, desiring but always dissatisfied and conflicted (Žižek 2006a: 80; Dean 2006: 99). This is why, Žižek maintains (1991: 103) outwardly 'permissive' societies such as ours also tend to be the most regulated: they command us to be fit and beautiful, to love our work or family, to avoid smoking and fat foods, and so forth.

One of the chief ways in which enjoyment is activated and maintained in late capitalism, especially when it comes to consumerism, is advertising. Advertising induces us to enjoy (Coke's 'Enjoy!' slogan says as much), binding us to continuous shopping. Yannis Stavrakakis (2006) argues that the Lacanian understanding of advertising differs significantly from the rational consumer behaviour model, which assumes we can make rational choices that maximize our personal advantage, and the mainstream critical Left model, which sees advertising as often duping us. The Lacanian position holds that, contrary to what the Left model assumes, we are not so passive or ignorant when we shop; we may know that we are being manipulated, but we nonetheless buy. This is because advertising *seduces rather than dupes* us; it appeals to our passions rather than our reason (as the rational choice model assumes) and so stimulates and re-engineers our desires (Stavrakakis 2006: 86).

For Lacan, enjoyment comes into being because of a constitutive lack, and human desire is precisely a desire for what is lacking. Stavrakakis notes how advertising plays on this link, that is, 'on the *manipulation* of the dialectic between lack and desire' (2006: 90; cf. Böhm and Batta 2010: 355). Branding and product promotion, accordingly, stimulate desire by constructing a social fantasy around the product, a fantasy that promises to fill our lack, fulfill our dreams, and meet our dissatisfaction. We are presented with magical commodities, such as (RED)'s auratic, celebrity-endorsed products, that cast a spell on us and set off our desire. What we buy when we consume the product is not so much the physical object, but the mystique surrounding it, the fantasy of helping, caring, saving. As Baudrillard emphasizes, we don't necessarily have to buy the rhetoric, but we do buy the enjoyment: 'Without "believing" in the product ... *we believe in the advertising that tries to get us to believe in it*' (1996: 166; cf. 64, 167, 173; 1998: 33; Stavrakakis 2006: 92). Advertising, in this sense, may well cause consumption, but it also becomes an *object* of consumption (Baudrillard 1996: 164).

But the social fantasy we are promised is fleeting and temporary. The object consumed turns out to be the sublime *objet petit a* (i.e. the 'it' in Coke's 'This is it!' or Nike's 'Just do it!'), impossible to hold or possess, never quite delivering on what we expect. As pointed out earlier, capitalism exploits this frustration, this putting off till later, to ensure its material reproduction. Advertising's social fantasy must remain an unfulfilled promise both to enable commodity fetishism and subjectivize us as desiring-machines. Hence Baudrillard argues that consumption has little to do with needs satisfaction and more with creating an uninterrupted cycle of enjoyment–disappointment (1996: 204; cf. Stavrakakis 2006: 95). This explains why the likes of Product (RED) must continuously offer new brands, personalized choices, and differentiated products, to keep us coming back for better and more. It also explains why, during times of crisis, no less than our political leaders enjoin us to shop, as did George W. Bush and Tony Blair after the 9/11 attacks. McGowan thus writes, 'When symbolic authority explicitly demands that we enjoy ourselves and warns us against restraining our enjoyment, we can be sure we have entered into a different kind of world [i.e. a society of enjoyment]' (2004: 36).

If enjoyment under late capitalism binds us to unceasing consumerism, it means not just that commodities become more important than people or social relations, but also that we start to delegate our beliefs to these commodities (cf. Pfaller 2005: 114). Žižek writes, in this regard, that 'it is as if ... [people's] beliefs, superstitions and metaphysical mystifications, supposedly surmounted by the rational, utilitarian personality, are embodied in the "social relations between things". They no longer believe, *but the things themselves believe for them*' (1989: 34).

We noted the same phenomenon in Chapter 1 in relation to humanitarian celebrities, but the argument appears particularly germane here: charity shopping is geared precisely to enabling us to transfer and displace our humanitarian urges onto, say, (RED) products (and the mystique created around them). With an easy and hassle-free push of a button, our purchases can care and save for us, and by doing good can redeem us as well. Charity consumption is thus able to incorporate a righteous and moral calling, a powerful fantasy of salvation, allowing us to channel our enjoyment into the campaign to save others (Kingsbury 2008: 53).

But if charity consumer goods believe for us, the important implication is that the ideology of humanitarianism is exteriorized and materialized. (RED) products become the material support for our belief in the need to do our cosmopolitan social duties. This reiterates again Žižek's important point that ideology is not merely about cultural values, customs, or prohibitions, but is radically externalized in things (1989: 40): we construct material reality ideologically, so that, in this case, it is integral to our lives as (charity) consumers, embodied in the things we buy, touch, eat, and live and work with every day. In this sense, by believing for us, charity goods become the material support for our unconscious (Žižek 1989: 40–41). We have delegated our philanthropy to them, so now they can do our charity work for us without us even having to know. This outsourcing of our beliefs makes the ideology of charity not weaker (because it has been delegated), but more powerful (because it now operates unobstructed).

The long and short of it once again is our depoliticization. If charity goods believe for us, do philanthropy for us, then we can sit back safe in the knowledge that the Third World or AIDS-stricken Africans are being 'saved'. The consequence is our transformation into passive spectators: charity consumerism has relieved us of our responsibility to act, to help change the world, perhaps even to *think* about helping change the world; instead, we can now watch and enjoy Bono and company do good. No wonder, as pointed out earlier, that our citizenship is circumscribed by our consumerism; that we remain oblivious to the socioenvironmental relations of production embedded in our shopping; and that our charity consumption helps 'save' Africans, but thankfully at a safe distance from us – mediated, anaesthetized, and exoticized by celebrity-heroes for our viewing pleasure.

Conclusion

Thus, today's global corporate philanthropy emerges, not from fundamental kindness on the part of such entrepreneurial giants as Gates and Soros, or some privileged Western capacity to care for the Other, but out of socioeconomic necessity. As pointed out earlier, charity is a basic ideological constituent of global capitalism, integral to the logic of the system itself. It is not an illusion or diversion, meant to distract us from what is really happening; rather, it points to real and important global problems (poverty/inequality, HIV/AIDS, authoritarianism), but only partially or indirectly reveals or admits to them. Charity is like the tip of the iceberg, making visible only its symptomatic pinnacle, but disavowing the large mass (i.e. the systemic violence) beneath. It acts as a sort of palliative care for the worst manifestations of exploitation, thus helping to stitch up structural inconsistencies and social antagonisms. In this sense, it is not meant to help the poor as much as save the rich, that is, avoid catastrophe or revolt, and legitimate, maintain, and advance global capitalism.

This is why charity enables what I have called 'decaf capitalism'. It allows corporations to engage in social devastation and pollution, while supporting good causes such as anti-poverty projects or reforestation and solar energy initiatives. It presents capitalism with a human and caring face, while the structural violence and inequality upon which this capitalism depends continue unabated. This is also why charity itself is marketed and branded: charity shopping empowers us all to purchase philanthropy online or in the store, and so enjoy becoming heroes-for-a-day. Rather than being the exclusive preserve of the rich, humanitarianism is thus democratized, although in the process we are (further) pulled into the lair of consumerism.

By helping to decaffeinate capitalist abuses, by commanding us to indulge in consumerist excess, global charity fastens us to neoliberal capitalism. It helps naturalize the 'business model', so that the latter can be unquestioningly applied to philanthropy as much as state health programs. When powerful actors, ranging from Microsoft to Bono or Gates, repeatedly present capitalism as a panacea for social ills, we listen. We tend to believe because, as Žižek says of our postpolitical ideological landscape, the 'Other supposed to know' believes (1997: 107). There might well be a few problems associated with the business model (pollution, poverty, corruption, etc.), but we ultimately trust the word of our entrepreneurial and cultural icons when they say these are minor exceptions, removable through technological means or better business practice. In this sense, not only is neoliberal ideology recommended to us by our sociocultural leaders, but it is also presented as *non-ideological*, as merely a question of good technique or neutral and pragmatic policy. Besides, we are told, what are the alternatives? Totalitarianism? Fundamentalism? Terrorism? The most common ideological trope, as we know, is this assertion of a dangerous, backward, and fanatical 'outside', in contrast to a pure 'inside' (i.e. neoliberal capitalism), distinguished by common-sense, wealth creation, and freedom. The effect once again is to prop up liberal capitalism as true and inevitable, that is, as the only game in town.

But if global capitalism secures our consent to the point of its incontestability, then it makes change unthinkable. The market economy remains depoliticized, its proper functioning requiring only 'wise' policy and tinkering at the edges. If we take liberal capitalism as given, moreover, then our ability to imagine other sociopolitical possibilities is forestalled. Instead, other than voting, the main choice offered to us is consumption, which becomes a substitute for politics. Accordingly, progressive causes and rebelliousness are packaged for our delectation by the likes of Nike or Dell, and we feel good about being able to do good while consuming.

Several further troubling implications ensue. To begin, by shopping, we are fundamentally unfree 'even as choices multiply and ever more experiences seem available for the taking' (Dean 2006: 191). On the one hand, as stressed earlier, 'free choice' is accompanied by a whole set of injunctions and regulations (you *must* enjoy, you need exercise every day, don't smoke, don't eat fried foods, etc.) that result in guilt and anxiety. The excesses of a society of enjoyment often mean the impossibility of really enjoying because there appear to be no limits either to enjoyment or its resultant constrictions. On the other hand, excess and permissiveness concede to an unrestrained superego, which can no longer postpone enjoyment, instead demanding instant gratification (Sharpe and Boucher 2010: 151; cf. McGowan 2004: 30). The result is a narcissistic, anti-authoritarian, and often belligerent personality, and in turn, a breakdown in decency and civility. Žižek points out that it is precisely to such permissiveness and perversion that today's religious fundamentalists and ethnic nationalists are responding, underlying once again how the latter political phenomena are integral to global capitalism, not outside or opposite to it, as liberals tend to claim (2008a: 9, 14).

By shopping, moreover, we end up turning further inwards – doing 'good' perhaps, but only in an atomized and self-enclosed way. Personal change, obedience, and apathy begin to feel much more appealing and fulfilling (i.e. enjoyable), whereas collective political activity looks messy and requires effort and struggle (i.e. constantly reminding us of our lack) (McGowan 2004: 139). We thus recoil at the public sphere and retreat to the private realm, shielded as it is from the dimension of the Real. In fact, as McGowan explains, in the neoliberal society of enjoyment, the state is seen no more as a guarantor of mutual sacrifice and repository of collective enjoyment; rather, it is viewed suspiciously as a threat and a thief: 'In giving money or control to the state, one is not performing a socially necessary sacrifice; instead, one is allowing the state to enjoy in one's stead ... [Hence] our attitude towards it tends to be hostile' (2004: 181).

Finally, the isolated and private act of shopping yields to a greater sense of fear, suspicion, and paranoia. McGowan writes that 'Security – securing one's private enjoyment – becomes the predominant way of interacting with the public' (2004: 171). We should note, in this regard, the increasing and widespread resort to security systems, security dossiers, cameras and closed-circuit television (CCTV), anti-terrorism squads, and travel bans for 'terrorists'. The proclivity towards safeguarding our enjoyment means an abhorrence to any risk or danger, consistent both with the post-9/11 securitization of the world and the often overblown public panic over the spread of SARS, mad-cow disease, and bird flu. Richey and Ponte argue that it may also be consistent with Product (RED)'s fetishization of HIV/AIDS, 'the fear factor that if not controlled in developing countries, AIDS could have a greater impact in rich countries' (2008: 715).

Of course, not all of these wider sociopolitical implications can be laid at the feet of either corporate philanthropy or charity shopping. But both certainly form part of the panoply of global capitalist practices, and they help illuminate continuing and novel neoliberal trends.

3

'SPECTACULAR NGOS': ACTIVISM WITHOUT ACTION?

> A man comes home early from work one day, only to find his partner in bed with another man. 'Why have you come home early?' the partner cries out furiously. 'How dare you sleep with someone else?' snaps back the man. To which the partner responds: 'I asked you first. Don't try and wriggle out of the problem by changing the topic!'
>
> (adapted from Žižek 2008a: 11)

In addition to spawning humanitarian celebrities and corporate philanthropy, the spread of late capitalist celebrity culture appears to have given rise of late to what I will call 'spectacular' humanitarian NGOs: organizations such as Médecins Sans Frontières (MSF)[1] or the Save Darfur Coalition that seek not just celebrity endorsements but celebrity status themselves, as a way of increasing fundraising and reach. The highly mediated and celebritized character of these organizations has provided added urgency to their humanitarianism. Their drive to 'act' and to 'act now', or rather their desire to be *seen* to be acting now, is akin to what Žižek calls 'obsessive neurotic' behaviour (2006a: 26), in which there is engagement in frenetic activity, precisely in order that nothing too threatening should happen (Daly 2010: 15). There is much brouhaha and spectacle – slick relief missions to save those in dire need, corporate partnerships to help increase development resources, even calls for military action to save genocide or disaster victims – but such busy-ness (and business) ultimately serves the preservation and furtherance of the neoliberal global order. As in the above joke, the NGO 'show' prevents changing the topic, focusing on the immediate and outward crisis, not its deeper politics. We thus have a paradox, wherein the possibility of meaningful sociopolitical change is foreclosed through spectacular acts and hyperactivity. In short, as Glyn Daly puts it, 'an activism without action' (2010: 15).

Of course, not all NGOs are ideological and depoliticizing in this way. There are thousands of NGOs worldwide, engaging in myriad activities from health advocacy to gender and development, several of which do critical-political work (as part of broader social movements, for instance). My focus in this chapter is mainly on transnational humanitarian NGOs, a sector dominated by Western-based BINGOs (big international NGOs) such as MSF or Oxfam, who carry out global advocacy, development, and emergency operations in an attempt to save human life (cf. Duffield 2007: 33). Yet, I would venture to say that, to the extent that NGOs participate in, and contribute to, the global neo-liberal hegemony, much of what I have to say about transnational humanitarian NGOs applies equally to other types of NGOs.

Spectacular NGOs

In *Society of the Spectacle* (1983), Guy Debord makes the case that the spectacle has become a central feature of late capitalism. Our media-based societies privilege the field of the audiovisual, whose organizing principle is the production and consumption of commodity-images: 'The spectacle is *capital* to such a degree of accumulation that it becomes an image' (Debord 1983: #34). True, the spectacle as political theatre has been deployed for centuries in all societies – think of the Olympics in classical Greece, the military campaigns of the likes of Darius the Great or Genghis Khan, and the public hangings of the European Middle Ages (Kellner 2004). But what has changed in late capitalism is the scope, depth, and intensity of the spectacle, facilitated by the late twentieth-century rise of the information economy. Douglas Kellner (2003, 2004) shows how 'megaspectacles' are now the defining events of our times – from the pervasive commodity-spectacles of McDonald's or Nike advertisements throughout our urban scapes, to media coverage of the 1991 Gulf War, Michael Jackson's trial, Princess Diana's death, the 9/11 attacks, or the shock-and-awe bombings of Iraq. As underlined in Chapter 2, we are increasingly witnessing the consumerization and entertainmentization of society and economy.

Debord saw his critique of the society of the spectacle as supplementing Marx's critique of commodity fetishism (cf. Chapter 2). His concern was directed at the added social alienation and reification brought about by the consumption of commodity-images; hence his now famous thesis: 'The spectacle is not a collection of images, but a social relation among people, mediated by images' (1983: #4). When relations between people are mediated by commodities-as-images, we have a kind of 'permanent opium war' (1983: #44) in which we become increasingly submissive and depoliticized. We tend to be mesmerized by media images and headlines, passively and uncritically consuming them.[2] The result is that we are more and more alienated from the direct and active reproduction of our lives.

We shall tease out the implications of the Debordian critique later, but let me first underline the relationship of the society of the spectacle to (humanitarian) NGOs. Indeed, NGOs have succumbed to spectacularization, too, unable to escape the pervasive logic of 'infotainment' and the commodity-image. Increasingly, they depend on the media for their functioning and survival. As Bernard Kouchner, co-founder of MSF and former French Foreign Minister, declares, 'Without the media, there is no important humanitarian action, and this in turn, feeds the papers' (quoted in Keenan 2002: 4). In the progressively more crowded and competitive humanitarian field, media exposure is essential to mobilizing awareness and garnering public support and donations.

Band Aid/Live Aid in 1984–85, and particularly Live 8 and the Make Poverty History campaign in 2008, are usually seen as pioneering the NGO-organized 'megaspectacle' (cf. Chapter 1). Yet, MSF is one of the first NGOs to have harnessed the media to publicize its medical missions, starting with the late 1960s Biafran blockade, but especially during and after the Rwandan genocide of 1994. It is MSF, as we shall see, that almost single-handedly brought the genocide to the media's (and the world's) attention. Similarly, of late, there is the example of the Save Darfur Coalition, which successfully harnessed the media to advance one of the largest transnational campaigns in recent years. Bringing together a broad network of mainly US anti-genocide and human rights organizations, college and school students, African-American church groups, and pro-Israel and Jewish groups, the Coalition organized a spectacular global campaign, especially during 2004–7, advocating for international intervention in Darfur (cf. Mamdani 2009; Haeri 2008: 35; Hassan 2010: 99; Flint and de Waal 2008: 180). Mahmood Mamdani calls it 'undoubtedly the most successful organized popular movement in the United States since the movement against the Vietnam War' (2009: 70).

The effectiveness of public outreach by the likes of MSF or Save Darfur depends on carefully planned and staged media campaigns. Save Darfur, for example, is well known to have employed several full-time staff for fundraising, and to have hired a top Washington, DC advertising agency (M + S Services) for its campaign (cf. Mamdani 2009: 23). Mainstream advertising in newspapers, magazines, and TV is a must, as are fundraising events (charity galas, auctions, runs, walks, fashion parades). But lately, NGOs have also been investing in slick website design and social media campaigns (e.g. webcasts, online ads, community blogs). The use of digital photography and video is crucial here: images, more than words, allow them to quickly and dramatically communicate devastation and distress. Accordingly, the Save Darfur website fastidiously documents alleged atrocities in the region (torched houses, rape, violence) with the help of photos, films, and satellite imagery. The point, in the Debordian vein, is to construct spectacle by selling media-friendly and sensationalized commodity-images.

Of course, wooing the mainstream press is a key part of any NGO media strategy. MSF, like most other humanitarian NGOs, deploys press officers on all of its missions, 'whose job it is to compete for media attention as well as to dramatize the situation in question' (DeChaine 2002: 360). Of late, reflecting the practice made famous during the 2003 Iraq invasion, journalists have been invited to 'embed' themselves with NGOs to witness humanitarian operations first hand (Cottle and Nolan 2007: 867). Most often, media packages are made available, pitching stories to a range of news services. Briefings are tailored to press requirements for, say, 'human' stories or in-depth commentary. Sometimes, stories are sold to emphasize the 'home' connection (to make a disaster more palpable to the home audience) (Cottle 2009: 154–55). A Reuters editor even offers the following tips to NGO communications staff when important stories are deemed to have been forgotten or overlooked (quoted in Cottle 2009: 151–52): 'keep in dialogue with the media', 'put a number on it' (e.g. provide death tolls), 'bring in the big names' (i.e. celebrities), 'make it visual' (i.e. 'nothing sells a story like a good picture').

Increasingly, NGOs are branding themselves. Like in the corporate sector, brands are vital to raising profile in the highly competitive global NGO field. Brands and logos create product recognition (cf. Chapter 1), in this case enabling NGOs to increase public/media familiarity, identification, and loyalty. The trendsetter here again is the Make Poverty History campaign, which as we noted in Chapter 1, logoized and spectacularized issues of poverty and debt. Most humanitarian NGOs have now followed suit: MSF trades on its Nobel Prize-winning image, but also on the idealism of its volunteer medical staff, whose motto is to 'Care For and Testify' (*témoigner*); the Red Cross rides on its reputation as trustworthy and neutral; and Oxfam and Save Darfur aim at promoting global community 'to overcome poverty and suffering' (Oxfam) and speak out against the 'atrocities in Darfur' (Save Darfur) (Cottle and Nolan 2007: 866–67; http://www.msf.org; http://www.oxfam.org.uk; http://www.savedarfur.org).

Celebrities play a big part in such branding, allowing NGOs to integrate glam with humanitarianism, or 'buzz' with 'biz' as some have characterized it (cf. Collier 2007: 4). Taking advantage of corporate marketing's free-floating association of stars with products, lifestyles, and values, NGOs use celebrity to add allure and reach to their activities. Celebrities help endorse campaigns, provide testimonials, offer 'expert' knowledge, and make fundraising appeals (cf. Brockington 2009; Brockington and Scholfield 2010: 552; Igoe 2010: 379). Several celebrities allow their own image or brand to be used for NGO fundraising products (T-shirts, mugs, photos, mementos, etc.). Oxfam has 'Celebrity Ambassadors' (e.g. Colin Firth, Scarlett Johansson, Chris Martin) it can call upon to endorse a range of causes (cf. Oxfam America 2011). And Save Darfur's campaign hinges largely on donations and support from a long and impressive list of celebrities, including Don Cheadle, Mia Farrow, George Clooney, Matt Damon, and Brad Pitt. Even artists and intellectuals such as Harold Pinter, Seamus Heaney, Günter Grass, Jürgen Habermas, and Tom Stoppard were roped in for their support at one point in the campaign (Mamdani 2009: 55–56). No wonder that, as Flint and de Waal report, Save Darfur's engagement of stars 'ensured that press coverage stayed at the astonishing level of about 500 articles per month throughout 2005 and beyond' (2008: 184).

Because NGOs resort to corporate marketing, branding, and celebrity product endorsements, the distinction between NGOs and private business is becoming increasingly blurred. In fact, direct NGO corporate ties, which used to be the exception only two decades ago, are now the norm. Many humanitarian NGOs nowadays even proudly display the logos of their corporate 'sponsors' or 'partners' on their websites: World Vision carries the logos of such companies as Barrick Gold, IBM, Verizon, Procter & Gamble; Save the Children: Bulgari, Ikea, Google, Merck, Microsoft; CARE: Gap, PotashCorp, MasterCard, Encana, Walmart, Coca-Cola; and so forth. All of this is a testament to the growing corporatization of NGOs.

The latest development is the state's encouragement of NGO corporate partnerships: for example, the Canadian International Development Agency has just announced a controversial multi-million-dollar grant for three NGOs (Plan Canada, World Vision Canada, World University Services Canada) to partner with Canadian mining firms (Rio Tinto, Alcan, Iamgold, Barrick Gold) on development initiatives in Latin America and Sub-Saharan Africa. The controversy mainly concerns the fact that some of these firms have recently been involved in labour and human rights disputes (Nutt 2012; Leblanc 2012).

Most likely, this trend of NGO corporatization is part of the logic of the neoliberal global order, in which to function as global players requires the adoption of corporate identities and practices. It is no accident that the very structure of global monopoly capitalism, dominated by a handful of huge corporate brands such as IBM, Microsoft, or Walmart, is now reproduced in the global humanitarian NGO field: it, too, is dominated by a coterie of BINGOs such as Oxfam, Red Cross, World Vision, and MSF. To function and compete as spectacular global organizations, they must be large, powerful, and evidently, corporate.

It is important to note that the spectacularization of NGOs happens not just because NGOs need and use the corporate media, but also because the media need and use them. The press often rely on humanitarian NGOs for news because the latter have a reputation for impartiality, and they work on the front lines in far-away and often exotic places (global emergency hot-spots, war zones, refugee camps, etc.). Humanitarian crises are eminently newsworthy; they offer sensational stories about destruction, suffering, and triumph, with easily identifiable victims and heroes/heroines. NGOs are ideally placed to help relay and construct these stories, in fact frequently acting as news scouts. In his analysis of the 2004 Asian Tsunami, for example, Scott Watson notes that the media placed NGOs such as the Red Cross in an 'authoritative position' to speak on issues of human emergencies and how best to respond to them (2011: 13). Similarly, François Debrix argues that during the Rwanda crisis of the early 1990s, it was only after the MSF 'witnessed' and 'discovered' evidence of genocide that 'photo-journalists, TV crews, humanitarian volunteers of all kinds and "benevolent" politicians' flocked into the country. In a way, Rwanda only became a global spectacle 'once MSF gave it a globally recognisable and eye-catching label, that of genocide'. Hence 'the key moment ... is not when the media take over. It is rather when international medical assistance specialists intervene ... ' (Debrix 1998: 841–43).

Therefore, it is not just that humanitarian NGOs rely on celebrities to build their reputation, influence, and public support; it is also that they have become celebrities in their own right, using the global media to sell messages and commodity-images, and are sought out by this same media to help identify and construct newsworthy stories. In this regard, one commentator aptly characterizes MSF staff as the 'glamour boys and girls of the aid business' (Di Giovanni, quoted in DeChaine 2002: 356). Like their global corporate and media partners, humanitarian NGOs such as MSF have transformed themselves into charismatic brands; they are now central to what Debord calls the 'society of the spectacle'.

The new humanitarianism: the imperative to 'act' and to 'act now'

Since the end of the Cold War, there has been an explosion of international NGOs, particularly development and humanitarian ones, leading to the rise of what is termed 'global civil society'. In large measure, this is due to the ascendancy of neoliberalism, which has seen NGOs fill the many gaps created by government cutbacks and privatization. But in part, it is also the result of the intensification of globalization and the information economy, which has opened up possibilities for greater 'borderlessness'. Not content with doing only aid and development work, NGOs have carved out an increasingly more activist and interventionist role for themselves in the global arena. This trend is what has been called 'the new humanitarianism'.

Central to the new humanitarianism is a security discourse, which divides the world, not so much along the lines of wealth vs. poverty as it used to, but more in terms of stability vs. threat. Mark Duffield argues that the security discourse is constructed on the basis of the metaphor of the 'borderlands' (i.e. the Third World), an imagined geographic space of instability, excess, and social breakdown, which poses a threat to the metropolitan areas (2001: 309).

The borderlands are depicted as violent and unpredictable, or at least always a potential danger; they are the source of many of the problems seen to plague global security, including drug trafficking, terrorism, refugee flows, and corrupt/weak/rogue states.

Accordingly, the point of international intervention is to tame and manage instability. In this scenario, poverty, corruption, and refugee flows are to be feared much more than alleviated. Development and humanitarianism are seen not as problems of reducing inequality or protecting the most vulnerable, but as technologies of security, which function 'to contain and manage underdevelopment's destabilizing effects' (Duffield 2007: ix, 24).

The practical outcome of this new humanitarianism is a significant shift away from respecting national sovereignty and towards external intervention in the Third World: it means neglecting international law, or obeying the 'higher' moral law of humanitarianism, under the guise of the 'responsibility to protect' (cf. Mamdani 2009: 274; Watson 2011: 5). In other words, new humanitarianism has increasingly become neoimperialism, allowing the West to 'transform conflicts, decrease violence and set the stage for liberal development' (Duffield et al. 2001: 269). Not just a Third World country's foreign policy, but now also its domestic economic or human rights situation is seen as a credible threat (Duffield 2001: 311), recalling colonialism's 'civilizing mission' to eradicate 'barbaric' Third World cultural practices such as widow-burning or infanticide. More often than not, the form of external intervention is military, that is, armed intervention parading as humanitarian rescue mission. The post-9/11 War on Terror has only escalated this trend, enabling the possibility of 'unending war' to secure the borderlands (e.g. Iraq, Afghanistan) (Duffield 2007: 131). Illustrative of unending war is the following list, compiled by Watson (2011: 4), enumerating the countries for which humanitarianism has been used to justify military intervention in recent years: Somalia, Haiti, Bosnia, Angola, Mozambique, Kosovo, East Timor, Sierra Leone, the Democratic Republic of Congo, Liberia, Zaire, Sudan, Côte d'Ivoire, Iraq, and Afghanistan.

NGOs are firmly enmeshed in this security–humanitarian network. For the past two decades particularly, the private–public linkages between Western states, UN agencies, private firms, militaries, and NGOs has grown. In fact, as Duffield puts it, the securitization of development/humanitarianism 'has been of central importance for legitimising the growing involvement of non-state actors' (2001: 312; cf. Watson 2011: 3–4). And NGOs have become not just accomplices in this network, but key players. Mamdani goes so far as to argue that the new humanitarianism is the 'twin of the War on Terror' (2009: 274), with groups such as Save Darfur as pivotal facilitators. NGOs have pushed for and capitalized on the vast resources directed at emergency and security operations around the globe. Many such operations (e.g. in Afghanistan, Haiti,

Bosnia) have been ambitious and well coordinated, with relief agencies working alongside military or peacekeeping campaigns.

The imperative to 'act' and to 'act now' is central to these NGO campaigns. To be sure, beginning mainly in the post-World War II era, organizations such as Oxfam, ActionAid, and MSF were *created* to respond to global crises, ranging from armed conflicts and epidemics to 'natural' or man-made disasters. Whether we are talking about the 1949 Palestinian refugee situation, the 1967 Nigerian civil war, the 1984–85 Ethiopian famine, or the more recent 2005 Pakistan earthquake, emergencies have become an opportunity for humanitarian NGOs to function and even expand. Indeed, they have been able to justify and aggrandize themselves based on what Duffield refers to as a 'permanent emergency regime' (2007: 25, 47–49, 219). All of them rely on a 'threat-urgency narrative' to 'legitimize their functions' (Watson 2011: 9); it is this narrative that allows them to identify and categorize the disaster (e.g. as an impending famine or a pressing refugee crisis), as well as publicly highlight the humanitarian duty to save lives or assist 'populations in distress', as MSF puts it (http://www.msf.org).

One of the most poignant recent examples of the construction of emergency discourse is that of the Save Darfur Coalition, especially during the 2004–7 period. The Coalition relied on highly charged rhetoric to issue its emergency call for international intervention. The first move, as Mamdani underlines (2009: 64–65), was to categorize the conflict in the Darfur region as racially motivated: the government-armed 'Arab Janjaweed militia' were reportedly perpetrating violence against 'black-skinned non-Arabs'. Such stereotyping became pervasive in Western public discourse and was often repeated by the mainstream press, including *The Washington Post* (Mamdani 2009: 64; cf. Hassan 2010: 98). Mamdani notes (2009: 6) that this ethnicized/racialized framing has its origins in the colonial tradition of racializing the peoples of Sudan for political purposes (i.e. as a divide and rule strategy); it is a framing that, in the contemporary global conjuncture, only served to reinforce the discourse of the War on Terror, demonizing Islam and Arabs, and pressing for immediate counter-terrorist action.

The Coalition's second discursive move was to characterize the Darfur situation as 'genocide' (despite evidence to the contrary, as we shall see below). It is the deployment of this culturally and politically charged term that, almost single-handedly, brought together such a large and diverse range of US-based organizations that made up the Coalition (see above), while catching the attention of the media and politicians alike (cf. Save Darfur Coalition 2011). After Save Darfur's 'genocide alert' in 2004, events quickly gathered pace: a student-led divestment campaign was organized, a large Save Darfur Rally To Stop Genocide was held in Washington, DC, and an impassioned plea (by George Clooney) was made to the UN Security Council for international intervention. In 2007, the rhetoric was ratcheted up. The Coalition criticized China for its strong support of the Sudanese government, with a campaign that included taking out full-page advertisements in *The New York Times* and Mia Farrow denouncing the upcoming Beijing Olympics as the 'Genocide Olympics'.

The overall effect of this emergency discourse was to exercise tremendous pressure on political leaders in the US and around the world. Secretary of State Colin Powell testified in front of the Senate Relations Committee that genocide was being committed in Darfur. The US Congress agreed, pushing for political and economic sanctions for Sudan. Meanwhile, the UN Security Council referred the Darfur case to the International Criminal Court, sent UN peacekeeping troops to Sudan, and following China's change of position on the Council in the face of public pressure, established a larger joint UN–African Union peacekeeping mission, with financial support from the US Congress (cf. Flint and de Waal 2008: 181, 280; Haeri 2008: 35–37).

One of the most troubling features of this NGO emergency discourse is its tendency towards militarization and war. The imperative to act 'now' tends to provide added impetus and rationale for militarized intervention. We are familiar with NGOs providing relief work in war zones, in which they must sometimes coordinate with warring factions to deliver aid programs. We are also familiar with the use of army troops in non-military crises such as the Asian Tsunami in 2004 or Hurricane Katrina in 2005 (to keep law and order, or help NGOs distribute food aid). Increasingly, as Watson argues, 'states and the international community have institutionalized a militarized response through the establishment of specialized military entities such as the United States Foreign Disaster Assistance or the Canadian Disaster Assistance Response Team' (2011: 9).

But what is relatively new and noteworthy is the call *by* humanitarian NGOs for military intervention – a phenomenon described by the paradoxical concept, 'humanitarian war'. It is a concept that, as Vanessa Pupavec notes, NGOs themselves helped legitimate, especially through their demands for military intervention in the Balkans during the 1990s (2006: 263). Thus, MSF appealed for military action in Bosnia in the mid-1990s, while Save the Children lobbied Western governments for armed intervention in Kosovo in the late 1990s (Pupavec 2006: 255). Since that time, several other similar calls have been made. Of particular note are Oxfam's demand, in relation to the Darfur situation, for a broader interpretation of the UN Charter on the principle of non-interference to include intervention, and Save Darfur's outright plea for a no-fly zone and Western military action. In fact, 'Out of Iraq and Into Darfur' became a common Save Darfur slogan. Pupavec points out, in this regard, that NGOs were quick to criticize the failure to obtain UN Security Council authorization for military intervention in Iraq, but were only too willing to ignore such authorization when they demanded military intervention in Kosovo and Darfur (2006: 266).

If rhetorical demands for action raise the stakes, resulting in the militarization of the new humanitarianism, so do media demands for spectacle. The media-tization of NGO emergency work – that is, the drive not just to act now, but also to be *seen* to be acting now – adds greater urgency. NGOs may well be responding to save lives, but they are also playing to the global media and public. MSF's *témoignage* (witnessing) after all, is about witnessing not just on behalf of disaster victims, but also *for* the media/public. This recalls our earlier arguments about the entertainmentization of humanitarianism – the pressures to create 'megaspectacles', to satisfy seemingly insatiable appetites for suffering, death, and disaster. The militarization of emergency work only supplies further fuel to this fire, aiding and abetting the spectacularization of violence and war. In this regard, Henry Giroux contends that we are witnessing a new phase in the society of the spectacle, that of the '*spectacle of terrorism*' (2006: 26). According to him, a 'visual culture of shock and awe has emerged', which celebrates violence in the form of night bombing raids, hostage takings, and beheadings, or the destruction of public buildings (2006: 21, 24).

The pressure to create spectacle, then, means that spectacular NGOs are not simply observers or objective relays in delivering humanitarian aid; they are full-fledged actors, identifying emergencies and constructing them for public consumption (cf. Keenan 2002: 5). Add militarization to this mix, and you move from the imperative to *act now* and *be seen to be acting now*, to an imperative to be seen to be acting now, *militarily if needs be* (or *preferably?*).

The systemic and symbolic violence of spectacular NGOs

> Three friends are having a drink at the bar. The first one says, 'A horrible thing happened to me. At my travel agency, I wanted to say "A ticket to Pittsburgh!" and I said "A ticket to Pissburgh!"' The second one replies, 'That's nothing. At breakfast, I wanted to say to my partner "Could you pass the sugar, honey?" and what I said was "You dirty fool, you ruined my life!"' The third one concludes, 'Wait till you hear what happened to me. After gathering the courage all night, I decided to say to my spouse at breakfast exactly what you said to yours, and I ended up saying "Could you pass me the sugar, honey?"'
>
> *(adapted from Žižek 2004b: 61)*

Often, the most traumatic situations are not necessarily the outwardly perceptible ones (i.e. the gaffes of the first and second interlocutors in the joke), but the less obvious ones (i.e. the repressed content in the outward politeness of the third). As Paul Taylor suggests, telling are the moments 'in which nothing of substance is said ... in that non-utterance resides all manner of psychologically destructive forces' (2010: 93).

And so it is with spectacular (humanitarian) NGOs: it is most often in these organizations' non-utterances that ideological violence is to be found. The spectacle of NGO humanitarianism is revealing not simply for what it shows, but more importantly for the violence it often ignores, takes for granted, or disavows. Žižek distinguishes two types of violence: (i) 'subjective violence', which is directly visible and identifiable (e.g. emaciated babies, physical destruction in the wake of a hurricane); and (ii) 'objective violence', which is less immediately perceptible (2008a: 1–2). Objective violence is itself made up of 'systemic violence', which refers to our often slow yet steady social oppressions (e.g. gender exclusion, wage discrimination, the daily grind of alienating work), and 'symbolic violence', the violence inherent in our systems of representation (e.g. the way in which an image of a starving child can hide as much as it reveals). The crucial point for Žižek is that objective violence is what is required for the 'normal' functioning of our social and economic systems. In other words, systemic and symbolic violence is the background against which subjective violence happens: objective violence 'may be invisible, but it has to be taken into account if one is to make sense of what otherwise seem to be "irrational" explosions of subjective violence' (Žižek 2008a: 2). Accordingly, I'd like to highlight the systemic and symbolic violence of humanitarian NGOs, violence which serves as backdrop to their spectacle.

The systemic violence of humanitarian NGOs stems, at least in part, from the very nature of their work – short-term emergency operations that attempt to rescue people from immediate danger, but make no attempt to address the broader or underlying causes of such danger. As MSF's James Orbinsky readily admits, MSF action 'takes place in the short term' with limited objectives in the wake of a crisis, 'but does not itself attempt to solve the crisis' (2000: 10). The problem is that such an approach is premised on what was earlier denoted as a 'permanent emergency regime': rather than working themselves out of a job, NGOs depend (and count) on more and more crises. They have every interest in global neoliberal capitalism's continued production of emergencies, which enables and legitimizes their spectacular humanitarianism. In this sense, the NGO-ization of humanitarianism (and development) may have less to do with finding effective solutions to problems than a way of keeping the humanitarian business in business.

True, some humanitarian NGOs do carry out broader 'development' programming, alongside their short-term relief and advocacy work. For example, MSF organizes a campaign to make cheaper generic drugs more readily available to Third World countries (cf. http://www.msfaccess.org), and Oxfam runs a host of projects in gender equality, health, and education around the world (cf. Oxfam UK 2011). But as pointed out in Chapters 1 and 2, most of these initiatives are depoliticized; they steer clear of, say, anti-capitalist/anti-racist critique, or unionization of workers (or women), in favour of tamer and non-threatening areas such as mainstream human/gender rights and education. As Issa Shivji contends, in Sub-Saharan Africa issues of equality and equity are banished to the 'realm of rights, not development'; that is, rights are a question of NGO 'advocacy', 'not a terrain of people's struggle' (2006: 35). Moreover, many NGO development projects (e.g. job training, micro-credit) are ultimately an attempt at integrating subaltern groups into global capital; as James Petras puts it (1999: 432), they help corner 'a new segment of the poor' (e.g. young people, marginalized women, landless farmers, the urban poor), binding them to market entrepreneurialism. The result once again is a reaffirmation of the status quo, whose systemic violence is the basis for humanitarianism. And so the cycle continues ... (I am not, of course, suggesting that humanitarian advocacy/relief and development should not happen, or that people must not be assisted in disasters; the problem is the significant institutional interests in people's ongoing suffering or dispossession, and the enormous investments made in addressing the symptoms rather than the cure.)

This myopic and status quo approach is integral to the symbolic politics of humanitarian NGOs, too. The spectacularization of their relief and advocacy work is notable for what it includes as much as what it excludes. There is, first, the tendency (underlined earlier) to 'sell' stories and images that are visually and sound-byte friendly. Spectacles involving celebrities, poverty-stricken people, crying mothers/children, gun-toting soldiers, or war-ravaged landscapes tend to be given priority. Most often, the resulting sensationalized images/stories are serialized and repeated to achieve maximum public and media spread and exposure. As one NGO media person puts it, 'the misery of the victims of famine, flood, war, and plague must be underlined, perhaps even exaggerated, if [the organization] is to attract sufficient public attention' (quoted in DeChaine 2002: 361). In this regard, MSF has been criticized for its sensationalized stories, causing some to pejoratively characterize the organization's press officers as 'catastrophe babes', 'whose motives are said to be driven more by the market than by the crises' (DeChaine 2002: 360). Such tendencies illustrate well the symbolic violence noted above, fetishizing and commodifying the outwardly visible (i.e. 'subjective violence') in the service of the society of the spectacle.

More often than not, the stories and commodity-images produced by NGOs resort to classic hero narratives, in which the NGO-as-hero/celebrity overcomes adversity (obstacles, enemies, crises) to save hapless victims. All the characters are clearly identifiable: the saviour-heroes are the aid workers, human rights advocates, and volunteer doctors/nurses; the enemies/adversaries are 'natural' disasters, or corrupt and authoritarian governments/leaders (e.g. the Janjaweed militia and President Al-Bashir, in the case of the Save Darfur narrative); and the victims are women, children, and dispossessed communities. Robert DeChaine states, for instance, that MSF's credibility as a humanitarian agency hinges at least in part on 'its ability to establish a perception of its volunteers as courageous, ideologically pure, morally committed agents of change. They are saviors, champions of the voiceless, who knowingly and willfully face the morally unrighteous enemies of humanity' (2002: 362).

The creation of victims is key, and the humanitarian spectacle manages to never run out of them. Debrix argues that what transnational humanitarian NGOs such as MSF create when they intervene across state boundaries are 'spaces of victimhood', both spatial and symbolic: 'Under the guise of reaching "victims" the world over, MSF constructs new spaces – humanitarian zones – inside which individuals in distress are identified as "victims", are sorted out, and become recognisable as generalised examples of human drama' (1998: 827). The establishment of refugee camps, famine sanctuaries, and the like, are meant to clearly demarcate these spaces, so that the victims can be triaged, categorized, treated, managed.

The people shepherded into these zones tend to be constructed as passive beneficiaries. Rarely do they have a voice; most often, it is the NGOs that speak and 'witness' for them. In the Darfur debacle, for example, there was a notable absence of any articulate Sudanese or indeed Darfurian voices; as Salah Hassan points out, the discourse was dominated by 'Western celebrity activists, aid workers, and other self-appointed experts and spokespersons, thus reconfiguring the "white man's burden" in a significant way' (2010: 97). Faced with such persistent victimization, it should hardly be surprising that NGO saviour-heroes have sometimes been received by disaster 'victims' with hostility rather than thanks, as in the case, for example, of Somalia in 1992 or Iraq after the 2003 invasion (Watson 2011: 14).

Kate Manzo (2008) underlines how often humanitarian NGOs resort to the use of child iconography (usually close-ups of single children's faces). Think of the 1960s 'Biafra child', the 1980s 'Ethiopia child', or the current-day Plan/World Vision/Save the Children poster child. Child imagery has become the face and brand of NGO humanitarianism (cf. Chapter 1). Here too, the child tends to be depicted as victim, with children's commodity-images deployed to evoke innocence, dependence, suffering (Manzo 2008: 636). Frequently, the child is meant to stand for the Third World, crying out to be helped and saved. Such paternalism only reproduces colonial tropes of infantalization of the colonies to rationalize Europe's 'civilizing mission'.

The production of these black-and-white stories and images, with plainly identifiable heroes, adversaries, and victims, makes for the ideal humanitarian morality tale. Drama and sensationalism permit clear and simplified messaging, enabling the audience to take sides, claim moral indignation at the situation, and feel good about its support for NGO humanitarianism. Mamdani likens this to a kind of pornography, which in the case of Save Darfur yielded a highly moral movement that appealed to people's self-righteousness rather than political analysis (2009: 56–57; cf. Flint and de Waal 2008; DeChaine 2002: 358–59). Moral campaigns tend towards depoliticization, opting (as we have seen) for short-term, managerial, and emergency/militarized solutions. Pupavec contends that moral advocacy avoids 'the stresses and responsibilities of implementing assistance programmes on the ground ... In other words, advocacy can in some cases represent a disingenuous flight from responsibility for social problems, rather than deeper engagement with them' (2006: 266).

The problem with the moral spectacle is precisely that it is less concerned with analysis and understanding than with taking sides and issuing calls to action. Manichean tales simplify, mystify, and ignore the often highly complex politics of emergencies. The focus on the outwardly visible and the spectacular, on special effects and sound-bytes, avoids layered, substantive, and media-*un*friendly investigation. Sensationalized media reports tend to decontextualize and homogenize, telling the story for its universal message, not its specific content: thus, for instance, earthquake 'victims' stand as 'global victims', so that the disaster 'is made into the general condition of humankind' (Debrix 1998: 841, 843). Media/NGO stories tend to linger on the photogenic, privileging physical destruction. In the case of the 2004 Asian Tsunami, Watson finds that the disaster was presented in the media as 'natural', 'unpreventable', 'indiscriminate', or 'random', when in fact the physical destruction and human suffering had as much to do with human activity and social systems (e.g. use of poor building materials, especially in poorer neighbourhoods): 'the physical evidence is used to tell a particular story – one that, in essence, speaks for itself in a way that is de-historical and de-political' (2011: 14–15).

What is left out of the NGO/media stories are the *un*-photogenic details, the 'boring' particulars of the daily grind of people's lives, the recurring patterns of alienation or marginalization. Historical knowledge is a no-no: 'spectacular time' militates against 'historical time', because the former must organize information 'through the media as dramatic events that are quickly displaced and forgotten' (Stevenson 2010: 162). When there *is* interest in details, the media usually home in on the personal (i.e. issues of identity, individual tragedy, etc.) or the gory (i.e. violence), rather than broader politics. In the 2004 Asian Tsunami, Watson finds that the media tended to fetishize human-interest stories (e.g. personal and family tragedies), devoid of any social or political context, and to sometimes suggest that 'victims' were responsible for their own plight (2011: 14). Moreover, all tsunami 'victims' were treated the same, ignoring the fact that local residents and Western tourists were differently impacted, and that local women and children, in particular, were the worst affected: the 'human-tragedy component served to tie all the human victims together: Westerners and locally affected populations ... [thus obliterating] the different sources of vulnerability for the two groups' (Watson 2011: 14–15). Similarly, in the Hurricane Katrina crisis, Tierney et al. (2006) find that the media focused almost exclusively on issues of looting, poverty, and racial tensions, and had almost nothing to say about recurring state cuts for infrastructure and social services in the worst affected, low-lying, and mainly poor black neighbourhoods. Concentrating on 'secondary malfunctions' and 'subjective violence' – poverty, crime, corruption, individual trauma – as opposed to the 'objective violence' of, say, inequality and broader political economy, is a recurring ideological strategy that we have observed before. 'Under the guise of exposing global trauma and injustice in spectacular detail, genuine consideration of the key political and economic causes is displaced' (Taylor 2010: 131).

Such tendencies to ignore key details or broader contexts are integral to the types of photos or films produced by NGOs. Invariably, these are either large-scale images (i.e. aerial or wide-angle shots) of landscapes and neighbourhoods, or close-ups of individuals and faces. This toggling between the bird's eye view and the shrunk/miniaturized view, as Jim Igoe argues,

> allows for the simultaneous presentation of problems that are so large they demand the attention of the whole of humanity, while identifying specific groups of people who are their perpetrators ... Missing from these presentations are the complex and messy connections and relationships that are invisible in both the open-ended vastness of spectacular [landscapes] and the compelling specificity of prosperous villagers.
>
> *(2010: 382)*

It is not just the broader contexts of emergencies that spectacular humanitarianism ignores; it is also that some emergencies tend to be neglected altogether. During the Asian Tsunami, for example, the Western press focused almost exclusively on known tourist locations across the region, overlooking the devastation in 'lesser-known countries and localities' (Cottle and Nolan 2007: 879). The other, more telling recent example here is the Congo, where over four million people have died over the last decade, but which has received little attention from the press. Žižek writes in this regard that:

> The Congo today has effectively re-emerged as a Conradian 'heart of darkness'. No one dares to confront it head on. The death of a West Bank Palestinian child, not to mention an Israeli or American, is mediatically worth thousands of times more than the death of a nameless Congolese.
>
> *(2008a: 3; cf. Mamdani 2009: 63)*

The various manifestations of symbolic and systemic violence outlined above are revealing of the *ideology* of spectacular NGOs. For what is ideology, in the

Žižekian sense that we mean it, other than the production of spectacular images and smooth spaces (i.e. humanitarian zones) to cover up the Real (broader political economy, long-term political alternatives, Western complicity)? The glossy photos and sensational headlines help create pure, untarnished, and moral humanitarian fantasies to be commodified and sold. The smooth spaces (refugee camps, etc.) help manufacture artificial humanitarian sanctuaries where 'victims' are categorized, controlled, and ultimately served up as advertisements for the likes of MSF, Save Darfur, or Save the Children (cf. Debrix 1998). The NGO/media spectacle helps to unify and stabilize reality, disavowing anything that disturbs the humanitarian dream-fantasy, is discomforting to the public, or threatens the neoliberal global order. Outwardly visible, subjective violence may well be shown, or even fetishized, but that it is symptomatic of a dirty underside, a broader underlying objective violence, is glossed over.

Of course, spectacular NGOs hide behind their faux objectivity and non-partisan humanitarianism to repudiate any accusations of political ideology. Yet, as we have seen, their very presentation of reality through their stories and images is already an ideological construction of it (cf. Taylor 2010: 83). They create (the public view of) emergencies and disasters in advance, so that 'reality' and the audience's perception of it are one and the same (cf. Žižek 1994b: 15). Thus, Debord writes, 'For what is communicated are *orders*: and with perfect harmony, those who give them are also those who tell us what they think of them' (1990: 6).

Anti-theoretical activism

> S/he who can does, s/he who cannot creates an NGO!
>
> *(after George Bernard Shaw)*

Žižek refers to the underlying moral tone of humanitarian work, its sense of righteousness and haste, as a 'hypocritical sentiment of moral outrage': 'There is a fundamental anti-theoretical edge to these urgent injunctions. There is no time to reflect: we have to *act now*' (2008a: 6). As noted earlier, this situation is compounded when NGOs play to the media/audience, since the spectacular tends towards the dramatic and sensational, and hence towards the entertainment value of fast action and expressive moral indignation. The problem with such anti-intellectualism is that it prioritizes shock-value rather than critique, doing rather than questioning: 'Don't think, don't politicize, forget about the true causes of poverty, just act, contribute money, so that you will not have to think' (Žižek 2010a: 4).

The imperative to 'act now, think later' is based on a set of false dualisms – acting/thinking, theory/practice, reason/emotion, mind/body, abstraction/

concreteness – prioritizing the first term. The resulting proclivity is to get bogged down in programs, strategies, or spectacles without stopping to adequately consider initial assumptions or broader issues (e.g. about the purpose of the activism or spectacle). Thus, when something goes amiss, the tendency is to address it through more and better practice/spectacle, not fundamental questioning.

Such empiricism has political ramifications, too. To privilege 'doing' (as opposed to thinking) is often to unquestioningly accept the status quo, for instance, a situation of gender or social inequality. The lack of a critical stance can mean, as underlined earlier, simplifying or ignoring broader relationships between, say, local communities and global socioeconomic power structures (cf. Shivji 2006: 41–42). Similarly, to privilege 'what works and what does not' is to downplay such important political questions as 'what works for whom?' and 'whose interests are being served?' The danger of fetishizing activism is that it tends to posit a 'pure' practice that can proceed without bias or theoretical abstractions, independent of, and unfettered by, political concerns about justice and legitimacy.

Žižek often refers to Hegel's counter-intuitive argument that even though our usual inclination is to think of the 'concrete' as real and the 'abstract' as general, the opposite is in fact the case: it is the immediate, on-the-ground reality that is 'abstract', so that to make it 'concrete' is to draw out the complex universal context that makes it meaningful (cf. Žižek 1999a: 90–91). Thus, when NGOs focus on doing without thinking, on moral outrage instead of questioning, on 'ground realities' devoid of context or history, their work is abstract in its very concreteness. The 'actual' and the 'empirical', or the 'image' and the 'spectacle', can be false, in the same way that fetishizing 'subjective violence' can be (cf. the previous section).

The Save Darfur campaign illustrates this problem well. For it is a campaign, as I have already mentioned, that prioritized spectacle and celebrity to grab public attention regarding the plight of Darfurians, calling not just for immediate action by the West, but military intervention. Mamdani states the campaign privileged 'doing over knowing' by substituting 'moral certainty for knowledge' and feeling 'virtuous even when acting on the basis of total ignorance' (2009: 3, 6; cf. Hassan 2010: 97). Flint and de Waal, similarly, refer to the campaign as 'high-decibel activism' which 'created a simplistic moral fable that portrayed the crisis as a battle of good and evil' (2008: xii, 184). Rather than carefully considering the Darfur situation before acting, the Save Darfur advocates relied on the 'evidence of their eyes' avoiding 'any discussion of context. But by letting pictures and interviews do the talking, they … opened an entire movement to "the CNN effect"' (Mamdani 2009: 7).

But what specifically did Save Darfur not get right? A lot, it seems. The framing of the conflict as a racialized one involving violence perpetrated, as stated earlier, by light-skinned Arabs against Black Africans was ill informed and ideological. Mamdani and others (cf. Flint and de Waal 2008: 186–87; Haeri 2008: 40) point out, first, that there are 'Arabs' on both sides of the conflict:

> whereas the adversary tribes along the north-south axis were usually 'Arab' and 'non-Arab', those along the south-south axis were 'Arab' on both sides. The work of the Save Darfur movement – and the media in its wake – has had the effect of obscuring the south-south axis in the conflict so as to present the violence as genocide unleashed by 'Arab' perpetrators and 'African' victims.
>
> *(Mamdani 2009: 16)*

Moreover, the Darfur conflict has happened not along racialized lines but mostly over land. The region has a long history of land conflicts and ecological degradation (desertification, drought), making arable land scarce and pitting the land-wealthier tribes against the land-poorer and landless ones (Mamdani 2009: 4, 236ff.; Hassan 2010). Yet, this crucial land dimension was notably absent from the analysis of Save Darfur and the mainstream media. A simplified racialized discourse, instead of a more considered political economy investigation, catered better to the spectacularized character of the Save Darfur campaign. It also played into the War on Terror discourse, given the latter's proclivity towards the demonization of Muslims/Arabs: 'The harsh truth is that the War on Terror has provided the coordinates, the language, the images, and the sentiment for interpreting Darfur' (Mamdani 2009: 71).

In addition, Save Darfur's naming of the conflict as 'genocide' was glaringly misinformed. Genocide refers to the slaughter of one people by another, yet there was no credible evidence of this in the region. The 2005 report of the UN International Commission of Inquiry on Darfur found that, while heinous crimes had been committed, the government of Sudan had not pursued a policy of genocide (Edozie 2009: 663; Flint and de Waal 2008: 182–83; Mamdani 2009: 2). Save Darfur's death figures, furthermore, were notably inflated,[3] much higher than those reported by the WHO, for example, which found that many fatalities were caused not by war but diarrhea and poor sanitation (Mamdani 2009: 25; Flint and de Waal 2008: 186). In fact, at the peak of Save Darfur's global campaign against 'genocide', fatality rates in the region had actually declined (Haeri 2008: 42; Mamdani 2009: 33, 55). As a result, in 2006, the US Government Accountability Office rebuked Save Darfur for overblown rhetoric and mortality rate reports, while on-the-ground UN and NGO staff accused the movement of 'genocide hysteria' (Flint and de Waal 2008: 186; Flint 2007: 539; Mamdani 2010: 139).

The effect of the campaign's overly simplified and inflated discourse was to depoliticize the Darfur issue. Mamdani points out (2009: 140) that there was no real concern to educate people or encourage public debate (in contra-distinction, for instance, to the anti-Vietnam War campaign in the US, in which debate, conferences, and teach-ins were quite widespread). Instead, Save Darfur spent tremendous effort and resources on advertising campaigns, and on trying to document atrocities or find proof of genocide. Rather than pushing for political solutions to the crisis (e.g. domestic mediation/negotiation), moreover, Save Darfur advocated for external military intervention. The campaign's moral spectacle appeared more inclined towards revenge than politics, 'punishment rather than peace' (Mamdani 2009: 16; Haeri 2008: 41). Mamdani correctly wonders why a mass movement against the war in Iraq, of the same size and force as that against Darfur, was not organized in the US and else-where, especially given that civilian death rates in Iraq far outweighed those in Darfur (2009: 5–6, 70). Medina Haeri responds, not surprisingly, that it is because the Darfur conflict was 'sensationalized and overly simplified in order to appeal to the broadest possible segment of the population' (2008: 40). Mamdani agrees, adding that 'Indeed, the lesson of Darfur is a warning to those who would act first and understand later' (2009: 6).

False activity and seduction

As argued at the outset of this chapter, the hyperactivism of humanitarian NGOs is ideologically revealing for what it masks: it is akin to the behaviour of the obsessive neurotic, who talks all the time in therapy, afraid that any moment of awkward silence will lead to threatening questions from the therapist. Žižek calls this 'false activity':

> Therein resides the typical strategy of the obsessional neurotic: he is frantically active in order to prevent the real thing from happening, so that nothing will change … obsessional neurotics talk constantly, inun-dating the analyst with anecdotes, dreams, insights: their incessant activity is sustained by the underlying fear that, if they stop talking for a moment, the analyst will ask them the question that truly matters – in other words, they talk in order to keep the analyst still.
>
> *(2006a: 26; cf. 1999b: 105–6, 110)*

What Žižek is underlining here is that we sometimes act, not in order to change something, but rather in order *not* to change something. The threat today, he claims 'is not passivity, but pseudo-activity, the urge to "be active", to "participate", to mask the nothingness of what goes on' (2008a: 217; cf. 2006a: 26).

Like the obsessive neurotic, humanitarian NGOs both *act on* and *act out* emergencies, lurching from one crisis to the next, displaying what one analyst has called 'hyper-active attention deficit disorder' (Ferguson, quoted in Pupavec 2006: 265, 257; cf. Donini 2002: 260). Such frantic pseudo-activity is integral to the global 'permanent emergency' regime that we referred to earlier (cf. Duffield 2007). NGOs count on, sustain, and indeed help produce emergencies; they have internalized and institutionalized a perpetual mode of crisis management, which aims not at dealing with long-term, underlying causes, as noted previously, but addressing only the short-term, visible symptoms. What humanitarianism of this kind does is cater only to bare life and survival; by trying to avert famine, suffering, or imminent death, it ignores long-term social regeneration. Thus, Jenny Edkins states, 'Relief is aimed at *preserving life of the biological organism* rather than restoring the means of livelihood of the community' (2000: 39, 146).

Let us remember as well that NGOs are playing *for* a spectacle, so that their activism requires a public, and takes on significance only because of the presence of the media. Žižek's (heterosexist) joke about Cindy Crawford, who is shipwrecked on a deserted island with a 'poor peasant', illustrates this point well:

> After having sex with him, she asks how it was; his answer is, great, but he still has one small request to complete his satisfaction – could she dress herself up as his best friend, put on trousers and paint a moustache on her face? He reassures her that he is not a secret pervert, as she will see once she has granted the request. When she does, he approaches her, gives her a dig in the ribs and tells her with the leer of male complicity: 'You know what just happened to me? I just had sex with Cindy Crawford!'
>
> *(2006a: 10)*

Like the peasant, spectacular NGOs need to be *seen to be doing* in order to do. They require the media gaze and recognition for their activism to be meaningful and worthwhile (cf. Dean 2006: 11). To add to my earlier formula, they need to be able to *act for* so as to *act on* and *act out* emergency humanitarianism.

This recalls Žižek's notion of interpassivity (cf. Chapter 1). Unlike 'interactivity', in which one is active through the other (i.e. one delegates one's activity to another), 'interpassivity' describes a situation in which one is passive through the other, that is, one concedes one's passivity to the other so that one can remain actively engaged: it is a situation in which '*I am incessantly active*, and sustain my activity by the other's passivity' (Žižek 1999b: 110). In like manner, NGOs are (spectacularly) active as a result of the media gaze, because we, as audience, are (passively) watching. There is a sexualized dimension here, which Žižek expresses thus (albeit, once again, in heterosexist fashion): the NGO may be likened to the pervert, who assumes the position of the pure instrument of the Other's jouissance: for the (male) pervert, the sexual act (coitus) involves a clear division of labor in which he reduces himself to a pure tool of her enjoyment; he is doing the hard work, accomplishing the active gestures, while the woman, transported in ecstasy, passively endures it and stares in the air.

(1998: 11)

There are several ideological operations at play here worthy of consideration. First, it is significant that the NGO, like the pervert, never publicly acknowledges that it is performing for the audience; there would be too much shame (and sham) in this, which is why it must be disavowed. Rather, the pretense (or ideological fantasy) is that the NGO always acts out its humanitarian work this way and that the media 'objectively' reveals to us the 'real NGO', *au naturel*. The fact that emergencies are produced and staged by NGOs − in the sense discussed earlier of identifying the crisis, (re)presenting it to the public, etc. − is thus hidden from view.

Second, if the NGO acts because it must be *seen* to be acting, then it is the performance, much more than the content of the performance, that matters. The society of the spectacle after all is a performative society, where exhibitionism and appearances trump meaningful social or political relationships. What matters, then, is putting on a spectacle, continuously and ubiquitously. No wonder that the humanitarian field is in a constant state of emergency, and that NGOs are hyperactive. The regime necessitates an incessant search for more and more drama, stories, commodity-images.

Third, not only are the humanitarian disasters staged and manufactured for the sake of the spectacle, but so is the sense of urgency. The imperative to 'act' and to 'act now', as discussed earlier, is part and parcel of the compulsion towards pomp and moral outrage, and can even tend towards militarized shock-and-awe. Cameras, news programs, 'expert' commentators, and TV anchors and talking heads, all feed off the pseudo-urgency that pervades humanitarian discourse.

Finally, and perhaps most importantly, if all (or mostly all) that matters is performance, then NGOs don't really need to do too much, as long as they *look* like they are. Their pseudo-activity gives the misleading impression that we are progressing towards a better and more caring society, yet nothing substantial or structural is actually happening. *Plus ça change, plus c'est la même chose.* NGO humanitarian work is fundamentally depoliticizing, intent more on manufacturing spectacles and celebrating the status quo than engaging in genuine sociopolitical transformation. In this sense, the frenetic activity of NGOs is, paradoxically, passive: it is outwardly dynamic but politically reactionary. Critical work is neglected or postponed in favour of ritual performance. Long-term struggle is sacrificed to short-term fame.

But on the other side of this 'interpassive' NGO spectacle is us, the audience. Recall that, in the interpassive relationship, NGOs cede their passivity to the audience; they are active in order to keep *us* still. We, in turn, delegate our activity to them. We become humanitarians on the cheap, watching, supporting, or consuming the spectacle of their relief/advocacy work. Our charitable duties are therefore outsourced (in the same way that they were with humanitarian celebrities in Chapter 1 and Product (RED) in Chapter 2). For Žižek, such ideological outsourcing is akin to what happens when we compulsively record TV programs:

> the immediate effect of owning a VCR [or PVR] is that one effectively watches *fewer* films than in the good old days of a simple TV set. One never has time for TV, so, instead of losing a precious evening, one simply tapes the films and stores them for future viewing … [It is] as if the VCR is in a way *watching them for me, in my place.*
>
> *(2006a: 24; cf. Pfaller 2003; van Oenen 2008: 3)*

In like manner, NGOs do our charity work for us. We remain passive humanitarians, but can go about our daily life, content that they are performing good deeds.

One of the problems with the late capitalist society of the spectacle is that we lead such busy lives, so often overwhelmed by work, family, and life's many other demands. Delegating some of our activity and beliefs is one way of unburdening ourselves (van Oenen 2008: 11). The hyperactivity of humanitarian NGOs is thus counteracted by our relative inactivity. We can sit back and relax while the humanitarian spectacle unfolds before our eyes, bombarding us with images, messages, and products to be consumed and savoured. But we are passive only to a point: of late especially, the Internet and social media allow and invite us to interact and participate, despite our busy lives (cf. Dean 2010; van Oenen 2008: 9). We are enjoined not simply to make donations or passively consume product-images, but also to provide our feedback by 'chatting', responding to blogs, or taking part in instant 'polls' (e.g. on how we feel about the latest humanitarian disaster). Yet such 'empowerment' is restricted, since our feedback is most often limited to pre-determined topics, and in any case is never binding on the NGO. Perhaps more important is that what this pseudo-participation does is tie us to the humanitarian regime: we become invested in it, even if we are mostly bystanders. In this sense, as Jodi Dean points out, we 'contribute to our own capture' (2010: 34).

Enjoyment (*jouissance*), of course, is an important part of such ideological capture. First, there is the excitement of the humanitarian spectacle. The media/NGOs thrive from our indulgence in the drama – the identification and staging of crises, the repetition of headlines and images, the urgent calls for action and support, the invitation for our comments on blogs/social media. The thrill lies in both our (pseudo-) participation in the game and the speed of it all, which Dean aptly denotes as the 'circulation of enjoyment' (2010: 27).

Next, there is the gratification of unburdening ourselves by delegating our humanitarianism to an Other. Although we may disavow it, we derive a certain satisfaction from outsourcing our beliefs (cf. Pfaller 2005: 114; van Oenen 2008: 5). We are content in the knowledge that the charity work is being done, and that it is being done by an 'other supposed to know' (i.e. the NGO-as-celebrity/expert). There is, moreover, a voyeuristic pleasure in witnessing the unfolding of other people's troubles from afar. Secure in our homes and communities, we may well emote with their plight, but we nonetheless feel contented and privileged not to be in their shoes.

Finally, there is the sheer *frisson* of giving. We are instantly gratified in becoming humanitarians-for-a-day through our donations, support, or charity consumption. By giving, we also take pride in joining a community of (Western) donors, benevolently contributing to people's humanitarian rescue. And not to be forgotten is the symbolic recognition and 'thank you' we receive from both the NGO and the recipient. Daly puts it this way:

> the [ideological] suture is effected in this way of staging the gaze of the Other in such a way that our own gaze is returned to us. As one charity [World Vision] puts it, 'you get to see and feel the difference your support makes, through the eyes of your sponsored child and their regular letters and photographs'. Thus what is sutured is the very fantasy about the Other's fantasy.
>
> *(2010: 8)*

Now it is possible, of course, that we don't or can't enjoy in this way, even though the discourse of humanitarianism is constantly telling us that we should. We may blame our inability to really enjoy, for example, on convenient others: 'If only the Third World would get its act together, I would enjoy'; 'why do we have to help those people? Can't they help themselves?'; 'if only they would stop making us Westerners feel so guilty and sorry for them'. Žižek refers to this as 'stolen enjoyment', through which we find scapegoats to overlook our own insecurity (1993: 203; cf. Dean 2010: 20). The fantasy of the theft of enjoyment is a screen for our inability to recognize our own structural contradictions, which in this case concerns our interest in preserving the global status quo, Western complicity in the production of emergencies, etc. In any case, stolen enjoyment *is* enjoyment. It is a yearning to enjoy despite not being able to, or a coveting of the Other's enjoyment. It is, in short, an enjoyment of missing enjoyment.

Thus, we are bound to the ideology of NGO humanitarianism not through manipulation as much as seduction (cf. Chapter 2). The economy of entertainment and enjoyment keeps us invested, even when we disidentify with the prevailing ideology. The problem is that, when we are so hooked to enjoyment, we search not for public action, but more (and more intensive) sensations (Stevenson 2010: 167). Even desperate appeals for humanitarian action do no political good, because 'the very urgency with which you the viewer/listener are asked to respond is the very thing that will prevent you from recognizing the causes (*objective violence*) of the scenario you are witnessing' (Taylor 2010: 179). Reflective politics and democratic dialogue are postponed in favour of speed, thrill, and instant gratification (cf. Keenan 2002: 1, 6).

The delegation of our beliefs to NGOs may seem like a way of disidentifying with humanitarianism, since despite the enjoyment of it all, a certain distance and remove is created. Yet, just the opposite is the case. As Robert Pfaller argues, outsourcing beliefs 'makes them even stronger than they were before' (2007: 37). This is because ideology functions precisely by proxy: by displacing our beliefs onto the NGO, we are externalizing and institutionalizing them, that is, making ontological what was previously subjective (2007: 37). We take for granted, for instance, that the NGO knows what it is doing (as celebrity/ expert), and that it is doing its job well, despite the fact that neither supposition is necessarily guaranteed or true. The NGO stands, then, as fetish, as objective embodiment of our ideological beliefs. By ceding our activity to it, we are acquiescing to its authority, which as we have seen, tends towards political conformism.

Therefore, the hyperactivity of humanitarian NGOs is matched by our relative inactivity. They outsource their passivity to us, and in fact require our political inactivity in order to sustain their spectacular humanitarianism. We, in turn, delegate our activity to them, and in fact require their spectacular activism to fuel our enjoyment. What emerges, then, is an ideological complicity: we cannot hold only NGOs responsible here: they may well play the dominant role (along with celebrities, corporate philanthropists, etc.) in manufacturing the ideological fantasy of humanitarianism, but for it to take hold and sustain itself, the audience must be part and parcel of the picture: we must be seduced by their performance and outsource our beliefs.

Scouting for new capitalist frontiers: disaster capitalism

We have already commented on the increasing corporatization of NGOs – their resort, for example, to corporate marketing, branding, and sponsorships. We have also alluded to how NGOs act as 'news scouts' for the corporate media, helping break news stories on crisis situations around the globe. But a relatively new trend in the NGO community is the integration of these two functions – corporatization and scouting. Indeed, NGOs are increasingly becoming agents of capital, sometimes acting as scouts for global capitalist penetration. Partly this is due to the hegemony of global neoliberalization that NGOs are enjoined to, and in fact, to which so many owe their very existence (given the explosion of civil society organizations during the dawn of neoliberalism in the 1980s/1990s). Most NGOs now work unabashedly within a neoliberal framework, having adopted the techniques of 'new public management', including the use of 'market mechanisms' such as performance indicators and benchmarking. Many NGOs have benefited from the structural adjustment regimes imposed in much of the Third World, especially Sub-Saharan Africa, as a result of which several 'now exercise significant control over the design and delivery of core economic and welfare functions of the state' (Duffield 2007: 80). Despite an initial reluctance to embrace the liberalization of markets (for ideological reasons), most NGOs appear to have now come on side, a situation James Petras characterizes as a push for privatization 'from below' (1999: 431). In much of Africa, such opening up of the economy to the private sector has translated into a reliance on foreign capital as the main engine of growth (Shivji 2006: 35).

But in addition to supporting market liberalization, NGOs have assisted in opening up new frontiers for capital. As touched on earlier, outreach to socially and geographically marginalized communities (refugees, migrants, displaced communities, indigenous people, youth, women, landless peasants, small farmers, urban slum dwellers) has helped better integrate them into the global economy. Education and job training programs help provide a ready army of cheap labour for the private sector. And the adoption of micro-credit and micro-enterprise programs (including by the likes of Oxfam and Christian Aid) has shifted 'the responsibility of self-reproduction from states to people reconfigured as social entrepreneurs' (Duffield 2007: 152; cf. Pupavec 2006: 261, 264).

While much more research is required on this phenomenon as it relates to the humanitarian sector, there is a burgeoning literature on it relating to the environmental NGO field, which I take as revealing of broader global trends. Brockington and Scholfield (2010), for example, show how conservation NGOs in Sub-Saharan Africa are integral to the spread of capitalism there. Large, mostly Northern-based NGOs such as Nature Conservancy, Wildlife Conservation Society, the Dian Fossey Gorilla Fund, and the Jane Goodall Institute are feeding a substantial global demand for nature-related photographs, films, and commodities. They are helping transform Africa's natural capital (forests, wildlife, landscapes) into 'symbolic capital and money', thus 'incorporating nature and wildlife into a broader capitalist system' (Brockington and Scholfield 2010: 552; cf. Brockington 2009; Igoe 2010). In so doing, these NGOs are preparing the ground for greater eco-tourism. Their growing presence on the continent has resulted in their ability to influence and lobby governments, not simply on conservation issues, but on broader policy-making relating to wildlife and land management, and environment and eco-tourism (including hotel and resort real estate development). Broadly speaking, then, NGOs such as these may be said to be helping identify new environmental areas for commodification. Thus, Paul Hawken, a proponent of 'natural capitalism' states:

> Ironically, organizations like Earth First!, Rainforest Action Network, and Greenpeace have now become the real capitalists. By addressing such issues as greenhouse gases, chemical contamination, and loss of fisheries, wildlife corridors, and primary forests, they are doing more to preserve a viable business future than are all the chambers of commerce put together.
>
> *(quoted in Daly 2010: 9)*

Perhaps one of the chief ways in which humanitarian NGOs are scouts for new capitalist frontiers is by way of 'disaster capitalism'. In *The Shock Doctrine*, Naomi Klein explains it this way:

> The history of the contemporary free market ... was written in shocks. Some of the most infamous human rights violations of this era ... were in fact either committed with the deliberate intent of terrorizing the public or actively harnessed to prepare the ground for the introduction of radical free-market 'reforms' ... I call these orchestrated raids on the public sphere in the wake of catastrophic events, combined with the treatment of disasters as exciting market opportunities, 'disaster capitalism'.
>
> *(2007: 23, 11, 6)*

Accordingly, disasters – ranging from tsunamis, earthquakes and hurricanes, to wars, market meltdowns, terrorist attacks, and political coups – help shock and 'soften up' societies, allowing political and economic elites to remove obstacles and create an ideological terrain conducive to neoliberal objectives. NGOs have very much become part of the ensuing 'disaster capitalism complex', helping provide emergency humanitarian relief, alongside multilateral and UN agencies, but also military and peacekeeping forces, private security firms, and policing.

Klein provides many examples to illustrate her argument. Notable for our purposes are the cases of Hurricane Katrina, the Iraq war, and the Asian Tsunami. What is striking about the first two cases is that the Bush government out-sourced many of the core welfare and security functions of the state to the private sector and NGOs: providing health care to disaster 'victims' and soldiers, intelligence gathering, security and law and order, prisoner handling and interrogation, etc. Katrina, much like Iraq, became the excuse to use US public funds to lay a corporate and NGO infrastructure across New Orleans/ Iraq, especially profiting private contractors such as Halliburton, Shaw and Bechtel (Klein 2007: 14, 519). As for the Asian Tsunami case, many affected areas had been caught up, previous to the disaster, in struggles between local communities, which depended on the land/sea for farming and fishing, and private developers, who were interested in real estate and tourism development. The tsunami facilitated gains for the latter across the region, allowing quick changes, for example, to zoning bylaws and building codes (Klein 2007: 496ff.; Watson 2011: 15). With local communities traumatized and disorganized in the wake of the disaster, and NGOs focusing on short-term emergency measures, neoliberal social and economic engineering was able to proceed unhindered.

Humanitarian NGOs may not always be directly involved in such economic shock therapy (although more research is required on this), but as an integral part of the global emergency regime, they are certainly complicit. What can perhaps be said more safely is that they surely have an interest in, and directly benefit from, disasters. They are the first to arrive on the scene, scouting and (mediatically) shaping the disaster, preparing the ground for the arrival of media, politicians, and business opportunists. In the post-disaster stages, even though they may not all (or not all of the time) straightforwardly advocate for neoliberal restructuring, their short-term and outwardly apolitical actions do not prevent, and sometimes even encourage, the opening up of new spaces for capitalist development. Then, once the neoliberal re-engineering has happened, they are only too happy to take over the welfare functions ceded by the state.

Postpolitics, panopticism, and the state of exception

Recall that postpolitics (or post-democracy) refers to the elimination of political debate, disagreement, and conflict, as a result of which liberal democratic politics is reduced to technocratic and 'expert' administration. Humanitarian celebrities such as Bono or Jolie, as we have seen in Chapter 1, are integral to this phenomenon, given their increasing influence on global policy relating to development, debt, famine, adoption, and the like. And so are humanitarian NGOs, particularly the large ones headquartered in the North (i.e. BINGOs). Staffed by mostly Western(ized), liberal/left-leaning, upwardly mobile, educated professionals (cf. Petras 1999: 430–32), they too wield enormous influence in global governance in such areas as emergency relief, development, disaster/conflict management, and so on. Like celebrities (and as celebrities in their own right), they add a veneer of populism to their newfound power, speaking and acting on behalf of global 'victims', the displaced, and the dispossessed. And even though they are 'non-governmental' organizations, their active participation in the global disaster complex, as we have noted, has absorbed them into a web of mutual interests connecting them with donor states, UN agencies, recipient governments, the corporate sector, global media, and militaries (Duffield 2007: 28).

The spectacular hyperactivism of humanitarian NGOs embodies postpolitics because it reduces activism to spectacle, ensuring that nothing too much, and certainly nothing too threatening, happens to global order and security. NGOs' concurrence, if not outright collaboration, with neoliberal governance, coupled with their increasing partnerships with the corporate sector, translates into an acceptance of global capitalism as the 'natural' socioeconomic horizon. Thus, implicitly if not explicitly, NGOs share with global economic and political elites a basic consensus on liberal democratic capitalism. The result is that their activism consists, in true postpolitical fashion, of technocratically managing an already accepted socioeconomic consensus. If there is debate or disagreement, then it is over, not political fundamentals, but technical arrangements – how rapidly to act, whom best to coordinate with, which beneficiaries to target.

One of the key reasons for which NGOs are able to act as managers of a pre-determined consensus is because, as Petras maintains, they tend to 'emphasize projects not movements' (1999: 434). Projects are atomized and artificial environments, often imposed from outside and notably divorced from broader power structures. Hence, NGOs are able to 'focus on "survival strategies" not general strikes; they organize soup kitchens not mass demonstrations against food hoarders, neoliberal regimes or US imperialism' (Petras 1999: 432). (This is why, I would argue, that the NGOs that tend to be meaningfully political/ critical are the ones that grow out of, and maintain their ties to, social/protest movements and broader Left oppositional politics.)

Even public participation, now all the rage within the NGO community, consists of consulting 'stakeholders' once the key decisions have already been made (cf. Kapoor 2002; 2008: ch. 4). Audience inclusion is stage-managed in the safety of the workshop or refugee camp, cut off as these are from the political vagaries of the outside world, with the NGO-as-facilitator selecting participants, and deciding who will speak and for how long. Participation is restricted, moreover, to relatively safe program areas such as health or education, excluding more controversial areas/topics such as land ownership, socioeconomic inequality, or workers' rights. 'Consensus' is thus achieved by omission and depoliticization under the guise of openness and participation.

It is worth dwelling on the panoptic dimensions of such managed consensus. Foucault (1984: 239ff.) defines panopticism as the pervasive surveillance of people in contemporary societies (e.g. in the form of TV monitoring, the creation of social security dossiers, or more recently, 'security assessments'), to the point where even those who may rebel against it, end up internalizing it. Rather than fostering information exchange, then, the information society/ society of the spectacle can stifle, censor, discipline, and normalize people. Spectacular humanitarian NGOs may thus be said to be helping lay the ground for a global surveillance infrastructure – a *1984*-like 'global panopticon' – to promote and monitor the established neoliberal consensus.

After all, not only are people herded into 'humanitarian zones', where they are triaged and managed, but they are also monitored by security guards and filmed and photographed by CCTVs, TV crews, and photojournalists alike. In the course of participating in NGO programs, moreover, people succumb to myriad disciplining mechanisms. One such mechanism is the 'new public management', which includes techniques such as performance measurement. While the ostensible (neoliberal) purpose of these is to help improve efficiency and financial accountability, their accompanying proclivity is to help better police people, thus expanding the reach of NGOs/donors/states into the everyday life of camps and communities. The other disciplinary mechanism is the participatory forum mentioned above, where consensus is easily staged. The aphorism, 'a consensus means that everyone agrees to say collectively what no one believes individually', applies well here, given the notable panoptic dimensions of participatory gatherings. For example, people may censor themselves under the watchful eye of their peers, or play to the public, or say only positive things (and leave out criticism) to please the funder.

Lest we take such panopticism as a kind of Western conspiracy, there is a notable Žižekian twist here, which complicates the story: there is a kernel of *enjoyment* in panopticism, a libidinal kick that comes from surveillance mechanisms and bureaucratic routines. Accordingly, NGOs may derive satisfaction from following institutional rituals; security officials and the media may delight in their newfound ability to monitor migrant/refugee/community activities; husbands and fathers may see participation/performance measurement as a way of keeping tabs on their wives or daughters; elites may take panopticism as an opportunity to manage dissent; NGOs and funders may voyeuristically get off on watching and monitoring people; and everyone may savour the panoptic production of gossip and rumour about colleagues, friends, and neighbours. Thus, we all end up subjecting ourselves to, enjoying, and even consenting to our own panoptic capture.

Equally concerning is the politics of fear associated with current global humanitarianism, to which NGOs are closely affiliated. Particularly since 9/11, the spectacle of war and terror has produced a climate of fear and suspicion (of terrorists, extremists, Muslims, and generally, Others). The visual theatre of war/terror aestheticizes raw violence, and as Giroux notes, produces both the 'spectacle of terror' and the 'terror of the spectacle' (2006: 31). Hoskins and O'Loughlin go so far as to argue that the media have become 'weaponized' and that television is now an actual constituent of terrorism (2010: 2; cf. Cottle 2009: 123). Humanitarian NGOs are complicit in this, as we have underscored. Their repeated appeals for emergency and sometimes military action, their de facto collaboration with military and security forces in the delivery of aid, their alliance with the media in producing spectacle – all contribute to the militarization of global politics.

A significant problem is that militarization and the politics of fear tend to mollify the public. Insecurity and anxiety help in rallying the masses against common enemies, appealing to our sense of national unity. We are thus softened (coerced?) into accepting the dominant power structures, that is, the postpolitical consensus. Disagreement, dissensus, and protest are seen as a threat to national unity and security. Hence, the spectre and spectacle of violence ends up devaluing critical thinking and democratic debate in favour of quick, emergency responses. Giroux avers, in this regard, that a 'cinematic politics of the visceral has replaced a more measured and thoughtful commentary on human suffering and alienation' (2006: 24).

A dangerous outgrowth of such conservatizing and conformist politics is the resort to authoritarianism. Of late especially, we have witnessed the establishment of extraordinary measures by putatively democratic governments around the world to deal with 'emergency' situations. These range from the use of torture and the suppression of internal critics to the curtailment of people's democratic rights and the institution of military tribunals for 'enemy combatants' (e.g. at Guantánamo) – all in contravention of international human rights codes but justified on the basis of security.

For Giorgio Agamben, these 'states of exception' used to be exceptional, but they have increasingly become the dominant model of governance (2005: 2). To be sure, in the global humanitarian field, the declaration of emergencies has often been exercised *as* a state of exception. In particular, as discussed earlier, the 'new humanitarianism' has provided the means to ignore international law in favour of external intervention. Such a practice has eroded the principle of equality among sovereign states, challenging the legitimacy of Third World governments, and allowing Western powers to intervene as required around the world (Pupavec 2006: 263). Mamdani points out the glaring contradiction: 'I am no apologist of sovereign governments, but so long as we live in a world constituted by sovereign powers, I insist that any attempt to qualify or restrict sovereignty be applied across the board to all powers' (2010: 140). Otherwise, the declaration of a state of exception is nothing more than imperialism masked as 'humanitarianism'.

In many ways, the functioning of today's transnational humanitarian NGOs *depends* on the state of exception. On the basis of the 'new humanitarianism', these NGOs begin by demanding 'unhindered access' to victims of civil strife, war or famine, often undermining if not challenging the legitimacy and social responsibilities of Third World governments. Then, once granted access, they establish humanitarian zones, which are the very embodiment of the state of exception. The people herded in these zones may well be provided with much-needed food, medical care, and basic amenities, but they tend to be constructed as passive recipients, with the NGO speaking for them to represent their needs and desires: 'Suddenly the unelected, often unaccountable and usually foreign aid workers become judge, juror and politician ... ' (Fox 2001: 281; cf. Watson 2011: 13). More to the point is that a hierarchy of victims is constructed, with some seen as more deserving than others. In this regard, Duffield writes, 'between saving the starving child or helping the poor child [or poor farmers or female-headed households] – whatever the final choice, a sovereign power over life is being exercised' (2007: 51; cf. 2001: 272; Fox 2001: 275; Debrix 1998: 838–39). Humanitarian zones thus become the ultimate depoliticizing, postpolitical sanctuaries, in which NGOs reduce people to 'bare life' and exercise the prerogative of life and death. Indeed, for emergency relief to happen, Duffield maintains, 'people must be taken out of politics' and be 'reduced to a life of exception ... ' (2007: 44).

Conclusion

Spectacular humanitarian NGOs are thus a case of depoliticized activism, of conformist action devoid of meaningful critique. In their quest for celebrity and spectacle, they end up valuing the photogenic, the moral, and the short-term (subjective violence) over the long-term and the structural (objective violence). The result is a lot of glitzy performance but little critical politics. In their effort to be global actors, they end up corporatizing their activities, partnering with business and corporate media, and readily taking over state welfare functions. The upshot is a cozying up to the neoliberal consensus. In their ambition to urgently respond (and be seen to be urgently responding) to emergencies, they end up creating and depending upon a state of permanent global emergency. The result is a movement towards the securitization and militarization of politics, with notably conservatizing, panoptic, and authoritarian tendencies. And finally, in their determination to save lives, they institute humanitarian zones as de facto states of exception, retaining unaccountable power. The consequence is the positioning of aid recipients as voiceless victims.

But when activism is reduced to a commodity-spectacle, when it closes down political contestation and attempts to naturalize the socioeconomic status quo, then there is no word for it other than ideology. Spectacular NGO humanitarian activism is a cover for the advancement of the neoliberal global order, helping to put a human face on the latter's production of crises and inequities. The spectacle, in this sense, is a screen, an ideological fantasy that zooms in on the caring side but pans away from the grimy foundations.

CONCLUSION

What is to be done?

I despise the kind of book which tells you how to live, how to make yourself happy! Philosophers have no good news for you at this level! I believe the first duty of philosophy is making you understand what deep s--- you are in!

(Žižek quoted in Brown 2010)

Do not be afraid, join us, come back! You've had your anti-communist fun, and you are pardoned for it – time to get serious once again!

(Žižek quoted in Douzinas and Žižek 2010: back cover)

Of late, Žižek (2008b: 420–29; 2010a: x; 2010b: 212) has identified four key antagonisms of contemporary global capitalism: (1) the looming ecological crisis, which brings us face-to-face with the end of human life; (2) the privatization of intellectual property, which threatens human knowledge and cultural systems; (3) the socio-ethical perils of an uncontrollable and privatized biogenetic revolution; and (4) the emergence of new social apartheids and exclusions (urban slums, illegal migrant labour, etc.). While all four antagonisms need to be acknowledged and addressed, according to Žižek, it is the last one which is crucial: the antagonism between the Included and the Excluded is intrinsic to the broader global capitalist system that also generates the other three. Without confronting the issue of social apartheid, none of the other antagonisms can be properly tackled. 'One can sincerely fight to preserve the environment, defend a broader notion of intellectual property, oppose the copyrighting of genes, without confronting the antagonism between the Included and the Excluded' (Žižek 2010b: 214–15).

Celebrity humanitarianism is an ideology that aims precisely at *not* confronting the antagonism between the Included and the Excluded. Recall

Žižek's contention that reality is always constructed on the basis of exclusions, gaps, or inconsistencies, and the function of ideology is thus to help cover up these holes. Celebrity humanitarianism is just such a cover-up. It may well provide funds for, say, poverty projects, but as we have seen, it fails to tackle the broader politics of inequality – a wider politics that would bring out the antagonism between the Included and the Excluded, implicating the celebrities themselves in the production of social apartheid. Celebrity charity work may well bring media attention to recurring humanitarian crises, but as we have underlined, the media spectacle tends to focus only on the 'subjective' violence – an outward violence that is symptomatic of an underlying structural violence, which the spectacle conveniently obscures.

Celebrity humanitarianism, in this sense, is not intended to save the Excluded so much as the Included. It aims at stabilizing, if not advancing, the global capitalist order, helping to deflect attention from the latter's inherent structural violence – inequality, unevenness, dispossession. It attempts to naturalize capitalism, presenting it as the only game in town, and showing its neoliberal variant as neutral, pragmatic, and *non*-ideological. And it helps construct the social fantasy of a humanized and 'caring' capitalism, a phenomenon I refer to as 'decaf capitalism': this is the ideological landscape in which the brutal forms of social exclusion upon which capitalism depends are mitigated by attending to their worst manifestations through welfare or charity; and where ecological devastation and ruthless business practices can legitimately stand alongside the promotion of green policies and corporate social responsibility.

But the ideology of celebrity humanitarianism is propagated not just by celebrities and their corporate and media backers; we, the audience, as I have argued, are also deeply implicated, since we help sustain the ideological fantasy. Our beliefs in the 'good works' of celebrities, our often unquestioned trust in their authority to influence public policy or promote neoliberal solutions – all help propagate the political economy of celebrity culture. Our enjoyment of (celebrity endorsed) charity shopping enables us to do our bit for the 'poor' and become humanitarians-for-a-day; yet at the same time, it further binds us to consumer capitalism. We are thus seduced by celebrity humanitarianism and its accompanying neoliberal capitalist arrangement, and hence complicit in our rapture and capture.

One of the disturbing outcomes of these ideological manoeuvrings, as underlined throughout this book, is depoliticization. When charity work turns principally on spectacle and show, the tendency is to valorize dramatic stories and moral arguments, sound-bytes and photogenic images, and quick and short-term solutions, often at the expense of a broad, complex, and long-term politics. When celebrities unilaterally represent the Excluded (the Third World, orphans, disaster victims, subaltern women, people living with HIV/AIDS), when they speak and 'witness' for them, the result is the construction of voiceless and passive victims.

Several implications follow. One is the de facto positioning of celebrities as powerful and influential public figures, thus contributing to what we have referred to as a 'postdemocratic' (or 'postpolitical') landscape. Humanitarian celebrities have joined the ranks of our often unaccountable political elites, helping determine, as previously noted, global policy on debt, famine, adoption, health, poverty reduction, or emergency relief. A second implication is the radical depoliticization of the global capitalist economy. By being enticed into consumer fetishism, by allowing others to prescribe solutions that buttress the neoliberal status quo, we end up disavowing just how much capitalism rules our (and celebrities') lives. Finally, celebrity humanitarianism helps avoid catastrophe or revolt by positioning us (as well as the Excluded) as docile citizens. To the extent that we are active, it is mainly as consumers or voters, and to the extent that we care for others, it is mainly by outsourcing our beliefs to celebrities or charitable NGOs. The result is acquiescence and allegiance to the status quo, and a relative inability to imagine alternative political horizons.

Ideology critique and 'traversing the fantasy'

So what is to be done? Žižek's answer is that ideology critique, of the kind I have attempted to undertake in this book, is a first key step. It involves two complementary procedures: (1) carrying out a 'symptomal reading' of ideology by examining how it is produced and what it is trying to hide, ignore, disavow; and (2) extracting the ideological kernel of enjoyment and belief (Žižek 1989: 125).

The first of these is about deciphering how the ideological field (of signifiers) is constructed, locating its nodal points (i.e. its master signifiers, for example, 'humanitarianism', 'activism', 'poverty', or 'Third World'), and identifying its Real (its gaps, contradictions, antagonisms, exclusions). Celebrity charity, as we have noted, is one such nodal point, a kind of sublime object that people accept on faith because it is 'good' (it saves people) and is associated with the glamour and authority of celebrities. There is a subliminal logic at play here that is circular and self-reinforcing: charity is good because celebrities are associated with it, and celebrities are good because they do charity. Carrying out ideology critique involves questioning and unravelling the mystique of this sublime object (and logic). It also means asking what the use of such terms as 'humanitarianism' serves to render invisible or unutterable (i.e. in this case, the linkages between the Included and the Excluded).

In many ways, the social fantasy constructed by the discourse of charity is that neoliberal capitalism is a stable and harmonious whole, but is being prevented from reaching its destiny by the Excluded (the poor, HIV/AIDS, debt, the Third World, etc.). Hence the need for charity. The implication is that removing poverty, debt, etc. (as opposed to inequality) will allow the neoliberal order to stabilize and return to its natural, harmonious state. Dismantling this social fantasy, as I have tried to do, involves showing that the Excluded are nothing but a 'fetishistic embodiment of a certain fundamental blockage' (Žižek 1989: 127). That is, the Excluded are not simple deviations, degenerations, or abnormalities, impeding the system's normal functioning, they are *integral* to the system's functioning; they are 'the points at which the "truth", the immanent antagonistic character of the system, erupts' (Žižek 1989: 128).

But identifying the holes within our knowledge systems is not nearly enough. This is because of what Žižek calls the 'fetishistic disavowal', according to which we can know, but still continue to do. The problem is evident, for example, in celebrities humorously mocking their own charity work yet persisting in their charity pursuits, or critical audience members decrying product advertising but still engaging in (charity) shopping (cf. Chapters 1 and 2). The strength of ideology, according to Žižek, lies precisely in allowing us a certain ironic distance, which makes us think we know better and can rise above ideology. In contrast to those such as Noam Chomsky who maintain that exposing the 'facts' is sufficient to undermine power (cf. Žižek 2002a: 4), Žižek's point is that, most often, it is not a lack of knowledge that is the problem, but our unconscious commands and passions that bind us to ideology despite critical distance.

Acknowledging and tracking the desires and beliefs we invest in ideology, then, is a crucial second procedure. It means 'articulating the way in which … an ideology implies, manipulates, produces a pre-ideological enjoyment [and belief] structured in fantasy' (Žižek 1989: 125). This is where psychoanalysis proper enters the fray (although it is integral to all Žižekian ideology critique). Psychoanalysis tells us that we do not necessarily know our interests, and even if we do, we often do not necessarily act on them. Libidinal excess (*jouissance*) and unquestioned beliefs so often circumscribe our thinking and actions. This is why, despite our suspicions or despondence, we buy into the fantasy of celebrity humanitarianism, which helps screen our own lacks and anxieties (about social injustice, poverty, or our own inadequacies), and sets off our desires (e.g. to shop, to donate). This is also why we so frequently displace our beliefs onto Others (celebrities, charity commodities, NGOs).

Done well, this two-pronged Žižekian procedure can enable us to 'traverse the fantasy' (Žižek 2008b: 329ff.). Traversing the fantasy means integrating the knowledge gleaned from ideology critique by fully assuming its consequences. It means learning to disengage from the lure of sublime objects, social fantasies, and the rituals and false promises of our hegemonic social institutions (Žižek 1989: 33; cf. Healy 2010: 497; Sharpe and Boucher 2010: 13, 74). It means taking responsibility for our desires and enjoyment, striving to reorganize them. Žižek illustrates the point this way in relation to the 9/11 attacks in the US:

> Either America will persist in [asking] ... 'Why should this happen to us? Things like this don't happen *here*', leading to more agressivity towards the threatening Outside ... Or America will finally risk stepping through the fantasmatic screen that separates it from the Outside World ... making the long-overdue move from 'A thing like this shouldn't happen *here*' to 'A thing like this shouldn't happen *anywhere!*' This is the true lesson of the attacks: the only way to ensure it doesn't happen here again is to prevent it from happening anywhere else.
>
> *(2002b: 49)*

Similarly, in order to confront the Real of our humanitarian desires, to traverse the fantasy of celebrity charity, the lesson is to grasp that such charity has little to do with the celebrity's benevolent altruism; that the ideological figure of the humanitarian celebrity is, as I have argued, a 'way to stitch up the inconsistency of our own ideological system [i.e. neoliberalism]' (Žižek 1989: 48).

Žižek takes Yannis Stavrakakis to task for suggesting that one way to traverse the fantasy is to cede only to partial enjoyment (Stavrakakis 2007: 282). For Žižek (and Lacan), one cannot limit or transcend the fantasmatic, since excess is integral to human drive (2008b: 328–29; cf. Daly 2010: 19). Rather than trying to tame *jouissance*, Žižek in fact suggests precisely the opposite: 'To "traverse the fantasy" ... paradoxically means *fully identifying oneself with the fantasy*' (2008b: 329). You come to terms with the fantasy by fully assuming it, submitting to it. One possibility here is over-identification: you challenge an ideological apparatus by acting out its disavowed enjoyment or fastidiously complying with its ideals. Jodi Dean imagines, for example, workers protesting against their employers by adhering strictly to employment contracts, clocking in and out of work exactly on time, not agreeing to any extras (e.g. over-time); or a disgruntled bus driver 'closing the doors in the face of commuters in order to follow the schedule to the letter' (2006: 167; cf. Sharpe and Boucher 2010: 83). Thus, over-identification with a regime's stated rules is adhering to them while, at the same time, contesting them, and so destabilizing their fantasmatic ground.

But traversing the fantasy is no easy feat. It requires tremendous struggle and effort, since it entails nothing less than changing the subject (her enjoyment, beliefs, identifications, attachments) in the process of assuming responsibility for her fantasy. There will be many forms of resistance along the way – habit formations, institutional rituals, commodity fetishism, superegoic commands to enjoy – and we will need to become 'fully conversant with [these] modes of resistance if we are to ever either overcome them, or at least reach a responsible accommodation with their intractable existence' (Taylor 2010: 24). There may, for instance, be fantasies (e.g. daydreaming, sexual, or violent fantasies) that we secretly really enjoy but would cause us enormous discomfort and shame to have to admit to publicly (Žižek 1989: 74). Re-arranging our desires and refounding our most treasured beliefs, in other words, is easier said than done, and Žižek would be the first to admit there are neither guarantees nor easy and fool-proof solutions.

Of course, Žižek has in mind a collective process of re-education of desire and belief that changes both subject and social fantasy concurrently. As Stephen Healy states, 'Traversing fantasy … is simultaneously a process of forming new languages, desires, subjectivities, and societies, transformatively affecting both [actor and acted upon]' (2010: 497). Most importantly, having fully taken responsibility for the social fantasy (of celebrity humanitarianism, neoliberalism), it is incumbent upon us to move towards a collective political act to found a new political order. Here is Healy again:

> It is not simply enough to show that capitalocentric visions of economic space are social constructions. We must attend to the pleasures of this fiction as well as emphasize the capacity of people to create new social relations, desires, and senses of self by traversing their fantasies and inhabiting economic space in a different (ethical) way.
>
> *(2010: 504)*

An uncompromising left politics?

But what does re-educating desire and belief mean in the context of celebrity humanitarianism? What kind of politics might it entail? There are, of course, many possibilities here, but my wager is that most fall into either of two categories of Left politics: reformist or revolutionary.

With regard to a reformist politics, the list is once again likely inexhaustible, but several key options come to mind on transforming the celebrity charity machine:

i   Encourage progressive celebrities to lead by example by publicly criticizing the global charity business, and rather than doing charity in the Third World, engage in direct political work in the West (i.e. the celebrities' own backyard) to make corporations, governments, NGOs, and global financial institutions (World Bank, IMF, WTO) more democratic and accountable to the Excluded/Third World.
ii Organize boycotts of (celebrity endorsed) charity products, fundraisers, and foundations.
iii Give 'radical' gifts: rather than donating to the mainstream liberal charities, including celebrity endorsed ones, give to radical political organizations (e.g. trade unions, workers' collectives, alternative media organizations, radical green/feminist/queer/indigenous peoples' organizations, etc.).

iv Give anonymous gifts: make donations in such a way as to keep the identity of the donor anonymous. This will help eliminate the donor's quest for public or media recognition and spectacle. But it would likely require intermediary organizations (to aid in channelling such gifts), which would themselves need to be highly accountable to the Excluded/Third World or else they would simply reproduce the work of already existing mainstream NGOs and multilaterals (cf. Kapoor 2008: 90–94).

v Make the state more accountable: rather than relying on privatized, neoliberal, and postdemocratic forms of charity, 'bring the state back in' so as to ensure that private individuals and organizations do not make and implement what are properly public decisions.

While seemingly progressive, the problem with all of these options is that they don't adequately grapple with global neoliberal capitalism (of which celebrity humanitarianism is but one manifestation) and are hence specimens of incomplete or failed fantasy traversal. Firstly, they are piecemeal options that, rather than directly confronting the capitalist system and our libidinal investments in it, are oriented more at reforming the celebrity charity machine through a series of haphazard actions. A consumer boycott (option ii above), even if it were not to narrowly target celebrity charity products, will tend to ignore the larger issues of commodity fetishism, and do nothing to address the often far more problematic issue of the social relations of production (cf. Chapter 2). True, some options (particularly i and iii) may well be steps *towards* radical political transformation, but they would need to be part of a broader and coordinated panoply of Left oppositional politics.

Second, practically all of the options involve outsourcing politics to others (progressive celebrities, radical organizations, intermediary aid institutions, the state), rather than doing it ourselves. This merely reproduces the depoliticizing tendencies of celebrity humanitarianism that we have been so wary of throughout this book. As Žižek recently stated at the Occupy Wall Street demonstrations in New York, 'After outsourcing work and torture, after marriage agencies are now outsourcing our love life, we can see that for a long time, we have allowed our political engagement also to be outsourced. We want it back' (2011b). By outsourcing, we mistakenly believe that meaningful change can come from the very elites who have been the obstacles to change until now (options i, iv, and v above). How much radical change can we realistically expect from celebrities and aid organizations, even progressive ones, when they are so entrenched in the current neoliberal order? Moreover, while the state is supposed to represent the public, the late capitalist liberal democratic state most often does not, dominated as it is by postdemocratic elites. Radical politics needs, then, to break out of the 'confines of the market-and-state frame' and re-think the very functions and form of the state (Žižek 2010b: 219; Douzinas and Žižek 2010: ix).

And finally, and perhaps most importantly, many of the above options (particularly ii and iv) are a compromise with global capitalism. That is, they accept the status quo, attending to systemic problems (charity products, social inequality) only after the fact (through consumer boycotts or anonymous gifts). Not only does such a stance allow the unfettered reproduction of the system, but by so doing it also risks being co-opted by the system. As Žižek never tires of repeating, 'capitalism is capable of transforming its limit, its very impotence, in the course of its power ... the more its immanent contradiction is aggravated, the more it must revolutionize itself' (1989: 52). Thus, even the most radical ideas and political leaders – revolution, Che Guevara, Gandhi – have been successfully commodified by the likes of Apple or Ben & Jerry's. (I would not be surprised if the branding and consumption of 'anonymous charity goods' is the next big thing in global humanitarianism!) The challenge, then, is trying to oppose capitalism without getting entangled in the logic of capital itself; as Glyn Daly suggests, it means attempting to 'subvert the logic of subversion' (2010: 15; cf. Mcmillan 2011: 2).

Žižek has often been criticized for taking an uncompromising and all-or-nothing political position (cf. Sharpe and Boucher 2010: 26). Yet, he gladly embraces this criticism, stating that late global capitalism's uncompromising revolutionary movement needs to be met with an equally uncompromising revolutionary response: 'The lesson of the last decades, if there is one, is the indestructibility of capitalism ... Even the radical Maoist attempt in the Cultural Revolution to wipe out the traces of capitalism ended with its triumphant return' (Žižek 2008b: 339). Given the severe limits capitalism places on subversion, politics must shoot not for the possible but the impossible, and hence try to change, not the coordinates within the system, but the system itself (Žižek 2001: 121; 2010a: 420).

Žižek takes the Left to task (including the likes of Antonio Negri, Simon Critchley, Yannis Stavrakakis, and Ernesto Laclau) for its seemingly progressive and critical yet ultimately reformist politics that results in de facto acceptance of the capitalist liberal democratic order. Thus, for him, Third Way social democracy may well have emancipatory intentions, but it operates within the rules already laid down by neoliberalism (amounting to capitalism with a human face, or 'decaf capitalism' as we have called it). Similarly, Left politics of localized and everyday resistance (advocated, for example, by the Zapatistas or postdevelopment thinkers such as Gustavo Esteva) ends up avoiding direct confrontation of centralized state and corporate power by trying to create alternate local spaces of freedom (Žižek 2008b: 337–38). And the same holds true for those who place their faith in social movements: if the last few decades have shown us anything, it is that neoliberal capitalism has been able to co-opt them too, taming them by culturalizing and indeed commodifying their demands (by way of 'multiculturalism', and by niche-marketing products for the likes of gays and lesbians, young women, non-white communities, organic food lovers, etc.) (Žižek 1999a: 355).

For Žižek, all such Left positions manifest a secret desire that nothing too much must change. All tend to yield to a polite, unthreatening and half-hearted politics, and the proof of the pudding is that the status quo tolerates, accepts and even accedes to their demands. All deplore and criticize capitalism and its attendant penchant for inequality and unevenness, but ultimately all represent a silent acceptance of capitalism. The true political act (and traversal of the fantasy) must be to confront the Real of our times – Capital. It is only by repoliticizing the economy that problems of global inequality can be meaningfully addressed; and it is only through such repoliticization that we can meaningfully begin to address such issues as localism, queer rights, gender equality, environmental degradation, and racism (Žižek 1999a: 353–55).

A revolutionary politics is thus about the Left being adamant that an alternative to capitalist liberal democracy is imaginable, and not being limited into thinking otherwise. In this regard, Žižek (2011b) argues that, on the one hand, we live in societies where everything seems possible. In the domain of technology or sexuality, for instance, you can travel to the moon, become immortal through biogenetics, and freely engage in sex of all kinds. On the other hand, in the domain of society and economy,

> almost everything is considered impossible. You want to raise taxes by little bit for the rich; they tell you it's impossible [because we] lose competitivity. You want more money for health care, [but] they tell you, 'impossible; this means a totalitarian state.' There's something wrong in the world, where you are promised to be immortal but cannot spend a little bit more for healthcare.
>
> *(Žižek 2011b)*

Žižek notes (drawing on Fredric Jameson) that it seems easier to imagine the end of the world through ecological catastrophe than conceive of an end to global capitalism (2010a: 334).

What the Left requires, according to him, is a revolutionary spirit that will truly traverse the fantasy and have the courage to imagine a new global order. It means we must *over-identify* with such a fantasy, that is, stay true to our desire, and refuse to back off or make more compromises. Not surprisingly, Žižek recently urged people at the Occupy Wall Street gathering at Zuccotti Park not to 'be afraid to really want what you desire' (2011b). Sticking to our desire may mean risking a lot, but it also means assuming our responsibility and autonomy.

Bartleby politics

> Better not to act and be thought a fool, than to act and remove all doubt!
>
> *(after Mark Twain)*

It may seem paradoxical that Žižek issues a call to a radical politics, yet champions Bartleby. In Herman Melville's short story, 'Bartleby, the Scrivener: A story of Wall Street' (1853), Bartleby is a legal copyist who ends up refusing to do the work asked of him. His stock response becomes, 'I would prefer not to', displaying his unwillingness to conform to the demands and standards of Wall Street. Žižek follows Bartleby's example to advocate for a studied passivity, going so far as to write: 'I would prefer not to give to charity to support a Black orphan in Africa, engage in the struggle to prevent oil-drilling in a wildlife swamp, [or] send books to educate our liberal-feminist-spirited women in Afghanistan' (2006b: 383).

Yet, despite appearances, Žižek does *not* support political withdrawal *tout court*, and is *not* saying we should ignore the plight of African orphans, endangered wildlife, or Afghan women. After all, the Excluded are at the forefront of his mind, as underlined earlier, prompting his very call for radical change. Instead, he argues that, given the present global political–economic conjuncture, not to act is to take an important political stand: 'Better to do nothing than to engage in localised acts, the ultimate function of which is to make the system run more smoothly ... People intervene all the time, "do something" ... The truly difficult thing is to step back, to withdraw' (2008a: 217).

Žižek's challenge is particularly pertinent to the fields of global humanitarianism and development, which are founded on 'doing' – assisting, helping, saving the Third World. In Chapter 3, we compared this urge to 'act' to the discourse of the obsessive neurotic, whose frantic activity is an avoidance of the Real. We noted how such hyperactivity is magnified in the context of the 'spectacular NGO', where the drive is not merely to act, but to be *seen* to be acting, leading to often depoliticized humanitarian work, and indeed, further dispossession of the Excluded. Precisely in such situations, when *plus ça change, plus c'est la même chose*, a Bartleby politics is a radical step: 'it's better to do nothing than to contribute to the reproduction of the existing order' (Žižek 2010a: 399). In the case of Save Darfur, for example, refraining from feeding the media hype, and taking time to carefully *study* the Darfur situation rather than engaging in self-righteous calls for militarized intervention, would have much better served Darfurians. Žižek offers this advice:

> Is this not exactly what Lenin did after the catastrophe of 1914? He withdrew to a lonely place in Switzerland, where he 'learned, learned, and learned,' reading Hegel's logic. And this is what we should do today

when we find ourselves bombarded with mediatic images of violence. We need to 'learn, learn, and learn' what causes this violence.

(2008a: 8)

In a sense, Žižek is turning Marx's eleventh Thesis on Feuerbach on its head here: there are circumstances when, rather than contributing to the logic of the global order, we should refrain from trying to change the world and engage instead in serious critical analysis. (Of course, in the NGO world, even taking this modest step would require immense, and often highly unpleasant, adjustment and reorientation.)

The issue, for Žižek, is not only to refrain from helping to reproduce the neoliberal capitalist system, it is at the same time to desist from the types of participation that such a system *expects* of us (as Lefties?). As Daly points out (2010: 14), it is this interpellation of us as liberal democratic multiculturalists, called upon to donate to African orphans, endangered wildlife, or Afghan women, that we must resist. This conformist positioning of us, this knee-jerk elicitation to save the Other, to get involved, to be 'active' and 'productive', 'is the very mode of operation of today's ideology' (Žižek 2006b: 383).

A Bartleby politics thus disturbs the Order by refusing to assist in the latter's maintenance or expansion. It means not political inaction but (provisional) strategic withdrawal: Daly calls it 'aggressive-passivity' (2010: 15), whereby we recognize and carefully consider the current impasse, suspend our libidinal investments, and boldly declare 'we would prefer not to'. By so doing, we not only refuse the logics and grammar of the Order, but also resist the types of participation (or even resistance) that it sanctions.

Yet, a Bartleby politics *is* strategic; it's a necessary step to imagine new spaces of political possibility. Žižek refers to it, not as a preparatory stage for a more radical politics, but as the 'background' to an alternative order. It is 'how we pass from the politics of "resistance" or "protestation," which parasitizes upon what it negates, to a politics which opens up a new space outside the hegemonic position' (2006b: 381–82).

Dismantling capitalism: towards a democratic communism?

I began with a critique of celebrity humanitarianism and have ended up advocating a revolutionary overthrow of the neoliberal capitalist order! But if inequality and unevenness are integral to this order, and the role of celebrity charity is to help smooth out these ills, as I have argued, then dismantling the system (particularly capital) *is* the way out. Given capitalism's extraordinary capacity to continuously turn its limits into further opportunity, the reform of neither capital nor celebrity will get us (or has got us) far. If humanitarianism is to be at all meaningful, it must move away from the depoliticized and moral solutions offered by celebrities towards the much broader, and necessarily risky and messy, terrain of – yes! – a ruptural, revolutionary politics. In this sense, to be a humanitarian *is* to be revolutionary.

But if a revolution is to happen, it cannot do so on the basis of wishful or idealist thinking. Rather, Žižek insists that it would need to grow out of what he sees as the four main contradictions of our times (i.e. ecological crisis, privatization of intellectual property, biogenetic revolution, new social apartheids). Since there is no 'outside' to capitalism, radical change must occur from within, by exploiting capitalism's self-induced antagonisms. In this sense, Žižek's revolutionary communism is a 'utopia of the "Real"', as opposed to a utopia of the ideal (Mcmillan 2011: 13); it is based not on an *a priori* or abstract archetype leading to a kind of ethical socialism, but on a politics that emerges from the actual/historical deadlocks within neoliberal capitalism (Žižek 2010b: 211–12; Mcmillan 2011: 7). The decision to act comes from a compelling 'must', as opposed to an 'ought': 'it is not something we "ought to do," as an ideal for which we are striving, but something we cannot but do, since we cannot do otherwise' (Žižek 2006b: 334). For this reason, Žižek has resisted providing a communist ideological platform or a specific program of revolutionary action, choosing instead, as Chris Mcmillan puts it, to 'politicise a potential rupture within capitalism by insisting upon its communist potential' (2011: 17).

Žižek's idea of communism relies on political identification with the Excluded (i.e. the product of the fourth antagonism): 'it is only the reference to the Excluded that justifies the term communism' (2010b: 214; cf. 2008b: 428). Often denoted as 'the part with no part' (a term Žižek borrows from Jacques Rancière), the Excluded comprise all those expelled from our capitalist societies, typically facing a range of real and discursive barriers to meaningful social and political participation (e.g. slum dwellers, illegal migrants, subaltern women, the homeless, indigenous communities, sweatshop labour). They are ostensibly an integral part of our societies but are set apart. Žižek sees them as the universal class, because they reveal the universal truth of our global capitalist system: its very functioning and survival depends on their exclusion. In this sense, the particularity of the Excluded – the fact that they are social pariahs, out-of-joint in the social order, belonging to none of its subsets – is the condition of their universality (Žižek 2008b: 414; Mcmillan 2011: 6–7). Their abjection stands for what is wrong with the whole system. (This, after all, is why celebrity charity is ideology: it disavows what is universally true about the global order – its continuous production of a 'living dead'.)

While deeply opposed to the violent and authoritarian communism of latter-day Eastern Europe and present-day China, Žižek supports a re-worked and radically democratic communism: a communism that is committed to a collective project and puts the commons first (the same global commons that neoliberal capital privatizes, dispossessing all those who are to join the ranks of the Excluded). He affirms that the 'only sense in which we are communists is that we care for the commons. The commons of nature. The commons of intellectual property. The commons of biogenetics. For this, and only for this, we should fight' (2011b; cf. Douzinas and Žižek 2010: ix; Žižek 2010b: 213).

As to how we move towards communism, Žižek provides only a sketchy idea, surmising that, 'the new emancipatory politics [growing out of the current global antagonisms] will no longer be the act of a particular social agent, but an explosive combination of different agents.[1] What unites us is that … we are in danger of losing *everything*' (2010b: 213). He recognizes that such an act will require political organization by what he calls 'the Party' to help politicize and coordinate the collective effort (2002a: 189). Sharpe and Boucher have criticized him for implying a dangerous top-down, vanguardist politics (2010: 187; cf. Boucher and Sharpe 2010), although others (Dean 2006; Daly 2010) defend him against such an accusation, arguing that the role of the Party is to help politicize the collective outburst (cf. Žižek 2002a: 225). Jodi Dean writes, in this regard, that 'the Party does not function as a new Master … so much as it does as an analyst disturbing the natural course of a situation, serving as a catalytic object' (2006: 197).

In part, Sharpe and Boucher's critique (2010: 164, 182, 220) appears to be based on Žižek's advocacy of a 'dictatorship of the proletariat', which they see as further betraying the totalitarian tendencies of his work. But I think they are off the mark here: Žižek's use of such concepts as 'the Party' or 'dictatorship' is meant as a reminder to the Left to refrain from so easily discarding such concepts because of their negative associations with the likes of Stalinism. The idea, he writes, is 'not to reject terror *in toto*, but – to reinvent it' (2008b: 7). This means, as Daly suggests, rendering 'explicit the implicit terror and violence of our [current] socio-economic systems, and to wrest the execution of such terror and violence away from the private-corporate interests and to place them within the domain of the commons' (2010: 19). Žižek is thus resurrecting 'terror' and 'dictatorship' in the service of a democratic revolution. He writes, in this connection, that the dictatorship of the proletariat 'does not mean the opposite of democracy, but democracy's own underlying functioning … [It is] another name for the violence of the democratic explosion itself' (2008b: 412, 416). Hence, such dictatorship is 'a loving kind of terror' (Daly 2010: 20), aimed at such things as the repoliticization of the economy and the institution of 'strict egalitarian justice' (Žižek 2008b: 461). Indeed, Žižek's identification with those who are radically disenfranchised implies an unrelenting commitment to equality: for, 'Freedom cannot flourish without equality and equality does not exist without freedom' (Douzinas and Žižek 2010: x); yet at the same time, there can be 'no effective freedom without "terror" – that is, without some form of unconditional pressure that threatens the very core of our being' (Žižek 1999b: ix).

By 'proletarian' dictatorship, moreover, Žižek has in mind less the specific groups that make up the Excluded than what the Excluded represent: the universal violence and inequality of our current system that results in their subalternization. It is precisely their lack of position and out-of-jointedness that endows the Excluded with a universalism worth committing to (in their sub-alternity, for example, we can all recognize our own social alienation). Žižek asserts, in fact, that the dictatorship of the proletariat is '*not* a State-form in which the proletariat is a ruling class' (2010b: 220). This is because 'all other classes are (potentially) capable of reaching the status of the "ruling class," while the proletariat cannot achieve this without abolishing itself as a class' (Žižek 2008b: 414). Žižek has in mind, then, a new state form that embodies, not a bourgeois, liberal democratic logic but an unyielding commitment to the Excluded through what he calls 'new forms of popular participation' (2010b: 220). He thinks we get glimpses of this in the current Chavez and Morales socialist experiments in Venezuela and Bolivia, respectively:[2] each case is a kind of 'dictatorship of the proletariat', since it draws on the work of an array of social agents and movements, but always maintains a privileged link with

> the dispossessed of the favelas … although Chavez still respects the democratic electoral process, it is clear that his fundamental commitment and source of legitimation is not there, but in the privileged relationship with the poor. This is the 'dictatorship of the proletariat' in the form of democracy.
>
> *(2008b: 379, 427)*

But as always, there are no guarantees. No guarantees that the revolution *will* happen (given the tremendous psychoanalytic, institutional, and political resistance it implies), and even if it does, that the 'dictatorship of the proletariat' will not turn into another authoritarianism (indeed, there are more than hints of that in the Chavez experiment). We would need to be continually alert to the rise of such authoritarianism and do everything we can to prevent it. The point nonetheless is that we must venture forth, viewing the antagonisms of our current global order, not as unalterable, but as a new political opportunity. As Žižek often likes repeating (2010b: 210), borrowing from Samuel Beckett: 'Try again. Fail again. Fail better.'

NOTES

Introduction: celebrity humanitarianism and ideology

1 I use the term 'Third World' in this book well aware of its pejorative meanings. But given that the mainstream discourse of development and its accompanying terminology is so problematic, I find the term the least of evils (marginally better, in my view, than 'Global South', which tends to be the current politically correct *academic* term). I prefer it because of its anti-hegemonic connotations and origins – it became popular after the 1955 Bandung meeting of non-aligned countries, at which Third World leaders attempted to chart an alternative course to either the capitalist West or the communist Soviet Bloc.

2 In particular, Slavoj Žižek and Jacques Rancière. See Chapter 1 for details.

3 I have examined some of these institutional forms elsewhere (cf. Kapoor 2008: ch. 5).

4 Vighi and Feldner come up with the following formula to summarize this Foucault–Žižek debate: '*Historicism = Historicity – The Real*' (2007: 23).

5 For Lacan/Žižek, the superego, which commands us to transgress and enjoy, is the dark underside of the Ego Ideal, which solicits us, on the contrary, to be reasonable, to defer enjoyment.

1 Celebrities: humanitarians or ideologues?

1 In addition to being an economist at Columbia University, Sachs is closely associated with the United Nations, having been its Director of the Millennium Project (responsible for the Millennium Development Goals). He has often advised Third World and Eastern European 'transition' governments on issues of market liberalization and structural adjustment. He was the main advocate of the disastrous 'shock therapy' in Russia's transition to capitalism, and although he appears to have re-packaged himself as a 'populist' and 'advisor to the stars' since the 1990s, he still advocates a version of shock therapy for Africa: the need for massive aid infusion and debt reduction, big development projects, more trade (Sachs 2005a). Ironically, his earlier structural adjustment policies are the very ones that contributed to the current debt problems of much of Sub-Saharan Africa.

2 In 2011, Madonna was criticized for scrapping her long-heralded plan for a project to build a girls' academy in Malawi (for which the government had given her land), and for

firing the Board of her Raising Malawi charity. She has now announced plans to build ten schools in the country, but has come under further criticism for inadequate local consultation (Smith 2012).

3 None of these traits are necessarily lurid or embarrassing, but mainstream Western society appears to think so, and the media profits from fetishizing 'deviations' from the norm, which is why celebrities and their PR machines must ultimately find ways of compensating or conforming.

4 As far as I can tell, only two Live 8 performers (Paul McCartney and Pink Floyd guitarist Dave Gilmour) committed to giving the revenues from the increased music sales to charity (BBC 2005).

5 While the BBC claimed repeatedly that resources raised by Band Aid were used to buy arms (2010a), it has subsequently withdrawn these reports and issued an apology (2010b).

6 Arguably, Geldof and Bono's humanitarianism is also gendered, fitting well the masculinist role of super-organizers and super-managers of large events such as Live 8, for example.

7 The US and Canada (as well as Australia) have a deplorable history on the treatment of indigenous/aboriginal children, many of whom were forcibly separated from their families, sent to 'reform schools', and placed with white families, and this throughout the twentieth century, until as late as the mid-1990s.

8 One has to be careful not to take this argument too far afield though, as some nationalist leaders have marshalled eugenic arguments to stop international adoptions, claiming they deplete a country's gene pool (cf. Saunders 2007: 11–12).

9 George Monbiot (2005) asks, in this regard, 'Where, on the Live 8 stages and in Edinburgh, was the campaign against the G8's control of the World Bank, the International Monetary Fund and the UN? Where was the demand for binding global laws for multinational companies?'

10 The ad campaign has since been expanded (cf. http://keepachildalive.org/i_am_african), featuring other celebrities as well, such as Richard Gere, David Bowie, and Sarah Jessica Parker. Note that the ONE campaign in the US deployed a similar strategy for its 2005 series of TV ads on MTV and other channels. The ads focused on celebrities (Brad Pitt, Justin Timberlake, Orlando Bloom, Sean Combs, Antonio Banderas, Ellen DeGeneres, Susan Sarandon, and others), who spoke for 'poor' Africans, affirming that: 'we can beat' poverty, AIDS, and hunger in 'parts of Africa, Asia and even America' (MTV 2005).

11 Following sharp criticisms of this exclusion, a last-minute Live 8 concert was organized in Johannesburg, South Africa; and Bono made explicit efforts to forge links with Southern musicians such as Youssou N'Dour and Wyclef Jean, including them in subsequent charity concerts such as the 2007 Rostock Concert for Poverty in Germany.

12 Of course, I, too, am using the term 'Africa', even as I warn against its use. This contradiction speaks to the very limitations of language – of never being able to step outside of language, of enjoying no access to any privileged place outside it, and hence of having to critique language through language itself. But there is a crucial difference between my use of 'Africa' and the celebrities': unlike them, I use it aware of the risks of homogenization and exclusion of difference.

13 These analysts' own role in seeking to champion (and heroize) one celebrity over another is to be questioned, as it risks reproducing celebrity culture and 'postdemocratic' politics.

14 It may be argued that Žižek himself is a celebrity: of late, he certainly has become a global Left intellectual 'star'. But this is only in relation to other academics, not entertainment celebrities of the likes of Bono, who has comparatively far greater mainstream public exposure. Yet, there is a crucial difference between Žižek and Bono in this regard: the former is not (and chooses not to be) directly tied to the global corporate sector, whereas the latter most definitely is. Even so, Žižek would be the first to admit not being able to isolate oneself from global capitalism or the corporate media, itself

revealing of the prevalence of late capitalist celebrity culture. See Taylor (2010: 149ff.) for an analysis of Žižek's relationship to the media.

2 Billionaires and corporate philanthropy: 'decaf capitalism'

1 Note as well that the Gates Foundation has 'given away' free software to US libraries and schools; but this 'generosity' can be characterized more as a marketing tool (for Microsoft) than philanthropy as it helps build a clientele.

2 Paul Taylor remarks, in this regard, that 'the severity of periodic financial crises underlines the extent of the self-deception involved: a capitalist system that prides itself upon its non-idealistic, pragmatic values actively requires a mass suspension of belief in order to function' (2010: 87).

3 The Asian financial crisis is famous for prompting then Malaysian Prime Minister Mahathir to make anti-Semitic remarks about Soros, accusing him of causing the crisis. For his part, Soros admits being involved in the crisis, but not of precipitating it (1999: 208–9).

4 Christopher Holmes suggests that, contrary to the mainstream perception that hedge fund managers *find* markets to correct mispricings and expose weaknesses, they *create* markets by the very act of collectively correcting and outwitting others (2009: 441, 443). They are thus much more activist and direct than is usually portrayed, expanding the scope of markets and increasing 'the amount of risk available to be traded upon' (Holmes 2009: 446).

5 EU leaders have blamed derivative speculation as a major reason for raising Greece's borrowing costs to such high levels, mostly by betting that the country would default (Moya 2010).

6 The EU's current legislation in this direction, for example, falls short of an outright ban on 'naked short-selling', i.e. trading derivatives without actually owning the assets, which has been highly destabilizing (cf. Moya 2010). Of late, four EU countries (France, Italy, Spain, and Belgium) have banned short-selling, but only on banking stocks (BBC 2011b).

7 The latest twist is the call by such philanthropists as Warren Buffett to raise taxes on the mega-rich in the US, and an appeal by Bill Gates for Western political leaders to adopt a financial transaction tax to be used as a new source for foreign aid (Lobe 2011). Once again, this is an ideological attempt to rationalize capitalism: what Buffett and Gates are effectively saying is, 'let us continue to engage in ruthless financial speculation, let capitalism wreak havoc, but let us help sweeten the pot *after the fact* with state welfare and foreign aid'. The only (possibly) positive dimension here is the endorsement of a state tax, which would at least be publicly overseen (although in Gates's proposal, it would for all intents and purposes be handed over to the increasingly privatized foreign aid industry).

8 Starbucks has also been engaged in a bitter trademark dispute with the Ethiopian government, which is trying to boost farmers' incomes by protecting the names of Ethiopian coffee-growing regions that appear on Starbucks' packaging (cf. Magubane 2007a: 5).

3 'Spectacular NGOs': activism without action?

1 Known as 'Doctors Without Borders' in parts of the English-speaking world.

2 Note that a Žižekian reading of such depoliticization would argue, not so much that we are passive in front of the spectacle, or duped by it, as much as seduced by it through the operation of *jouissance* (enjoyment). See Chapter 2 on this point, and the section on seduction later in this chapter.

3 Save Darfur's death figures, based on a questionable US State Department 2005 study, were reported as just under 400,000, while a 2003 WHO finding put the figure closer to 70,000, a figure more or less corresponding to the findings of other studies, including the

State Department's own 'internal study'. For a fascinating examination of this 'numbers politics', see Mamdani (2009: 25ff.).

Conclusion: what is to be done?

1 An explosive combination of different agents could, of course, include Left celebrities and NGOs.
2 The cases of the Indian states of Kerala and Bengal are also illustrative here, each one having been governed almost without interruption since the late 1950s and 1970s, respectively, by a democratically elected communist government. Kerala, in particular, is often heralded as a successful 'model' of equitable development (although not without many of its own social problems), especially relative to the sea of inequality in the rest of the country.

BIBLIOGRAPHY

ABC News (2005) 'Angelina Jolie inspires international adoptions', 1 October.

Adair, S. (2010) 'The commodification of information and social inequality', *Critical Sociology*, 36(2): 243–63.

Adorno, T. (1990) *The Culture Industry: selected essays on mass culture*, London and New York: Routledge.

Agamben, G. (2005) *State of Exception*, Chicago: Chicago University Press.

Andrews, T. (2008) *Killing for Coal: America's deadliest labor war*, Cambridge, MA: Harvard University Press.

Aslanbeigui, N. and Summerfield, G. (2001) 'Risk, gender, and development in the 21st century', *International Journal of Politics, Culture and Society*, 15(1): 7–26.

Austin Statesman, (2007) 'Gates Foundation to maintain its investment plan', 14 January. Available at http://www.statesman.com/news/content/news/stories/nation/01/14/14gates.html (accessed 23 December 2008).

Barnett, M.N. and Weiss, T.G. (eds) (2008) *Humanitarianism In Question*, Ithaca: Cornell University Press.

Barron, L. (2009) 'An actress compelled to act: Angelina Jolie's *Notes From My Travels* as celebrity activist/travel narrative', *Postcolonial Studies*, 12(2): 211–28.

Baudrillard, J. (1996) *The System of Objects*, trans. J. Benedict, London: Verso.

——(1998) *The Consumer Society*, London: Sage.

BBC (2005) 'Donate Live 8 profit says Gilmour', 5 July. Available at http://news.bbc.co.uk/1/hi/entertainment/4651309.stm (accessed 23 March 2010).

——(2006) 'Live Aid 1985: how it all happened', July. Available at http://www.bbc.co.uk/music/thelive8event/liveaid/history.shtml (accessed 23 March 2010).

——(2010a) 'Geldof challenges BBC aid claim', 7 March. Available at http://news.bbc.co.uk/2/hi/8554048.stm (accessed 23 March 2010).

——(2010b) 'BBC apologises over Band Aid money reports', 4 November. Available at http://www.bbc.co.uk/news/entertainment-arts-11688535 (accessed 4 November 2010).

——(2010c) 'Financier Soros to donate $100m to Human Rights Watch', 7 September. Available at http://www.bbc.co.uk/news/world-us-canada-11218868 (accessed 20 March 2010).

——(2011a) 'Hedge funds "grabbing land" in Africa', 8 June. Available at http://www.bbc.co.uk/news/world-africa-13688683 (accessed 8 June 2011).

——(2011b) 'Four EU nations ban short-selling on banking stocks', 12 August. Available at http://www.bbc.co.uk/news/business-14500731 (accessed 15 August 2011).

Bello, W., Bullard, N., and Malhotra, K. (2000) 'Introduction' and 'Notes on the ascendancy and regulation of speculative capital', in W. Bello, N. Bullard, and K. Malhotra (eds) *Global Finance: new thinking on regulating speculative capital markets*, London: Zed.

Birn, A.-E. (2005) 'Gates's grandest challenge: transcending technology as public health ideology', *The Lancet*, 11 March. Available at http://physiciansforhumanrights.org/students/hhr-ed/gates-grandest-challenge.pdf (accessed 23 March 2010).

Bishop, M. and Green, M. (2008) *Philanthrocapitalism: how the rich can save the world*, New York: Bloomsbury.

Böhm, S. and Batta, A. (2010) 'Just doing it: enjoying commodity fetishism with Lacan', *Organization*, 17(3): 345–61.

Boltanski, L. (1999) *Distant Suffering: politics, morality and the media*, Cambridge: Cambridge University Press.

Boucher, G. and Sharpe, M. (2010) 'Introduction: "Žižek's communism" and *In Defence of Lost Causes*', *International Journal of Žižek Studies*, 5(2). Available at http://www.zizekstudies.org/index.php/ijzs/article/viewFile/258/336 (accessed 2 February 2012).

Brenner, N. and Keil, R. (2005) *The Global Cities Reader*, London and New York: Routledge.

Brockington, D. (2009) *Celebrity and the Environment: fame, wealth and power in conservation*, London: Zed.

Brockington, D. and Scholfield, K. (2010) 'The conservation mode of production and conservation NGOs in sub-Saharan Africa', *Antipode*, 42(3): 551–75.

Brown, H. (2010) 'Slavoj Žižek: the world's hippest philosopher', *The Telegraph*, 5 July. Available at http://www.telegraph.co.uk/culture/books/authorinterviews/7871302/Slavoj-Zizek-the-worlds-hippest-philosopher.html (accessed 10 January 2012).

Bryan, D. and Rafferty, M. (2006) *Capitalism with Derivatives: a political economy of financial derivatives, capital and class*, Basingstoke: Palgrave Macmillan.

Bunting, M. (2005) 'A day with Bono: "We have to make Africa an adventure"', *The Guardian*, 16 June.

BusinessWeek (2010) 'The 50 most generous philanthropists'. Available at http://www.businessweek.com/interactive_reports/philanthropy_individual.html (accessed 12 March 2010).

Caliari, A. (2007) 'Regulation of hedge funds: why is it a social security issue?', *Social Watch*, 52. Available at http://www.coc.org/system/files/Regulation_of_HedgeFunds2007%5B1%5D.pdf (accessed 12 March 2011).

Carmel, E. and Tjia, P. (2005) *Offshoring Information Technology*, Cambridge: Cambridge University Press.

Carr, D. (2007) 'Citizen Bono brings Africa to the idle rich', *New York Times*, 5 March.

Castle, S. and Jolly, D. (2008) 'Europe fines Microsoft $1.3 billion', *New York Times*, 28 February. Available at http://www.nytimes.com/2008/02/28/business/worldbusiness/28msoft.html (accessed 12 March 2010).

Collier, P. (2007) *The Bottom Billion: why the poorest countries are failing and what can be done about it*, Oxford: Oxford University Press.

Commission for Africa (2005) *Our Common Interest: an argument*, London: Penguin.

Connelly, C. (2007) 'Angelina – from the heart', *Marie Claire*, October.

Cooper, A. (2007) 'Celebrity diplomacy and the G8: Bono and Bob as legitimate international actors', Waterloo, ON: Centre for International Governance Innovation, Working Paper No. 29.

——(2008a) *Celebrity Diplomacy*, Boulder: Paradigm.

——(2008b) 'Beyond one image fits all: Bono and the complexity of celebrity diplomacy', *Global Governance*, 14: 265–72.

Cottle, S. (2009) *Global Crisis Reporting: journalism in the global age*, Berkshire: Open University Press.

Cottle, S. and Nolan, D. (2007) 'Global humanitarianism and the changing aid-media field', *Journalism Studies*, 8(6): 862–78.

Creswell, J. (2008) 'Nothing sells like celebrity', *New York Times*, 22 June.

Curan, C. (2010) 'Jay-Z's 99 problems', *New York Post*, 16 May.
Curtin, D. (2005) *Environmental Ethics for a Postcolonial World*, Oxford: Rowman & Littlefield.
Daily Telegraph (2006) 'View from Davos: Bono marketing his red tag badge of virtue', 27 January.
Daly, G. (2010) 'Causes for concern: Žižek's politics of loving terror', *International Journal of Žižek Studies*, 4(2). Available at http://www.zizekstudies.org/index.php/ijzs/article/viewFile/259/337 (accessed 20 April 2011).
Davidson, S. (2007) 'Angelina Jolie interview: Mama!', *Reader's Digest*, June.
Davis, D.B. (1975) *The Problem of Slavery in the Age of Revolution 1770–1823*, Ithaca: Cornell University Press.
Dean, J. (2006) *Žižek's Politics*, London and New York: Routledge.
——(2010) 'Affective networks', *Media Tropes*, 2(2): 19–44.
Debord, G. (1983) *Society of the Spectacle*, Detroit: Black and Red.
——(1990) *Comments on the Society of the Spectacle*, London: Verso.
Debrix, F. (1998) 'Deterritorialised territories, borderless borders: the new geography of international medical assistance', *Third World Quarterly*, 19(5): 827–46.
DeChaine, D.R. (2002) 'Humanitarian space and the social imaginary: Médeçins Sans Frontières/Doctors Without Borders and the rhetoric of global community', *Journal of Communication Inquiry*, 26(4): 354–69.
de Waal, A. (2008) 'The humanitarian carnival: a celebrity vogue', *World Affairs*, Fall.
DeWinter, R. (2001) 'The Anti-Sweatshop Movement: Constructing Corporate Moral Agency in the Global Apparel Industry', *Ethics & International Affairs*, 15: 99–115.
Dieter, H. and Kumar, R. (2008) 'The downside of celebrity diplomacy: the neglected complexity of development', *Global Governance*, 14: 250–64.
Dodd, R. (2002) 'The role of derivatives in the East Asian financial crisis', in J. Eatwell and L. Taylor (eds) *International Capital Markets: systems in transition*, New York: Oxford University Press.
Donini, A. (2002) 'The geopolitics of mercy: humanitarianism in the age of globalization', in E.W. Nafziger and R. Väyrynen (eds) *The Prevention of Humanitarian Emergencies*, Basingstoke: Palgrave.
Douzinas, C. and Žižek, S. (2010) 'Introduction: the idea of communism', in C. Douzinas and S. Žižek (eds) *The Idea of Communism*, London: Verso.
Drake, P. (2008) 'From hero to celebrity: the political economy of stardom', in S. Dricker and G. Gumpert (eds) *Heroes in a Global World*, Creskill, NJ: Hampton Press.
Duffield, M. (2001) 'Governing the borderlands: decoding the power of aid', *Disasters*, 25(4): 308–20.
——(2007) *Development, Security and Unending War: governing the world of peoples*, Cambridge: Polity.
Duffield, M., Curtis, D., and Macrae, D., (2001) 'Editorial: politics and humanitarian aid', *Disasters*, 25(4): 269–74.
Easterly, W. (2010) 'John Lennon vs. Bono: the death of the celebrity activist', *The Washington Post*, 10 December.
Edkins, J. (2000) *Whose Hunger? Concepts of Famine, Practices of Aid*, Minneapolis: University of Minnesota Press.
Edozie, R.K. (2009) 'Global citizens and Sudanese subjects: reading Mamdani's *Saviours and Survivors*', *African Affairs*, 108(433): 661–67.
Edwards, M. (2009) 'Gates, Google, and the ending of global poverty: philanthrocapitalism and international development', *Brown Journal of World Affairs*, 15(2): 35–42.
Eisenberg, P. (2006) 'The Gates–Buffett Merger isn't good for philanthropy', *Chronicle of Philanthropy*, 20 July.
Eng, D. (2003) 'Transnational adoption and queer diasporas', *Social Text*, 21(3): 2–37.
Erdogan, B.Z., Baker, M.J., and Tagg, S. (2001) 'Selecting celebrity endorsers: the practitioner's perspective', *Journal of Advertising Research*, 41(3): 39–49.

Eurodad (European Network on Debt and Development) (2005) 'Devilish details: implications of the G7 debt deal'. Available at http://www.eurodad.org/uploadstore/cms/docs/Overview_G7_debt_deal.pdf (accessed 17 February 2006).

Flint, J. (2007), 'Darfur: stop! confrontational rhetoric', *Review of African Political Economy*, 34 (113): 535–40.

Flint, J. and de Waal, A. (2008) *Darfur: a new history of a long war*, London: Zed.

Forbes (2011) 'The world's billionaires'. Available at http://www.forbes.com/wealth/billionaires (accessed 12 March 2011).

Foucault, M. (1980) 'Truth and Power', in C. Gordon (ed.) *Michel Foucault: Power/Knowledge*, New York: Pantheon.

——(1984) *The Foucault Reader*, P. Rainbow (ed.), New York: Pantheon.

Fox, F. (2001) 'New humanitarianism: does it provide a moral banner for the 21st century?', *Disasters*, 25(4): 275–89.

Frazier, M. (2007) 'Costly RED campaign reaps meager $18 Million', *Advertising Age*, 5 March. Available at http://adage.com/article?article_id¼115287 (accessed 15 July 2010).

Fridell, G. (2006) 'Fair trade and neoliberalism: assessing emerging perspectives', *Latin American Perspectives*, 33(6): 8–28.

Fridell, M., Hudson, I., and Hudson, M. (2008) 'With friends like these: the corporate response to fair trade', *Review of Radical Political Economics*, 40(1): 8–34.

Gailey, C. (2000) 'Seeking "baby right": race, class, and gender in US international adoption', in A.-L. Rygold (ed.) *Yours, Mine, Ours … and Theirs: international adoption*, Oslo: University of Oslo Press.

Gamson, J. (1994) *Claims to Fame: celebrity in contemporary America*, Berkeley: University of California Press.

Gates, B. (2006) 'Beyond business intelligence: delivering a comprehensive approach to enterprise information management', Microsoft Corporation Executive E-Mail. Available at http://www.microsoft.com/mscorp/execmail/2006/05–17eim.mspx (accessed 15 July 2010).

——(2008) 'A new approach to capitalism', in M. Kinsley (ed.) *Creative Capitalism*, New York: Simon & Schuster.

Gates Foundation (Bill and Melinda Gates Foundation) (2011a) 'Programs and partnerships'. Available at http://www.gatesfoundation.org/programs/Pages/overview.aspx (accessed 3 May 2011).

——(2011b) 'Foundation fact sheet'. Available at http://www.gatesfoundation.org/about/Pages/foundation-fact-sheet.aspx (accessed 3 May 2011).

Geldof, B. (2005) *Geldof in Africa*, BBC TV Series (6 parts).

Gillard, H., Howcroft, D., Mitev, N., and Richardson, H. (2008) '"Missing women": gender, ICTs, and the shaping of the global economy', *Information Technology for Development*, 14(4): 262–79.

Giroux, H. (2006) *Beyond the Spectacle of Terrorism: global uncertainty and the challenge of the new media*, Boulder, CO: Paradigm.

Global Fund (2011) 'Pledges and contributions (as of 31 March 2011)'. Available at http://www.theglobalfund.org/en/pledges/ (accessed 5 April 2011).

Goodman, M. (2009) 'The mirror of consumption: celebritisation, developmental consumption and the shifting cultural politics of fair trade', Environment, Politics and Development Working Paper Series, No. 8, Department of Geography, King's College London.

The Guardian (2005) 'Out of Gleneagles', 11 July.

Guilhot, N. (2007) 'Reforming the world: George Soros, global capitalism and the philanthropic management of the social sciences', *Critical Sociology*, 33(3): 447–77.

Haeri, M. (2008) 'Saving Darfur: does advocacy help or hinder conflict resolution?', *Praxis: the Fletcher Journal of Human Security*, 23: 33–46.

Hague, S., Street, J., and Savigny, H. (2008) 'The voice of the people? Musicians as political actors', *Cultural Politics*, 4(1): 5–24.

Harmes, A. (1999) 'Hedge funds as a weapon of state? Financial and monetary power in an era of liberalized finance', YCISS Occasional Paper No. 57, York University.

Harvey, D. (2006) *Spaces of Global Capitalism*, London and New York: Verso.

Hassan, S.M. (2010) 'Darfur and the crisis of governance in Sudan: a Left perspective', *South Atlantic Quarterly*, 109(1): 95–116.

Healy, S. (2010) 'Traversing fantasies, activating desires: economic geography, activist research, and psychoanalytic methodology', *The Professional Geographer*, 62(4): 496–506.

Hill, H. and Chu, Yun-Peng (2001) 'An overview of the key issues', in H. Hill and Y.-P. Chu (eds) *The Social Impact of the Asian Financial Crisis*, Cheltenham: Edward Elgar.

Holmes, C. (2009) 'Seeking Alpha or creating Beta? Charting the rise of hedge fund-based financial ecosystems', *New Political Economy*, 14(4): 431–50.

Hoskins, A. and O'Loughlin, B. (2010) *War and Media*, London: Polity.

Igoe, J. (2010) 'The spectacle of nature in the global economy of appearances: anthropological engagements with the spectacular mediations of transnational conservation', *Critique of Anthropology*, 30(4): 375–97.

Jolie, A. (2003) *Notes From My Travels: visits with refugees in Africa, Cambodia, Pakistan, and Ecuador*, New York: Pocket Books.

Kapoor, I. (2002) 'The devil's in the theory: a critical assessment of Robert Chambers' work on participatory development', *Third World Quarterly*, 23(1): 101–17.

——(2008) *The Postcolonial Politics of Development*, London and New York: Routledge.

Keenan, T. (2002) 'Publicity and indifference: media, surveillance, "humanitarian intervention"'. Available at http://roundtable.kein.org/files/roundtable/keenan.publicity.pdf (accessed 2 March 2011).

Kellner, D. (2003) *Media Spectacle*, London and New York: Routledge.

——(2004) 'Media culture and the triumph of the spectacle', *Razón y Palabra*, 39 (Abril-Mayo). Available at http://www.razonypalabra.org.mx/anteriores/n39/dkelner.html (accessed 20 May 2011).

Kiely, R. (2000) 'Globalization: from domination to resistance', *Third World Quarterly*, 21(6): 1059–70.

Killercoke (2010) 'Coke's crimes'. Available at http://www.killercoke.org/crimes.htm (accessed 2 May 2010).

Kingsbury, P. (2008) 'Did somebody say jouissance? On Slavoj Žižek, consumption, and nationalism', *Emotion, Space and Society*, 1: 48–55.

Klein, N. (2007) *The Shock Doctrine: the rise of disaster capitalism*, New York: Picador.

Krause, P. (1992) *The Battle for Homestead, 1880–1892*, Pittsburgh, PA: University of Pittsburgh Press.

The Lancet (2009) 'Editorial: what has the Gates Foundation done for global health?', 373, 9 May.

Leblanc, D. (2012) 'Miners show new way for CIDA', *Globe and Mail*, 30 January.

Littler, J. (2008) 'I feel your pain: cosmopolitan charity and the public fashioning of the celebrity soul', *Social Semiotics*, 18(2): 237–51.

——(2009) *Radical Consumption: shopping for change in contemporary culture*, Berkshire: Open University Press/McGraw-Hill.

Live 8 (2005) 'The story so far'. Available at http://www.live8live.com/whathappened/ (accessed 10 March 2010).

Lobe, J. (2011) 'Bill Gates to support "Robin Hood" tax', *Al-Jazeera*, 24 September. Available at http://www.aljazeera.com/indepth/features/2011/09/2011924125427182350.html (accessed 26 September 2011).

McChesney, R.W. (2008) *The Political Economy of Media: enduring issues, emerging dilemmas*, New York: Monthly Review Press.

McGowan, T. (2004) *The End of Dissatisfaction? Jacques Lacan and the Emerging Society of Enjoyment*, Albany: SUNY Press

——(2010) 'The necessity of belief, or, the trouble with atheism', *International Journal of Žižek Studies*, 4(1). Available at http://zizekstudies.org/index.php/ijzs/article/view/226/ 324 (accessed 1 March 2010).

Mcmillan, C. (2011) 'The communist hypothesis; Žižekian utopia or utopian fantasy?', *International Journal of Žižek Studies*, 5(2). Available at http://zizekstudies.org/index.php/ijzs/article/view/301/399 (accessed 2 February 2012).

Magubane, Z. (2007a) 'Africa and the new cult of celebrity', *The Zeleza Post*, 20 April. Available at http://www.zeleza.com/blogging/popular-culture/africa-and-new-cult-celebrity (accessed 2 March 2010).

——(2007b) 'Oprah in South Africa: the politics of coevalness and the creation of a black public sphere', *Safundi: the journal of South African and American studies*, 8(4): 373–93.

——(2008) 'The (Product) Red man's burden: charity, celebrity, and the contradictions of coevalness', *The Journal of Pan African Studies*, 2(6): 2–25.

Mamdani, M. (2009) *Saviors and Survivors: Darfur, politics, and the War on Terror*, New York: Doubleday.

——(2010) 'Context for those who would demonize', *SAIS Review*, 30(1): 139–43.

Manzo, K. (2008) 'Imaging humanitarianism: NGO identity and the iconography of childhood', *Antipode*, 40(4): 632–57.

Marshall, P.D. (1997) *Celebrity and Power: fame in contemporary culture*, Minneapolis: University of Minnesota Press.

Marx, K. (1867) *Capital: a critique of political economy*, vol. 1, trans. B. Fowkes, reprinted 1990, New York: Penguin.

Melville, H. (1853) 'Bartleby, the Scrivener: A story of Wall Street', reprinted by Project Gutenberg 2004. Available at http://www.gutenberg.org/cache/epub/11231/pg11231.txt (accessed 23 July 2010).

Monbiot, G. (2005) 'Africa's new best friends', *The Guardian*, 5 July.

Moya, E. (2010) 'Brussels proposes tougher regulation of derivatives market', *The Guardian*, 15 September. Available at http://www.guardian.co.uk/business/2010/sep/15/brussels-proposes-tougher-regulation-derivatives?INTCMP=SRCH (accessed 12 March 2011).

MTV (2005) 'One by one', TV advertisement, aired from April onwards.

Myerson, A. (1997) 'In principle, a case for more sweatshops', *New York Times*, 22 June. Available at http://www.nytimes.com/1997/06/22/weekinreview/in-principle-a-case-for-more-sweatshops.html (accessed 20 March 2010).

Nash, K. (2008) 'Global citizenship as show business: the cultural politics of Make Poverty History', *Media, Culture and Society*, 30(2): 167–81.

Negen, B (2009) 'The keys to successful cause marketing'. Available at http://www.onecoast.com/retailer/library-advisor-article-detail.asp?aid=1261 (accessed 23 March 2010).

New Internationalist (2006) 'Bob Geldof'. Available at http://www.newint.org/columns/worldbeaters/2006/01/01/bob-geldof/index.php (accessed 29 March 2010).

Nickel, P. and Eikenberry, A. (2009) 'A critique of the discourse of marketized philanthropy', *American Behavioral Scientist*, 52(7): 974–89.

——(2010) 'Philanthropy in an era of global governance', *Third Sector Research*, 19(8); 269–79.

Nutt, S. (2012) 'Do aid organizations take the corporate bait?', *Globe and Mail*, 25 January.

Oakland Institute (2011) 'Press Release: Understanding land investment deals in Africa', 7 June. Available at http://media.oaklandinstitute.org/press-release-understanding-land-investment-deals-africa (accessed 8 June 2011).

OED Online (2011) *Oxford English Dictionary*, Oxford University Press, December. Available at http://www.oed.com (accessed 12 December 2011).

Okie, S. (2006) 'Global health – the Gates–Buffett effect', *The New England Journal of Medicine*, 355(11): 1084–88.

O'Manique, C. and Labonte, R. (2008) 'Rethinking (Product) RED', *The Lancet*, 371, May: 1561–63.

Opalesque (2009) 'Investing – Soros Fund reports $4.2 bln holdings', 17 August. Available at http://www.opalesque.com/54134/soros%20fund/Investing_reports246.html (accessed 12 March 2010).

Open Society Foundations (2011) 'Frequently asked questions'. Available at http://www. soros.org/about/faq (accessed 12 March 2011).

Orbinsky, J. (2000) 'Protecting civilians in conflict: we must separate military from humanitarian action', *Doctors Without Borders/Médecins Sans Frontières Alert 5.*

Ortiz, A. and Briggs, L. (2003) 'The culture of poverty, crack babies, and welfare cheats: the making of the "healthy white baby crisis"', *Social Text*, 21(3): 39–57.

Oxfam America (2011) 'Celebrity ambassadors'. Available at http://www.oxfamamerica.org/ whoweare/celebrity-ambassadors (accessed 2 November 2011).

Oxfam UK (2011) 'Oxfam in action'. Available at http://www.oxfam.org.uk/oxfam_ in_action/(accessed 2 November 2011).

Petras, J. (1999) 'NGOs: in the service of imperialism', *Journal of Contemporary Asia*, 29(4): 429–40.

Pfaller, R. (2003) 'Little gestures of disappearance: interpassivity and the theory of ritual', *Journal of European Psychoanalysis*, 16 (Winter/Spring). Available at http://www.psychomedia. it/jep/number16/pfaller.htm (accessed 21 June 2011).

——(2005) 'Where is your hamster? The concept of ideology in Slavoj Žižek's cultural theory', in G. Boucher, J. Glynos, and M. Sharpe (eds) *Traversing the Fantasy: critical responses to Slavoj Žižek*, Aldershot: Ashgate.

——(2007) 'Interpassivity and misdemeanors: the analysis of ideology and the Žižekian toolbox', *International Journal of Žižek Studies*, 4(2). Available at http://www.zizekstudies. org/index.php/ijzs/article/viewFile/19/69 (accessed 24 March 2011).

Phillips, M. (2008) 'Tycoon philanthropy: prestige and the annihilation of excess', in D. Crowther and N. Capaldi (eds) *The Ashgate Research Companion to Corporate Social Responsibility*, Aldershot: Ashgate.

Piller, C., Sanders, E., and Dixon, R. (2007) 'Gates Foundation money works at cross purposes', *Los Angeles Times*, 7 January.

Ponte, S., Richey, L.A., and Baab, M. (2009) 'Bono's Product (RED) initiative: corporate social responsibility that solves the problems of "distant others"', *Third World Quarterly*, 30(2): 301–17.

Pound, M. (2008) *Žižek: a (very) critical introduction*, Grand Rapids, MI: William B. Eerdmans Publishing.

Product (RED) (2008) 'The (RED) manifesto'. Available at http://www.joinred.com/ manifesto/ (accessed 11 July 2008).

——(2011) 'The (RED) idea'. Available at http://www.joinred.com/aboutred (accessed 5 April 2011).

Pupavec, V. (2006) 'The politics of emergency and the demise of the developing state: problems for humanitarian advocacy', *Development In Practice*, 16(3–4): 255–69.

Rachman, G. (2007) 'The aid crusade and Bono's Brigade', *Financial Times*, 30 October.

Rajagopal, A. (1999) 'Celebrity and the politics of charity', in A. Kear and D. Steinberg (eds) *Mourning Diana: nation, culture and the performance of grief*, London and New York: Routledge.

Rancière, J. (1994) 'Post-democracy, politics, and philosophy: an interview with Jacques Rancière', *Angelaki*, 1(3): 171–78.

——(1998) *Disagreement*, Minneapolis: University of Minnesota Press.

——(2003) 'Comment and response', *Theory & Event*, 5(3).

——(2006) *Hatred of Democracy*, London and New York: Verso.

Randall, D. (2008) 'The truth about celebrity giving', *Forbes*, 24 November. Available at http://www.forbes.com/2008/11/24/oprah-philanthropy-celebrity-biz-media-cz_dkr_ 1124charitycelebs.html (accessed 29 March 2010).

Richey, L.A. and Ponte, S. (2008) 'Better (RED)™ than dead? Celebrities, consumption and international aid', *Third World Quarterly*, 29(4): 711–29.

Rimmer, M. (2010) 'The Lazarus Effect: the (RED) campaign and creative capitalism', in T. Pogge, M. Rimmer, and K. Rubenstein (eds) *Incentives for Global Public Health*, Cambridge: Cambridge University Press.

Rojek, C. (2001) *Celebrity*, London: Reaktion Books.

Rorty, R. (1998) *Truth and Progress. Philosophical Papers*, Vol. 3, Cambridge: Cambridge University Press.

Rosenman, M. (2007) 'The patina of philanthropy', *Stanford Social Innovation Review*, April. Available at http://www.ssireview.org/opinion/entry/the_patina_of_philanthropy/ (accessed 20 March 2010).

Sachs, J. (2005a) *The End of Poverty*, London: Penguin.

——(2005b) 'Who beats corruption?', Project Syndicate. Available at http://www.project-syndicate.org/commentary/sachs106/English (accessed 20 March 2010).

Saunders, R. (2007) 'Transnational reproduction and its discontents: the politics of inter-country adoption in a global society', *Journal of Global Change and Governance*, 1(1): 1–23.

Save Darfur Coalition (SDC) (2011) 'We are united to end genocide'. Available at http://www.savedarfur.org/pages/we-are-united-to-end-genocide (accessed 30 November 2011).

Shah, A. (2005) 'G8 Summit 2005 outcome'. Available at http://www.globalissues.org/TradeRelated/Debt/g8summit2005/outcome.asp (accessed 17 February 2006).

Sharpe, M. and Boucher, G. (2010) *Žižek and Politics: a critical introduction*, Edinburgh: Edinburgh University Press.

Shiva, V. (2005) *Earth Democracy*, London: Zed.

Shivji, I.G. (2006) 'The silences in the NGO discourse: the role and future of NGOs in Africa', *Africa Development*, 31(4): 22–51.

Singer, S. (2002) 'Warrior one', *Vogue*, October.

Smith, D. (2012) 'Madonna's new school pledge angers Malawi officials', *The Guardian*, 23 February. Available at http://www.guardian.co.uk/music/2012/feb/23/madonna-schools-pledge-angers-malawi-officials (accessed 5 March 2012).

Soros, G. (1999) *The Crisis of Global Capitalism: open society endangered*, 2nd edition, New York: PublicAffairs.

——(2002a) 'Against market fundamentalism: "the capitalist threat" reconsidered', in L. Zsolnai (ed.) *Ethics and the Future of Capitalism*, London: Transaction Publishers.

——(2002b) *George Soros on Globalization*, New York: PublicAffairs.

Spivak, G.C. (1988) 'Can the subaltern speak?', in C. Nelson and L. Grossberg (eds) *Marxism and Interpretation of Culture*, Chicago: University of Illinois Press.

Stavrakakis, Y. (2000) 'On the critique of advertising discourse', *Third Text*, 14(51): 85–90.

——(2006) 'Objects of consumption, causes of desire: consumerism and advertising in societies of commanded enjoyment', *Gramma*, 14: 83–105.

——(2007) *The Lacanian Left*, Edinburgh: Edinburgh University Press.

Stevenson, N. (2010) 'New media, popular culture and social theory', in A. Elliott (ed.) *The Routledge Companion to Social Theory*, London and New York: Routledge.

Stiglitz, J. (1998) 'Boats, planes, and capital flows', *Financial Times*, 25 March.

Stross, R. (1997) *The Microsoft Way*, Reading, MA: Addison-Wesley.

Swibel, M. (2006) 'Bad girl interrupted', *Forbes*, 178(1): 118–19.

Tanzi, V. (2002) 'Globalization and the future of social protection', *Scottish Journal of Political Economy*, 49: 116–27.

Tarnoff, C. and Nowells, L. (2005) 'Foreign aid: an introductory overview of U.S. programs and policy', Washington, DC: Congressional Research Service.

Taylor, P.A. (2010) *Žižek and the Media*, Cambridge: Polity.

Tierney, K., Bevc, C., and Kuligowski, E. (2006) 'Metaphors matter: disaster myths, media frames, and their consequences in Hurricane Katrina', *The Annals of the American Academy of Political and Social Science*, 604(1): 57–81.

UNDP (1999) *Human Development Report*, New York: Oxford University Press.

Upadhya, C. and Vasavi, A. (2008) 'Outposts of the global information economy: work and workers in India's outsourcing industry', in C. Upadhya and A. Vasavi (eds) *In an Outpost of the Global Economy: work and workers in India's information technology industry*, London and New York: Routledge.

Vanity Fair (2007) 'Africa Issue', July.

van Oenen, G. (2008) 'Interpassivity revisited: a critical and historical reappraisal of interpassive phenomena', *International Journal of Žižek Studies*, 2(2). Available at http://www.zizekstudies.org/index.php/ijzs/article/view/96/230 (accessed 23 April 2011).

Vighi, F. and Feldner, H. (2007) *Žižek: beyond Foucault*, Basingstoke: Palgrave Macmillan.

Waldinger, R. and Lichter, M. (2009) *How The Other Half Works: immigration and the social organization of labour*, Berkeley, CA: University of California Press.

Wallerstein, I. (1974) *The Modern World-System, vol. I: capitalist agriculture and the origins of the European world-economy in the sixteenth century*, New York: Academic Press.

——(1980) *The Modern World-System, vol. II: mercantilism and the consolidation of the European world-economy, 1600–1750*, New York: Academic Press.

——(1989) *The Modern World-System, vol. III: the second great expansion of the capitalist world-economy, 1730–1840's*, San Diego: Academic Press.

——(2004) *World-Systems Analysis: an introduction*, Durham: Duke University Press.

Watson, S. (2011) 'The "human" as referent object? Humanitarianism as securitization', *Security Dialogue*, 42(1): 3–20.

Williams, A. (2006) 'Into Africa', *New York Times*, 13 August.

World Development Movement (2006) 'Small change', June. Available at http://www.wdm.org.uk/sites/default/files/smallchange01062006.pdf (accessed 12 March 2010).

Youde, J. (2009) 'Ethical consumerism or reified neoliberalism? Product (RED) and private funding for public goods', *New Political Science*, 31(2): 201–20.

Zalik, A. (2004) 'The Niger Delta: petro-violence and partnership development', *Review of African Political Economy*, 101(4): 401–24.

Žižek, S. (1989) *The Sublime Object of Ideology*, London: Verso.

——(1991) *Looking Awry: an introduction to Jacques Lacan through popular culture*, Cambridge: MIT Press.

——(1993) *Tarrying With The Negative: Kant, Hegel, and the critique of ideology*, Durham: Duke University Press.

——(1994a) *Metastases of Enjoyment: six essays on women and causality*, London: Verso.

——(ed.) (1994b) *Mapping Ideology*, London: Verso.

——(1997) *The Plague of Fantasies*, London: Verso.

——(1998) 'The interpassive subject', *Traverses*, Centre Georges Pompidou. Available at http://www.lacan.com/zizek-pompidou.htm (accessed 22 May 2011).

——(1999a) *The Ticklish Subject: the absent centre of political ontology*, London: Verso.

——(1999b) *The Žižek Reader*, E. Wright and E. Wright (eds), Oxford: Blackwell.

——(2001) *On Belief*, London and New York: Routledge.

——(2002a) '"Introduction: between the two revolutions", and "Afterword: Lenin's choice"', in S. Žižek (ed.) *Revolution at the Gates: Žižek on Lenin, the 1917 writings*, London: Verso.

——(2002b) *Welcome to the Desert of the Real*, London: Verso.

——(2004a) 'From politics to biopolitics ... and back', *The South Atlantic Quarterly*, 103(2/3): 501–21.

——(2004b) *Organs Without Bodies: on Deleuze and consequences*, London and New York: Routledge.

——(2006a) *How to Read Lacan*, London: Granta Books.

——(2006b) *The Parallax View*, Cambridge, MA: MIT Press.

——(2006c) *The Universal Exception*, New York: Continuum.

——(2006d) 'Nobody has to be vile', *London Review of Books*, 28(7): 10.

——(2007) 'Censorship today: violence, or ecology as new opium for the masses'. Available at http://www.lacan.com/zizecology1.htm (accessed 15 February 2011).

——(2008a) *On Violence: six sideways reflections*, New York: Picador.

——(2008b) *In Defense of Lost Causes*, London: Verso.

——(2009a) 'First as tragedy, then as farce: the economic crisis and the end of global capitalism', paper presented at Royal Society for the encouragement of Arts, Manufactures and

Commerce (RSA), 24 November, London. Available at http://www.thersa.org/events/vision/vision-videos/slavoj-zizek-first-as-tragedy,-then-as-farce (accessed 10 March 2010).

——(2009b) 'How to begin from the beginning', *New Left Review*, 57, May–June: 43–55.

——(2009c) 'Brunhilde's Act', *International Journal of Zizek Studies*, Special Issue, Vol. 4. Available at http://zizekstudies.org/index.php/ijzs/article/viewFile/294/362 (accessed 20 February 2011).

——(2009d) *First as Tragedy, Then as Farce*, London: Verso.

——(2010a) *Living In The End Times*, London: Verso.

——(2010b) 'How to begin from the beginning', in C. Douzinas and S. Žižek (eds) *The Idea of Communism*, London: Verso.

——(2011a) 'Hegelian dialectic and Ernst Lubitsch's Ninotchka'. Video available at http://www.youtube.com/watch?v=wmJVsaxoQSw (accessed 12 December 2011).

——(2011b) 'Slavoj Žižek at Occupy Wall Street'. Video available at http://www.thepaltrysapien.com/2011/10/slavoj-zizek-at-occupy-wall-street/ (accessed 13 October 2011).

INDEX

Lightning Source UK Ltd.
Milton Keynes UK
UKOW05f0324130117
292003UK00005B/29/P

9 780415 783392